MAINE SPORTING CAMPS

GEORGE SMITH

Camden, Maine

Published by Down East Books
An imprint of Globe Pequot
Trade Division of The Rowman & Littlefield Publishing Group, Inc.
4501 Forbes Boulevard, Suite 200, Lanham, Maryland 20706
www.rowman.com

Unit A, Whitacre Mews, 26-34 Stannary Street, London SE11 4AB

Distributed by NATIONAL BOOK NETWORK

British Library Cataloguing in Publication Information Available

Library of Congress Cataloging-in-Publication Data Available

ISBN 978-1-60893-532-1 (paperback)
ISBN 978-1-60893-533-8 (ebook)

♾™ The paper used in this publication meets the minimum requirements of American National Standard for Information Sciences—Permanence of Paper for Printed Library Materials, ANSI/ NISO Z39.48-1992.

Printed in the United States of America

CONTENTS

Foreword

Magical Memories
—by Bill Green, TV6 news reporter and host of *Bill Green's Maine*

Maine sporting camps have been providing magical memories for well over a century. Historically, these camps yielded the big trout or deer, but most have changed with the times as we've redefined what an outdoors person is. Today, Maine sporting camps offer activities for a plethora of interests among people who enjoy healthier pursuits, come as part of a family and regrettably, stay for a shorter length of time.

George Smith is almost uniquely qualified to write this book. He is a serious and seasoned member of that old "hook and bullet" crowd, but cleans up nicely and can charmingly discuss any aspect of Maine, our history and the outdoors.

Where better to share such a meal than at one of Maine's great sporting camps? Part of the fun would be wonderful food spiced with a mix of amusing and amazing stories often based on George's own experiences or local stories that make each Maine camp legendary. In fact, in *Maine Sporting Camps*, George begins the conversation by not only recommending places to hunt and fish, but also pointing out which camps offer outstanding "non-consumptive" activities such as hiking, birding and Nordic skiing. Through such activities and conversations we share memories of the Maine Outdoors with others as well as with those who have come before.

If you want to know what visiting a camp is like or if you are looking for a camp to visit, this is a book for you. It's a historically significant field guide that gives us a wonderful accounting of these grand institutions of Maine.

George has thoroughly and meticulously researched this guide book and yet made it a pleasant read. You can use it to pick your next staycation, put it on a shelf to use for research, or leave it in your favorite reading nook for when you want to take your next back country trip without getting out of your comfortable chair.

If you've never visited a Maine sporting camp, you should do so. You don't have to bring anything except an open mind. You will be treated to scenes and experiences that will generate memories that last a lifetime, memories made at Maine Sporting Camps.

Introduction

History meets hospitality at Maine sporting camps today. While they were once rustic and remote, today's camps offer more comfort and convenience, but it is still the wild Maine outside the cabin door that attracts many of us.

The original attraction was bountiful fish and game and that is still true at some sporting camps, but many of today's visitors come to enjoy outdoor activities like birding and hiking, snowmobiling and snowshoeing. Some are just trying to escape the "real" world. And some of us come to eat!

It's a lot easier today to get to a sporting camp than it once was. Consider this description of the route to Camp Phoenix on Nesowadnehunk Lake in the North Woods, published in the March 1999 edition of *The Maine Sportsman*:

> There are two ways of reaching 'Sowadnehunk from stations on the Bangor and Aroostook (railroad); both routes themselves passing through good game country. The one by way of Patten, Shin Pond and Trout Brook Farm involves a fifty mile walk or buckboard ride over the roads, requiring about two and a half days' time. The trip by way of Norcross is shorter and even more picturesque, and may be covered in two days. A steamer running from Norcross to various points on Twin, Pemaeumcook and Ambajejus Lakes, will take the traveler fifteen miles on his way to Camp Wellington run by Seiden McPheters. At this point one crosses a half-mile carry on a jumper, and begins the ascent of the West Branch in canoes ... the last mile the canoe must be poled.

Getting there was part of the adventure, I guess! Maine once had more than 300 sporting camps. Nearly all are only memories today. I've got a stack of brochures here on the table of camps no longer in business.

Flagstaff Lake Camps in Eustis: Fifty weeks of the year belong to your job … but the other two are yours! Fill them brimful of the good things of life by vacationing at Flagstaff Lake Camps where the thrill of sport and scenery prevails throughout your holiday season—not any longer.

Black Bear Camps in Stratton: Black Bear Camps, nestled in the big pine woods of northwestern Maine on Flagstaff Lake, with its two hundred mile rugged shore line, are two miles north of Stratton and thirty miles from the Canadian boundary, and provide an ideal wilderness retreat for sportsmen and vacationists—long gone.

Round Mountain Lake Camps in Eustis: This ideal family resort is located in Northwestern Maine … in the wildest and most mountainous part of the state. These are genuine log camps with a central dining room where every attention is given to the quality of the food. Would have loved to stay here.

Cobb's Pierce Pond Camps. Wait! Cobb's lives on!

And that's the reason I wrote and Down East Books published this book. Amazing, life-changing, never-to-be-forgotten experiences are still available at historic Maine sporting camps.

Camp Phoenix

Let's begin with the story of Camp Phoenix, a sporting camp for almost a hundred years. In the late 1800s, hunters, anglers, and trappers began to flock to Camp Phoenix, located in Maine's remote northern forest full of moose, deer, and even caribou, with rivers and ponds teeming with huge native brook trout. Our state also attracted visitors looking to boost their spirits and health. Many came to these camps and stayed all summer.

As rail lines extended throughout the state it became easier (but not easy) to get to these sporting camps, where guides were ready to give guests the experience of a lifetime.

Over the years, Camp Phoenix's complex of buildings changed. The lodge burned; a better one was built. Cabins were constructed and moved.

And through it all, the place prospered. After Governor Percival Baxter created his stunning 200,000 acre park, literally out the back door of the camps at Phoenix, more hikers arrived to stay at the camp and enjoy the park and its forty-seven mountains.

Nevertheless, in 1988, Camp Phoenix was sold and turned into a condominium project where families own the camps individually and the land and out-buildings in common. A group of seven families purchased the large lodge.

My wife Linda and I purchased Cabin 3A in 1991, one of the best decisions we ever made. Our children grew up here and now return with our grandchildren. We drive 20 miles on the Perimeter Road in Baxter Park, then turn into our camp driveway. From camp, we can hike to many spectacular places in the park. And the lake is still the best native brook trout water in the state.

Thanks to Bill Horner and his wife Cookie, who also own a camp here, we have a wonderful history of Camp Phoenix, published on the 100th anniversary of the camps. Let's dip into Bill's book for a moment.

An ad in the 1917 issue of *In the Maine Woods* trumpeted the "Famous Camp Phoenix" offering "The best hunting and fishing opportunities in the Aroostook country. Comfortable cabins, outlying camps, guides, canoes and numerous waters to give variety. For the vacationist the surroundings are unsurpassed for resting and recuperation. Splendid canoeing, mountain climbing and woods tramps." Just in case that wasn't enough enticement, the ad reported "Our guests pronounce our table as unusually good and our *spring water* as being an attraction in itself."

The 1930s are considered by the Daiseys (who owned the camps for fifty-six years) as the heyday. The camp featured electricity, garden grown and livestock supplied food, isolation from the public, exclusive use of the entire lake, unparalleled trout fishing, live-in guides, and speedy access by car from Greenville. They had a large and loyal clientele who returned year after year.

The demise of traditional sporting camps has many causes, including a reduction in game animals and loss of quality fishing, and the fact that people are busier these days and no longer have weeks of time to vacation in the woods. Today, a three-day stay is a long one!

The camps featured in this book have made the adjustments and improvements necessary to keep up with the demands and expectations of its guests. And while I can only urge you to leave your computer and cell phone home, I know many of you want those services to be available wherever you go. You won't be out-of-touch at most of these sporting camps, but you will have the chance to get-in-touch with history and spend some time in magical Maine places.

Sporting Camp Challenges

The Maine Sporting Camp Heritage Foundation was very helpful as I researched the history of sporting camps and worked to understand how we lost so many. It is on the Foundation's website that I learned, "In 1904 there were at least 300 sporting camps in operation in Maine. By 2007, this number had dwindled to fewer than forty.

"Maine Sporting Camps face serious challenges to their survival," reports the Foundation. "Changes in land ownership and land management policies, high land valuations and taxes, lack of long term leases, increased government regulation, lack of affordable capital and encroaching development all threaten the future of Maine's remaining Sporting Camps ... Many camps have already been purchased by individuals and families, who then convert the camps into exclusive-use, private vacation properties."

I asked the owners of Maine's sporting camps to tell me about their challenges and boy, did I get an earful. Right at the top of the list was the loss of hunters and anglers, with the blame being cast widely to everything from coyotes to loss of habitat to poor fisheries and wildlife management. The loss of deer hunters over the last five years has been particularly painful. Deer nearly disappeared in western and northern Maine after two tough winters and our failure to protect critical deer wintering areas was a key factor. Consider this story.

On the porch of Claybrook Mountain Lodge in Highland Plantation are two carved "Buck Boards" listing the bucks and does that guests and guides have shot since the lodge opened in 1984. The Buck Boards tell the story better than I ever could.

Here are the harvest numbers for recent years: 2009-0, 2010-0, 2011-1, 2012-1, 2013-0. For many years, the November deer season was the busiest for the Drummonds. But things have changed. "The deer herd in our area has declined to such an extent that our (deer) season is the least profitable of the year," Greg tells me. A large deer wintering area just across the road from the Drummonds lodge was nearly clear-cut and no longer provides deer with the winter cover they need. So what is their busiest time of the year now, you ask? Its winter, when the camps are loaded with cross country skiers and the Drummonds serve weekend lunches to traveling snowmobilers.

Some folks, including the Drummonds, have smartly moved on to identify and cater to other outdoor recreationists. A few years ago the Drummonds turned Memorial Day weekend into a birding adventure, attracting so many guests that they added a second birding weekend last year. Greg Drummond, along with his friend Ron Joseph, a retired federal wildlife biologist, lead the birding weekend adventure. My wife Linda and I had a terrific time there on one of their birding weekends this year, identifying ninety-eight species of birds in two days.

Camp owners listed lots of other challenges, including taxes and regulations, described by one camp owner as, "death by a thousand cuts." Getting and keeping good staff (and not just at the remote camps) was a major problem. The cost and complexity of insurance was mentioned by many, as was rising food and other prices. A lack of advertising and marketing was high on many lists, one camp owner noting that "the state of Maine is focused more on the coastal areas for marketing of tourism and travel." That's true, but it's caused by the fact that tourists want to visit the coast, and the state's limited dollars must be used to let tourists know we have what they are looking for. And sadly, they are not looking to hunt and fish here.

Quite a few mentioned competition from online businesses that market private camps for rent, noting that those camp owners are not governed by the same taxes and rules. That issue was raised at the legislature in 2015 but no action was taken. Others pointed to nearby development or logging that changed the experiences at their camps. And one camp owner blamed his problems on Democrats!

Many camp owners complained about technology. "The biggest (challenge) is technology," one wrote. "We are a rustic sporting camp. We live in a time where most people are too caught up in their electronic devices ... Here we believe that a vacation is a time to remove yourself from all of that craziness—from the things that cause stress and headaches."

You can set aside all the stress in your life by visiting a traditional Maine sporting camp. And I'll guarantee one thing: You won't want to leave!

DEFINING A SPORTING CAMP

I had great difficulty in defining a sporting camp and asked many for help. Some favored the traditional camps with a lodge where meals are served to all guests and separate camps are provided for sleeping. That sounded good, at least as a starting point.

I first turned to legendary outdoor writer Bud Leavitt (now deceased), who reported in his *Bangor Daily News* column that a Maine sporting camp, "consists of a collection of cottages or camps, located in the vicinity of a central structure that houses a kitchen, dining room and something close to being called a recreation room. Originated in Maine, the term 'sporting' conveys the idea of a gay life of drinking and carousing ... and 'camp,' being singular, gives the impression of a single building. I imagine that 'sporting' became part of the name," wrote Bud, "because guides call their fishermen and hunters 'sports.'"

Here's what I found in a 1952 Bangor and Aroostook Railroad publication, *In the Maine Woods*. "Maine probably has the finest sporting camp accommodations to be found anywhere in the nation. While some are remote, they are, nevertheless, completely equipped to provide every comfort and convenience. You'll find them in all regional frequented by good fishermen, and they are an unfailing sign that in their vicinity the fishing is excellent.

"The most striking feature of a sporting camp is the central lodge, usually built of logs. In this log lodge is a main dining room and a large recreation room. Almost invariably a huge open fireplace built of field stone is the central attraction in the recreation room. Here the fishermen gather after a hearty meal and discuss the day's experiences.

"Surrounding the main lodge are individual log cabins or cottages, where fishermen, singly or in groups, may enjoy comfort and privacy.

These cabins are equipped with modern plumbing and every convenience essential to good living. Here one can be himself and do as he likes.

"These sporting camps, no matter how remote, are reached relatively easily by auto or by boat from a point where a train or other conveyance drops you."

Then I considered Camp Phoenix, which began as a single two-story building with the kitchen and dining room on the first floor and lodging on the second floor. Cabins were added over the years, while meals were still served in the lodge. In 1970s, owners George and Beryl Emerson added kitchens to some cabins, recognizing that some guests could not afford the traditional American plan with all meals provided.

Should I include lodges that have no camps? I turned to Maine's Department of Health and Human Services that licenses sporting camps to see how the state defines them—and discovered many that are not sporting camps at all. Some offer only single uses from bear hunting to kids' music. And elsewhere I discovered sporting camps that are not licensed as sporting camps but are licensed in other categories, including as restaurants. In some ways this was a treasure hunt, because for weeks I was discovering more camps wherever I looked.

The Maine Sporting Camp Association was a great help. The Association reports that "most camps consist of a main lodge (which may or may not have guest rooms) and cabins. Some also offer primitive outpost cabins. Some camps offer running water and electricity while others offer a true camping experience with a bathhouse and gas lanterns. Most camps offer a variety of meal plans to suit the needs of their sports." Yes, one of my favorite sporting camps still has outhouses (but indoor showers).

Then I posted, in my "George's Outdoor News" blog on the website of the *Bangor Daily News*, an announcement that Down East Books had asked me to write this book, and invited readers to tell me about their favorite sporting camps. I got swamped! And discovered more camps that were not on my list.

Finally, knowing this could not be a hundred thousand word tome, I started to narrow down the list. Out went most of the camps serving only a single purpose, like bear hunting. Some I removed because they were old and in poor shape, or suffering from other problems. And then there was the sporting camp owner who said he didn't want to be in the book!

Finally, if a sporting camp owner would not complete my survey/inventory, so I could tell you what to expect there, I did not include that camp in this book. Meeting your expectations is critically important to any camp owner and to me! I don't want you to have a bad experience at a Maine sporting camp. I did, as a compromise, include a list of sporting camps at the end of the book that did not return my survey, with their website addresses, so you can check them out yourself. And please don't assume every Maine sporting camp is listed here, because I am sure there are some I missed, even though I spent a lot of time looking!

I was particularly delighted with some of the stories submitted by long-time guests or guides of some of these sporting camps, and thank those folks for writing and sharing those stories. I am sure you will enjoy their stories as much as I did. You will also notice that my wife Linda joined me in writing about some of the camps. We used those columns in our "Travelin' Maine(rs)" weekly columns in central Maine's daily newspapers. You can access those columns on my website, www.george smithmaine.com.

And I am pretty sure you will want to closely examine the inventory of information for each camp. I know it is very important that your expectations be met, so I have tried hard to tell you everything you need to know to make that happen.

Long Way Out

Be thankful it is so easy these days to get to a great Maine sporting camp. Here's an old story about one man's journey to Camp Phoenix, as told by Henry LaPointe, a camp guide.

"Henry related that he'd been to the mouth of the West Branch to meet a Boston shoe shop owner who was elderly. The trip took several days to the mouth of Nesowadnehunk Stream. From here they must walk the remainder of the journey. The elderly man would fall asleep each time the party stopped to rest.

"Night came and Mr. LaPointe stayed with him while the others proceeded. Mr. Daisey sent horses and a jumper to haul him in. The night they arrived in camp the old man died. Thus his guide needed to return over the same long route out."

What a way to go.

Conclusion

Maine has led the nation in conservation of our special places and critical wildlife habitat. Over the last thirty years, nearly 3.7 million acres have been conserved by direct purchases or conservation easements. Most of this land is in the more rural parts of the state, where many of my favorite sporting camps are located.

When you are enjoying our state, please keep in mind that Mainers have spent a lot of money to provide us with spectacular recreational opportunities, to protect the habitat of our favorite wild critters, and to make sure these special places are always available.

Your patronage of a Maine sporting camp will also help sustain another one of our special places. Catch some wild trout. Hunt grouse, ducks, deer, bear, or (if you are lucky enough to get a permit) moose. Hike the mountains and woods. Canoe and kayak the rivers and streams. Swim in the lakes. Gaze at the sea. Eat like kings. Leave your troubles behind. And stay long!

The Sporting Camps

Favorite Camps

Bradford Camps

Bradford Camps are historic and traditional, upgraded for the comfort of guests, with wonderful hosts and a huge area to hunt, hike, fish, kayak and canoe, and enjoy nature and the stunning scenery. And the food is great too! It's a bit of a drive, but you can opt to fly in, and once you get there, you will not want to leave.

Owners: Igor and Karen Sikorsky; 20 Trafton Lane, Kittery, ME 03904. PO Box 729, Ashland, ME 04732; www.bradfordcamps .com, maine@bradfordcamps.com; (207) 433-0660.

Directions: 50 miles in from North Maine Woods Ashland gate. Munsungan Lake off Pelletier Road. Seaplane base. GPS coordinates: N46° 23' 00"/W69° 00' 00". Realty Road west out of Ashland to Pinkham Road to Pelletier Road to Munsungan Lake Road. Gravel road. See website for detailed driving instructions.

Description: 8 guest cabins with kitchens and full bathrooms on the water, lodge with library/game room and dining room. The cabins and lodge are the only buildings on the lake. Camps were started in 1890 and have had continuous upgrades while maintaining the traditional atmosphere of a remote sporting camp.

Prices: Base price is $185/night; kids under 18 are $93/night. Boats and motors $65/day.

Meals: Provided, served family style.

Activities: Fishing, hunting, moose watching, canoeing, lots of special opportunities including a shooting school and courses in GPS orienteering and backwoods skills.

Other: Guides are available for $220–$270/day. Hunting and fishing licenses available. Phone service available but not Internet. Pets allowed only in October.

Season: Year-round.

BRADFORD CAMPS ARE A STATE TREASURE

The six-hour drive from my home to the camps went quickly, with my friend, long-time now-retired guide Gary Corson, in the passenger seat. We shared stories and talked about fishing issues all the way, with one stop at Dysart's in Hampden for a great breakfast.

As we drove into the yard at Bradford Camps, we stepped out of the vehicle and back in time. Log cabins dotted the shoreline, made from logs that were floated across the lake more 100 years ago. In all that time, the camps have had only five owners. Igor and Karen Sikorsky knew immediately, after searching the state for years, that these were the camps for them, and they've been providing the age-old sporting camp experience for twenty years.

Igor is well acquainted with the sporting camp experience because he started going to Cobb's Pierce Pond Camps when he was 10. Traditions are important at sporting camps. I loved Karen's story about the lodge's beautiful living room. She and Igor moved the furniture around and long-time guests objected!

On the wall of the lodge, I recognized the famous photo of Will Atkins with a canoe full of moose heads. Atkins built the original camps here in the 1800s. And while the camps retain the old, including the gorgeous log siding, they offer modern day comforts including full bathrooms in each cabin. Gaslights and instant hot water are nice features, too.

Our cabin 5 had two large bedrooms and a gathering room with a woodstove. The windows looked out on Munsungan Lake and the mountain beyond. Chad, who helped us move our gear into the cabin and has worked here for twenty years, already had a fire going and the cabin, on this cool rainy day, was nice and warm.

When we first arrived, we walked to the lodge where guests were eating lunch. Within ten minutes, we'd met and been welcomed by Igor, Karen, all the staff, and even all the guests! Yes, this is a welcoming place.

Neither Gary nor I was anxious to fish in the downpour (and I do have to confess that I am a fair weather angler these days), so we spent the afternoon in the lodge's beautiful living room. As I got acquainted with Igor and Karen, and shared stories with them and other guests who had either arrived that afternoon or returned to the camps after a day of fishing, I found the afternoon flying by. I especially enjoyed perusing their wonderful collection of old books and hearing stories about some of the mounts on the walls.

CHALLENGES

Igor and I talked about the challenges facing sporting camp owners these days. Finding staff is right at the top of the list and he told me a funny story about one fellow who applied for a job at the camps, emphasizing that, "I would be great because I love fishing!" You would be wrong if you think working at a sporting camp gives you a lot of time to fish. Igor and Karen had, up to the first week in June, fished just once this year, for two hours. Last year they fished for four hours, total.

We also talked about how they've had to add outdoor activities and special events to make up for the loss of the traditional deer hunting business. They once hosted fifty deer hunters each fall. Today, almost none. They do get a lot of bird hunters in the fall, are especially busy with bear hunters, and also host moose hunters, but their summers are now busy with families and special events, and they are fortunate to still be a major destination for anglers. Most of those return each year, often several times a year. Ninety percent or more of their guests have been here before. Forty percent of their guests are Maine residents. Karen explained that, "every two weeks is a new season here," and looking at their schedule of activities, I had to agree. There's a lot going on here!

Before we knew it, the dinner bell was ringing. Yes, they have the traditional dinner bell. Chef Tiffany, originally from Dexter and now living in Portland in the off-season, is a great cook. This far off the grid, and more than 50 miles from a grocery store, you have to be imaginative and she is all of that. All of our meals were great and my very favorite dish was her beef stroganoff.

With other guests at our dinner table the first night, we shared stories about loons grabbing our trout. I told my story about the bat that picked my fly right out of the air. I had to reel it in to release it. Both Gary and I had also caught ducks while fly fishing. Warden stories were interesting too, some good, some bad. By the time the dessert arrived—home-made vanilla ice cream with chocolate cookies and hot fudge sauce—well, I shouldn't have done it, but I not only ate every bit of it, I licked the bowl!

And just to show you how tuned in the staff is to your every need, they keep the meals hot for guests who arrive late from fishing. Callie, our server, was very friendly and helpful, and Hannah, the Sikorsky's God-daughter, who just graduated from college, was also on hand to tackle any and all jobs. Breakfasts here are awesome and they'll pack you a lunch so you can spend your day fishing, hunting, and enjoying the woods and waters.

Fishing

Igor is a pilot and flew Gary and me into Big Reed Pond for a day of very special day of fishing. About a third of their guests actually fly in to the camps. Jim Strang of Millinocket offers that service.

As Gary and I flew back from Big Reed that afternoon, Igor gave us a tour of the region, and I was astonished by how many remote ponds and flowages are available for fishing adventures. Gary has guided on all of them and he and Igor shared stories about each water as we flew over. Boy, did I want to jump out and try every one! Many are accessible by car, sometimes with a short hike after the drive. And Igor flies his guests into them for a day of fishing. He has canoes stashed at many and cabins available at some. It would take a lot of visits to fish them all, but I discovered, while talking to the anglers who were at the camps at that time, that they all have favorites.

Anglers here are lucky because they still have good fishing for our traditional fish: brook trout, lake trout, and landlocked salmon. Many of their best brook trout waters are on the state's Heritage List and protected, offering rare opportunities to fish for our native fish (Maine has 97 percent of the native brook trout left in the United States). Gary Corson—along with the Sportsman's Alliance of Maine when I served as the organization's executive director—led the campaign to win legislative approval for the initiative to name the brook trout as our Heritage Fish and protect them in 300 waters that have never been stocked and still hold native brook trout. The guests at Bradford were very clear about their desire to catch native and wild fish. They don't come all the way up here to catch stocked fish.

One such guest is David, who has hunted and fished all over the world, but Bradford Camps on Munsungan Lake is the only place he's returned to, and he often comes here several times a year. David told us he likes to hike into remote ponds and Igor gives him a radio to check in. David has a special affection for the guides here. And his voice got excited when he told me about the 23-inch trout he caught on his 3-wt. fly rod. I'd be excited too!

GUESTS

One thing I love about sporting camps is that you get to meet so many interesting people and always leave with new friends. David, for example, arrived just after us and joined us in the living room that afternoon, sharing micro-brews with me. I have to admit, despite my affinity for Maine micro-brews, David's All Day IPA session ale from Founders in Grand Rapids, Michigan, was very good. David first came to Bradford to hunt grouse and still does, telling me grouse hunting is amazing here. Eventually, he started coming here to fly fish (and he has fished in a lot of other places, including some of my favorites in Montana).

Gary and I got up at 5:30 a.m. each of the two mornings there, and were welcomed into the kitchen where coffee was ready and Igor, staff, and some guests were enjoying the early morning. I could get used to this!

While we were in the living room the first afternoon, a guest came in from fishing, very excited. He'd caught his biggest brook trout ever, with his new Orvis 5-wt. rod. Another guest told me he plans to bring his five grandchildren here. "It's a good place to introduce them to hunting and angling in a comfortable and safe place," he said.

I really enjoyed one guest's story about the time he was bird hunting here and lost his dog. Igor took off in his plane and searched for the dog that night. They put out a kennel and the dog's blanket near where he'd last been seen, and someone found the dog and put him in the kennel.

David had a great story about a friend who landed forty fish someplace (not here), but came out of the water at the end of the day covered in leeches. And I was captivated by his stories of grouse hunting here, when he rarely ever sees another hunter. "If you are willing to walk," he said, "there are endless covers." Karen likes to talk with all new guests, before they arrive, to make sure they know what to expect and that their expectations are met. A good policy, for sure.

Leaving

On our final morning, Igor gave me a tour of the cabins, his workshop, the new $6,000 generator, the saw mill, and the bridge he built across the brook so Brad Hall, their neighbor, could walk over to visit. Brad's father once owned the camps and we had a great visit with him that morning. I was very interested to discover that Brad has solar power at his camp. His apple trees, like Igor's and Karen's, were devastated by hungry moose.

The ice house was particularly interesting. Every winter, Igor and six to twelve friends come up to cut the ice and store it under sawdust in the ice house. They stay in one winterized cabin that even has hot water. One guy brings his own beef. They cook. They snowshoe. They snowmobile in. They cut the ice into large blocks and swing them into the ice house with a special contraption. They used to have to lift them in by hand and I guess that was pretty tough. I stuck my hands into the sawdust and felt the very cold ice, understanding that it lasts until the end of October.

I laughed when we entered Cabin 8, everyone's favorite, at the end of the line of cabins, and then noticed Cabin 1 next to it. While some of the cabins have been relocated, they kept the cabin numbers for guests who always want the same cabin for their visits here.

Behind Cabin 2, a big old pine was hit by lightning one night while everyone was at dinner. The lightning went into the ground and connected to the gas line under the cabin and the tree caught fire. It burned for about a half hour, when a guest ran to the lodge and told Igor, "You've got to come now!" He shut off the generator, cutting off the propane, and the fire went out.

So many great stories here. And I perked up when they started telling stories about Jerry Bard, who worked here for twenty-five years, but before that, worked at Camp Phoenix, where I now own a camp. After 100 years as a sporting camp, Camp Phoenix was turned into a condominium. It reminded me of how lucky we are to still have Bradford Camps and the few dozen other sporting camps that have been able to transition to this new day and economy, while maintaining such a wonderful and timeless tradition.

Claybrook Mountain Lodge

LINDA AND I ENJOYED A TERRIFIC WEEKEND OF BIRDING HERE, WHERE the guides and guests, and our hosts Greg and Pat Drummond, delivered an unforgettable experience. This is a lodge that is cherished by Mainers, located in the woods, surrounded by mountains, with meandering brooks, remote ponds, and yes, lots of birds!

Owners: Gregory and Patrice Drummond; 61 Howard Hill Road, Highland Plantation, ME 04961; www.claybrookmountainlodge .com; (207) 628-4681.

Directions: The lodge is 11 miles north of North New Portland in Maine's west central mountain region, on a gravel road .7 of a mile off the Long Falls Dam Road. Take Route 16 from North Anson toward Kingfield. Leave 16 and turn onto Long Falls Dam Road. After 10 miles watch for Old County Road on the left. Old County Road can be entered from the south end or the north end. The only turn off Old County Road is Howard Hill Road 1½ miles from the south end or ⅓ mile from the north end. The lodge is on 150 acres of woodland with free access to more. There are no gates or fees involved in getting here. GPS coordinates: N45° 03' 36"/W70° 04' 52".

Description: Claybrook Mountain Lodge was built in 1984 with the first few years open only as a hunting lodge. Eventually staying open through winters, our cross country ski trails took shape creating great skiing from the lodge door, perfect for family fun. On land bordering a beautiful trout stream, with other bodies of water nearby, the camps are open spring and summer for fishing as well as fall hunting. Many come to relax on the front porch and soak up the view overlooking foothills of Maine's western mountains while enjoying a day of hiking or paddling.

The lodge offers 6 bedrooms with 3 shared baths on two floors. A comfortable gathering room on the first floor has a soapstone woodstove for ambiance as well as being the primary heat source. Comfortable furniture, a wide variety of books and games as well as a second floor living room create a homey atmosphere.

Prices: The cost is $110/person for one night's lodging with three meals. Guide fee is $250/day and includes whatever vehicles are needed. Canoe rental is $30/day and includes paddles and life jackets.

Meals: Modified American plan. Enjoy wholesome meals prepared in the kitchen and served in the cozy dining room. They serve a hot breakfast, a packed lunch, and a home cooked four course dinner. The cookie jar is always available as well as coffee and tea. Pat calls her meals wholesome New England home cooking with a twist. She utilizes fresh local vegetables when available and much of the fare is organic. In summer they use as much as they can from their own garden. Eggs are from their own hens, and they accommodate special dietary needs.

Activities: Cross country skiing, birding, moose calling, hunting and fishing, hiking and biking, paddling flat water.

Other: Internet but no cell phone service. No pets. No minimum stay except on winter weekends.

Season: Open year round with the winter season the busiest at this time.

FAMILY FUN AT CLAYBROOK MOUNTAIN LODGE
George

It was a birding adventure we will never forget and not just because we identified ninety-eight species of birds. Claybrook Mountain Lodge in Highland Plantation offers comfort, adventure, and fabulous food, but it's the family atmosphere created by owner/hosts Greg and Pat Drummond that keeps bringing guests back year after year.

The weekend we were there, there was a couple from Litchfield with their two grandchildren, Corey and Elise. The couple has been coming here for twenty-five years. On their first trips, before the lodge was built, they stayed in Greg and Pat's home. Everyone there for the birding weekend was from Maine and judging from the guest book, this is a place cherished by Mainers.

When Greg and Pat Drummond built and opened the lodge next door to their home in 1984, their first guests were deer hunters. And for many years, the November deer season was their busiest. But things have changed. "The deer herd in our area has declined to such an extent that our (deer) season is the least profitable of the year," says Greg. So what is their busiest time of the year now, you ask? It's winter, when the lodge is full of cross country skiers and the Drummonds serve weekend lunches to traveling snowmobilers.

A few years ago the Drummonds turned Memorial Day weekend into a birding adventure, attracting so many guests that they added a second birding weekend. Greg, along with his friend Ron Joseph, a retired federal wildlife biologist, leads the birding weekend adventure. We traveled throughout the area, stunning in its beauty, and stopped here and there to hike and identify the amazing array of birds.

After our Friday night dinner, I told Pat, who does everything in the kitchen from cooking to dish washing, that we were changing the column to focus on "Claybrook Mountain Restaurant." Pat could cook for the finest restaurant in Portland. Her food, much of it made from scratch, is so good. And there is lots of it, including a bottomless cookie jar.

After a vigorous day of birding, I sat outside next to the wood fire on Saturday evening as Greg cooked onions and steaks on the grill. Ron passed by with a basket full of eggs from the chicken coop, reminding me that Pat had said at breakfast, "You couldn't have had a fresher egg!" Highlights of the meals for me were cream of fiddlehead soup (Greg picked the fiddleheads) and gazpacho, three-bean salad, strawberry rhubarb pie with ice cream, the steaks, lemon thyme roasted turkey, French toast (with homemade maple syrup), and Pat's breads and muffins. I even loved Pat's homemade yogurt.

At Friday night's dinner Corey had told us his sister Elise "is really good at birding. She's a walking encyclopedia." And boy, he got that right. Elise was superb at spotting and identifying birds.

The lodge has six comfortable bedrooms, three baths, a lovely living room, and a porch where we all hung out. We're hoping to return for their moose calling weekend in September.

Linda

Ron Joseph, one of Maine's well known birders, was there for a weekend of birding during the spring migration, so of course when George suggested this for a travel column, I quickly agreed. As we sat down to a gourmet dinner cooked by Pat on Friday night, we started to hear stories of the adventures everyone around the table had already experienced here.

"What was our total of birds last year, Ron?" asks one guest. "106," he replies. I looked at George and our eyebrows went up. "Well, we want to set a new record," another guest responded. Competitive birding. I love it. I knew this was going to be a weekend to remember.

Even though the lodge is located in Carrabasset Valley, and you can see the beautiful mountains as you travel through the rolling hills, this does not feel like the busy Sugarloaf area that is nearby. When we arrived we found an idyllic country yard, complete with chickens running about. Claybrook Mountain is a very homey and welcoming place. When we arrived Greg and George chatted for a while out on the deck. The car wasn't unpacked so I grabbed my binoculars and sat in one of the chairs on the deck with another birder. The yard was buzzing with activity where the apple tree is a favorite landing spot for migrating birds.

The meals here are extraordinary. Walking into the kitchen I saw loaves of oatmeal bread, baked fresh by Pat every day. Dinner is a four course event. On Friday night we enjoyed homemade fiddlehead soup (so delicious), with a gourmet salad, roasted thyme and lemon chicken, carrots and whipped potatoes. Although each of us was beyond full, we were served my favorite for dessert, fresh strawberry rhubarb pie with ice cream. We ate until we were more than full and were told we'd be walking to look for woodcock.

We were in for a treat as Ron started calling owls. Young Corey joined him. The response from barred owls was amazing, especially when they broke out in their "monkey call." We all complimented Corey on his calling.

Many of us got up early each morning to get in an hour of birding with Ron before breakfast. After breakfast we hit the road for a full day of birding. I peppered Ron with questions about certain calls and hope I retained a fraction of what he taught me.

As a collective group we saw or heard ninety-eight species of birds. I call that an amazing two day adventure. Great birding, super friendly people, incredible food, in a magical setting. No wonder Claybrook Lodge has huge numbers of repeat customers!

AN ANGLING STORY FOR THE AGES

Greg Drummond told one brief story on Saturday morning as we were driving along Back Road in Lexington Township. It was so good that I sat down with him the next morning and asked for the entire story with permission to share it with you. Here it is.

Granville Bond lived in Wellesley, Massachusetts, and had a son Norris and grandson Bill. Granville was over 6 feet tall and very strong. He lugged 100 pound sacks of grain as a teenager and ended up owning that business. His wife died in her mid-sixties and Granville was devastated.

He hardly left the house. But when he was seventy-nine, his friend Silas told him they needed to go fishing. Silas contacted Maine's Fish and Wildlife Department for recommendations, and they ended up at Cobb's Pierce Pond Camps, where Greg was a guide and Pat was the cook. "The day he arrived was one of the luckiest days of my life," Greg said.

Granville came to Cobb's every year until he was eighty-nine. One year he came late, not realizing the camps were closed, so Greg stayed on with him and guided him for four days. Granville had strong political views and often argued politics with Greg.

Granville like to fish Kilgour Pond, but it was a difficult one mile hike in to the pond, and Greg suggested he not try to make it, but Granville insisted, saying "This might be my last trip up here." He had to take his leg brace off in some places and fell several times, but they made it to the pond. Greg launched the canoe and paddled around the pond. At 4 p.m. on this hot sunny day, having caught no fish, Granville was clearly exhausted. "It's time to leave for dinner," Greg told him.

But Granville wanted to stay. "Will they be mad if we arrive late?" he asked. So they stayed. Greg says he had no hope of catching anything, but Granville hooked a big trout. Unfortunately when Granville turned one way and Greg paddled the other, Granville tugged at the fish and it broke off. Then he hooked a second nice trout and that too broke off.

Not long after that Greg anchored near the edge of a weed bed and Granville caught a trophy brookie. "It was at least five pounds," said Greg. It made a long run and plunged into the weeds. Granville played him well, for a long time, then started working him toward the canoe. When he got the fish close to the canoe, his line was blanketed with weeds and they couldn't see the fish. But Greg managed to get the weeds off the line and the fish rolled up and sideways. It was huge and beautiful.

Greg grabbed the net but when he moved to dip it into the water, the fish spooked and made a quick dash, breaking the line. The trout settled under the canoe, and they sat there watching it. Granville was devastated. It was the biggest trout he'd ever caught after a lifetime of fishing in Maine. He returned to Cobb's two more years and never caught anything close to a brookie that big.

Granville had asked his son Norris to come to Cobb's with him many times, but Norris didn't, until Granville got into his late eighties. Then he and Norris came twice a year, once with Granville's friend Silas.

When Granville died, Norris called Greg to let him know, and told Greg he wanted to bring his son, Bill, to show him his grandfather's favorite fishing spots. "When Bill arrived, before I even saw him" Greg told me, "I heard his grandfather's voice. Bill sounded exactly like Granville and was the mirror image of him too, tall and strong.

"I took Norris and Bill to three ponds and then into Kilgour," Greg says. And at Norris' urging, Greg told Bill his grandfather's fishing stories, particularly the one about the huge trout that got away. No fish were rising, so Greg paddled over to the shore near where Granville had caught his whopper, and put a size 16 Maribou streamer on Bill's fly line, telling him to let it sink to the bottom.

Almost immediately, Bill announced that he'd caught bottom. But the bottom was moving away, the rod was jumping, and Greg recognized right away that Bill had a good one on. And Bill landed that trout, 21 inches long, fat, and weighing exactly 5 pounds.

Norris said, "Man, I wish Dad was here to see this." And they all burst into tears.

Macannamac Camps

MACANNAMAC CAMPS ARE SPREAD OUT ON THREE REMOTE LAKES about fifty miles northwest of Millinocket and still offer great hunting and fishing. But they are also provide a wonderful vacation get-a-way, as Linda and I discovered in July of 2015.

Owners: Josie and Dave Allen; PO Box 598, Millinocket, ME 04462 (mailing address only); www.macannamac.com; (863) 203-9529.

Directions: In North Maine Woods (with gate fees), nearest town is Millinocket or Ashland. I-95 exit 244, left to Millinocket. Follow Baxter State Park signs through Millinocket. Follow Macannamac sign to Golden Road. Travel to Mile 28 and turn right onto Telos Road. Follow signs next 40 miles to Haymock Lake and Macannamac Camp office.

Description: 7 housekeeping camps and main lodge. Located on Haymock, Spider, and Cliff Lakes. Haymock Lake camps have full bathrooms. Spider and Cliff Lake camps have outhouses. Fully equipped kitchens, private lots, and docks. Haymock Lake Lodge has 3 bedrooms and baths. Fully furnished log home. Summer rental and full American plan in lodge in fall season. All camps are winterized with wood heat.

Prices: Spider and Cliff Lakes, 2 adults minimum, $99/night or $95/night for 5 or more nights. Groups 3–10 adults, $30–$44/

person/night. Full utility housekeeping at Haymock Lake, 2 adults minimum, $109/night or $105/night for 5 or more nights. Groups 3–10 adults, $40–$54/person/night. Kids no charge. Luxury Lodge on Haymock Lake, 2 adults minimum, $175/night with 3 night minimum stay. American plan or modified American plan available October and November. Two adults minimum $150/day; children ages 7–18, $50/day, under age 6 free.

Meals: American plan 3 meals/day in October and November only. Modified plan includes supper only.

Activities: Fishing, hunting, exploring, relaxing.

Other: Minimum stay of 2 nights at outpost camps. All housekeeping camps require 2 adults minimum, with 18 or younger free. No cell phone or Internet service. Pets allowed.

Season: Year-round.

A TRIP INTO THE NORTH WOODS IS RELAXING AND RESTORATIVE

George

Macannamac Camps in the north woods are relaxing and restorative, the idyllic Maine we talk about but rarely experience. Fifty miles northwest of Millinocket, Jack McPhee built most of his log cabins in the 1980s on Haymock, Spider, and Cliff Lakes. He was a warden pilot, knew every lake and pond in the north woods, and selected these for their remoteness and great hunting and fishing.

Today, they are still busy in the spring and early summer, with anglers, and in the fall, when hunters flock here seeking deer, moose, and grouse. Open all winter long, Macannamac is also popular with ice anglers and snowmobilers. Ironically, they are least busy in July and August, when we visited. If you are looking for a summer getaway in the real Maine, put these camps on your list!

Most of Macannamac's guests come every year, many with family members or hunting/fishing buddies. I don't doubt, now that Linda and I have visited, that we will become regulars here. For one thing, I want to stay in every one of their seven camps.

Imagine you are the only ones in a cabin on a beautiful remote lake at the end of a road. That would be their Cliff Lake cabin. Picture yourself here with a small campfire, roasting marshmallow, on the cliff at water's edge—the place where a young fellow once caught a 4 pound lake trout and, just before he lifted it up out of the water, had it grabbed by a huge laker that wouldn't give up his meal. The young fellow hauled them both up the cliff. Yes, lifetime memories are made here.

I am especially drawn to their Macannamac Camp, one of four camps spread out on Spider Lake. It's the first cabin Jack built, with a wall filled with deer and moose antlers, including the set of antlers from Jack's first deer, shot when he was ten years old. Over the years I've heard many fishing tales from this lake, and boy, do I want to fish here.

Of course, I am thinking about returning with the group of guys I bird hunt with each fall, to rent the lodge on Haymock Lake, a gorgeous and very large building with a huge living and dining room and beds for up to a dozen people. There are many remote roads and trails where you can hunt without ever encountering another hunter.

Josie McPhee, Jack's widow, kept the camps going for nearly two years after his death, with lots of help from family members, eventually marrying the local game warden, Dave Allen, who recently retired from that job. They are a great team, keeping the camps updated and immaculate. I honestly have never been in sporting camps as neat and clean as these.

There are a few things you need to know. There is no Internet or cell phone coverage here (yes, trust me, this is a good thing). They do have a satellite phone. There are full baths in the Haymock camps, outhouses in the others. Full kitchens are available in all camps, and Josie serves meals to the lodge guests in the fall if they wish. Judging by the dinner she served us, most lodge guests probably sign up for Josie's meals! It's a bit of a drive on gravel roads but not at all difficult. You will travel on the North Maine Woods roads, paying a fee at the gate for that privilege. And you will never, ever, be more relaxed than you are here.

Linda

For those of you who love secluded getaways, Macannamac Camps offers a little slice of heaven. You can stay in their main lodge with a large group, or choose from two other camps on this beautiful property where owners Dave Allen and Josie McPhee live year-round. Haymock One, where we stayed, is a nice big log cabin with two bedrooms, a large living space and kitchen, and a full bathroom. We spent a lot of time sitting on the covered deck which overlooks a pristine piece of woods of stunning birch trees with the lake just beyond.

You'll find a canoe for your use and a private dock for each of the camps here. But if you want secluded and remote, select their other camps. These outpost camps are right near the water and offer the quiet peacefulness one finds in the true North Woods.

I enjoyed the drive on the Golden Road and the Telos Road. At some point we crossed into territory I had never seen before. The dirt road was in good condition but I was glad to be in the Subaru and not my little car. We stopped for a picnic at the Cribworks on the west branch of the Penobscot River, enjoying lunch on the cliffs above the rapids and the view and sound of the rushing water. That five hour trip, much of it on those dirt roads, let me appreciate just how vast the northern part of our state is! The North Woods system covers three million acres, so we were barely in it. Holy cow!

A few of my favorite things here were the peace and quiet, the fresh, clean air, sounds of birds I rarely hear at home, stunning views, and a tour of the area graciously given by Josie. Oh, and a bed so comfortable that I was astonished to wake up after 7:30 a.m. Welcome to the North Woods; feel free to slow down and sleep in.

FROM THE CABIN IN THE BIRCHES
—by Josie McPhee, 2014

It happens every year. When the first late fall night brings the sound of complete quiet; the lake water is frozen, a blanket of snow has arrived, the wind abates, and the night falls. It is absolutely amazing how awesomely quiet it is. And it amazes me every year! Even though it always comes, always happens, that first time each year is as wonderful as all the other times. Life is good when the simple pleasures never become ordinary.

It has been twenty years since I have been here at Haymock Lake and working for Macannamac Camps. It simply doesn't seem that it could be possible. And yet, in thinking of all the work, fun, beauty and hardship which has filled those years, it makes the reality of the number of years seem more real.

Being here that long, and having done all that I have, and enjoying and enduring life's experiences in such a place, was something very unexpected, unplanned, and unparalleled to any thought of what I saw as the future for me. And it has been worth it.

Life is full of surprises—that is what I have often heard people say. I suppose there is truth to the phrase, but perhaps it is more that life is simply full of changes, adjustments which are placed in front of us where our choices on our life's path are made. The so-called "surprises" I feel are well thought out plans that are laid before us, and as we make our choices the story begins to unfold into a long tale.

Some of the surprises are bountiful gifts full of pleasure and memory makers, and there are others that are terribly hard to bear. Perhaps one has finally arrived when the recollection of them all are seen as precious spots along the way, treasured and appreciated for how each event shaped our lives.

I am blessed with good health and a body that can move freely without impediment to work and play, a family of wonderful people that I know are always there, and a treasure chest of friends near and far that care and give of themselves to me in friendship, and all of which, family and friends, are my precious spots along the way.

A GOOD DAY AT HAYMOCK LAKE
—by Josie McPhee

It was a beautiful October day and I had settled in at our Haymock Lake office to greet arriving grouse hunting groups. One was an older gentleman and his son who had come to camp for the prior three seasons to hunt partridge. They were pleasant men, always giving high praise regarding the camps and the beauty of the land in the north Maine woods.

They pulled in by mid-afternoon for their three night stay at one of our camps on Spider Lake. After enjoying the report of their trip from their downeast home, I began the process of checking them in; writing out the receipt, giving them the camp lock combination, and validating their North Maine Woods vehicle permit.

While doing this, I asked if they wanted me to go ahead and write in their reservation for the next year. A silence filled the room, and I could see as I searched their faces of all but sheepish expressions that something was amiss. I quickly broke the silence by saying perhaps they had not planned to return the following fall.

The older gentleman, with a somewhat hanging head, conveyed to me they wouldn't be back, though they had greatly enjoyed their time at Macannamac. He went on to share the fact they had purchased a camp of their own.

I don't believe they were expecting my excited and joyous reaction! The next several minutes of conversation were full of how happy I was for them and there was nothing like having a camp of your own. I inquired about its location, and they shared that though it was not on a water source, it was a wonderful woods camp in an excellent grouse hunting area closer to their home. I told them about my personal camp in downeast Maine and how I loved it there as well.

By the end of our conversation they were far more relaxed. We returned to finishing the check-in process and transaction of payment for their stay. They paid in cash and placed it on the office desk. Before leaving, the older gentleman took a Macannamac business card which has the standard information on the front, and on the back is a reference to a scholarship fund which sends kids to conservation school sponsored by a local fish and game club. The members of the club had honored my late husband, Jack McPhee, by naming the scholarship fund for him.

As we walked out to their vehicle, I thanked them for coming again and expressed my joy for them and their camp purchase. Then they were on their way, traveling the final 13 miles to Spider Lake to enjoy a few days of grouse hunting.

I stepped back into the office, picked up the carbon copy receipt and cash, folded it up and placed it in the desk drawer. I returned to my tasks of the day and tending the office. By day's end, everyone due to arrive had checked through and I gathered the receipts from the desk drawer. Everyone had paid with a personal check except the older gentleman and his son. When inspecting the cash they'd left in payment, I discovered they had overpaid by $30.

Instead of all twenty dollar bills that would have made the payment accurate, one was a fifty dollar bill. I was absolutely mortified. How could I have been so careless, so unprofessional as to not have double checked their payment while they were in the office? My mind quickly went back to the excited conversation we had about their new camp and how I had failed to pay attention to verifying their payment. My mind raced—what if they discovered the missing fifty dollar bill? Would they think they had lost it? Even worse, would they realize they left it in their payment to Macannamac and I hadn't corrected the error?

I desperately needed to correct my mistake. Yet the demands of the following day wouldn't allow me to leave the office. I hoped perhaps they would stop by during the day while out hunting, and I would be able to right the wrong.

The following day came and went and I lived in anxiety. The next morning I took myself and the $30 to Spider Lake. Sure enough, they were not in camp. I wrote a note of apology, placed it in an envelope with their money, and left it in the door jamb of the camp. I could only hope they would receive my written apology as a sincere one.

The next day was their departure day. I thought of them pulling out of Spider Lake camp probably for the last time, and hoped they knew how I appreciated their presence at camp for four consecutive years. In the late morning, my English setter gave the alarm that someone had driven in the office driveway. As I approached, I could see it was the older gentleman's vehicle and my heart sank. I thought, no one ever stops in on their way home, ever! I was sure there was going to be a problem, and I couldn't blame them. The son was at the vehicle and I immediately asked if they had found the envelope. He said yes and that his dad was inside the office.

I walked in, spoke a quick greeting, and began to apologize for my neglect. Then I looked down at the gentleman's hands. There was the $30 and the business card he had taken three days before, with the scholarship information facing up. He looked at me with tender eyes and said, "You take this and give it to the folks that send kids to conservation school, in Jack's name."

I can't begin to express the feelings that flowed through me at that moment. Here stood a man I had had brief encounters with the past four years, and he took my mistake and gave it back to the Jack McPhee Conservation School Scholarship Fund. I know he saw the relief in my face and the appreciation in my eyes that flooded with tears.

As they drove away heading for home, I realized how goodness in people can manifest itself in countless ways, but the acts of kindness which arise from a merciful heart are the absolute best of all.

Libby Camps

LIBBY'S IS AN AWARD WINNING ORVIS ENDORSED LODGE IN BOTH FLY fishing and wing shooting magazines. This commitment to service and conservation has been recognized with Libby's receiving the 2006-2007 Orvis Endorsed Lodge of the year and the 2010 Maine Tourism Hall of Fame award, as well as being featured as one of the greatest fishing and hunting lodges in North America in numerous books and magazines. The camps have been owned for 125 years by the Libby family, now in the fifth generation.

Owners: Matt and Jess Libby; PO Box 810, Ashland, ME 04732; www.libbycamps.com; (207) 435-8274.

Directions: Located 45 miles southwest of Ashland, just north of Baxter State Park. Access via the Oxbow road through the Oxbow NMW checkpoint. From I-95: Take exit 264 and go north on Route 11 for 46 miles. Take a left onto the Oxbow Road, and follow for 12 miles where you come to the NMW checkpoint. Bear right after the checkpoint and follow Oxbow Road for 17 miles, Libby's driveway is on the left. GPS coordinates: N46° 18' 26"/W68° 50' 35".

Description: 10 guest cabins spread out on Millinocket Lake around the main lodge where everyone congregates for meals. Full bathrooms in each camp. Cabins built from 1890 to 2015.

Prices: Fishing: lodging $225/person/night, guide $300/day, seaplane fly outs from $170/person/flight.

Upland Hunting: $300/person/night guide with dog $470 per day. Bear: $2,200/person/week all inclusive; Moose: $1,750/person lodging, $2,800/person fully guided, $4,650/person VIP includes extra pre-scouting and flight time; Deer: $1,150/person unguided, $2,050/person guided per week. All prices per week.

Meals: All meals provided in the main lodge. Breakfast is order what you like, lunch is sandwiches packed for the day, supper is served family style.

Other: 2-night minimum during fishing season, 3-night minimum for upland. Internet service but no cell phone service. Pets allowed.

Season: May 15–September 30 for fishing, October 1–November 15 for upland birds, November for deer, January 17–March 15 for snowmobiling.

THE ULTIMATE OUTDOOR EXPERIENCE
—by Matt Dunlap, Maine Secretary of State

The first time I went to Libby Camps north of Baxter State Park, I didn't realize how far off the beaten path it was until the post-dinner fellowship had given way to the shroud of night and the call of sleep before a few days of bird hunting and trout fishing.

We finally stopped telling stories to let the night enfold us, and lying in bed under a pile of quilts, the silence was striking. Nothing. No street noise, no electrical appliances, no far-off neighbor's dog barking at a skunk in the trash. Just deep, cavernous quiet.

It's a part of the outdoor experience I don't take for granted. I remember bear hunting one fall, and while sitting in a tree stand waiting for something to happen, pulling out my smart phone and whiling away some time responding to a few emails. After a couple of hours, it dawned on me that I was virtually sitting at my desk—albeit 20 feet in the air.

Since that realization, I drink in the quiet of the outdoors. It's restorative in many aspects of the human experience, and while I'm lucky in that it's fairly accessible to me as a roustabout Maine sportsman, I consider the camp fees at Libby Camps to be a strong bargain, given the experience you get. Matt Libby and his wife Ellen run the camps now, but they're grooming the next generation to take them over in a few years, as has been the family tradition going back many decades. (Since this has been written Matt and Ellen's son Matt and his wife Jess have taken ownership of Libby Camps while Matt and Ellen own and manage the outlying camps.)

Standing on the threshold of the primal boreal forest, the sportsman has plenty to drink in while there. My personal favorites, aside from the fantastic hunting and fishing, are counted in the myriad small things. "What kind of sandwich would you like for your lunch?" Ellen asked me my first morning. I looked over the list of what she could do, and the roasted turkey—not a cold-cut, processed turkey sandwich, but cooked at camp—and homemade cranberry jelly sandwich with cheese still warms my heart all these years later.

It's hard to go wrong when bird hunting with a guide in northern Maine. Don Kleiner, a former president of the Maine Professional Guides Association with whom I shared lunch while sitting on a wind-blown hemlock tree near where we'd spend the afternoon fishing, mentioned to me he'd be doing some guiding at Libby's one fall. That sparked a plan in my head.

I like to hire a guide once in a while. While I like to think of myself as a seasoned outdoorsman, hiring a guide affords me the opportunity to learn new tricks and techniques about hunting and fishing—plus I get to support an industry I care a lot about. Making a full-blown excursion out of it and going to a sporting camp had never occurred to me before, and I had hunted and fished with Don enough to become a big fan of his guiding skills. After a couple of conversations, I booked a trip for the first week of October.

The seasons of Maine are kind to the sportsman. There's something to do practically every day in the woods and on our waters, which are still as primal today as they have been since the retreat of the last glacial ice around 10,000 years ago. Northern Maine is famous for its hunting and fishing, and for the bird hunter in the early season, there are opportunities to do both. That's what I got to do.

We spent our mornings hunting upland birds, where I had ample opportunity to disgust the dogs with my poor wing shooting. I didn't blame them for expecting more of me for their hard work, but when you don't put in the time on a skeet range for a few years, you learn to enjoy the more esoteric aspects of hunting, like the sheer adventure of it. But Don and I had lots of laughs.

At Don's advice, I had brought my fly rod, and we spent our afternoons in a series of canoes, flipping Muddler minnows for aggressive brook trout. It was so much fun, I decided to take advantage of Matt's Orvis dealership and equip myself with another world-class fly rod and reel. I've used it many times in the years since I bought it on a whim, and every time I take it out of the case and fight a trout or salmon with it, I'm pleased yet again for the impulse of that moment.

Our evenings were punctuated with the pleasant camaraderie of dinner, when the other hunters and anglers sat in the dining room regaling each other with the day's adventures. We all came from different places and walks of life, and all walked lightly after shedding the burdens of our workdays. In the dining hall, we could just be sportsmen. And there's so much relief in that. Ellen's cooking didn't slow the good feelings down, either.

But later into the evening, when it was nearing time to bed down, I would stand on the porch of my cabin and just listen. Occasionally, there would be the far-off warble of a loon, or some other creature of the night. But overwhelmingly, it was quiet. The quiet of the wild is restorative to the soul, a reminder that cell phones, computers, and phone messages only take away, they never fulfill. Nothing can fulfill the soul like a hunting and fishing trip in far, wild Maine, and no one can hold the door open for that adventure like Libby Camps.

Outpost Camps

Owners: Matt and Ellen Libby; 197 Haystack Road, Castle Hill, ME 04757; www.libbyoutpost.com; (207) 551-8292.

Directions: 10 locations on remote lakes and rivers within the North Maine Woods (road fees apply), all located from the northern boundary of Baxter State Park to the Reality Road, west of Oxbow to the Allagash Wilderness Waterway. All accessed on private gravel roads or by seaplane.

Description: All outpost cabins are log constructed located on a lake, pond, or river. Cabin ages range from 5 to 80 years. Fully equipped housekeeping cabins with outhouses.

Prices: Range from $30 to $125/person/night depending on nights and number of people.

Meals: Kitchens available in all camps.

Other: No cell phone or Internet service. Pets allowed. 2-night minimum.

Season: Year-round.

Appalachian Mountain Club Camps

GORMAN CHAIRBACK LODGE AND CABINS

THE APPALACHIAN MOUNTAIN CLUB OWNS MORE THAN 70,000 ACRES just east of Greenville, and has invested heavily to upgrade the traditional sporting camps there. They are now in the process of upgrading their third camp, Medawisla Wilderness Lodge. Linda and I enjoyed a winter trip to Gorman Chairback, and I took retired fisheries biologist John Boland to Little Lyford for a fall fishing trip.

Directions: These directions take you to Gorman Chairback, and to reach Little Lyford, just keep going. *Road Conditions:* The access roads to AMC's Maine Wilderness Lodges are dirt logging roads subject to the impacts of wet weather conditions, particularly during early spring and late fall. Please note that until road grading occurs in these regions, conditions are rough and may not be passable in cars with low ground clearance. For up-to-date information, contact AMC Reservations or the AMC Greenville Office.

Summer Directions to Gorman Chairback: Located approximately 20 miles east of Greenville and 15 miles west of Route 11 outside of Brownville. Limit your speed to 25 mph and yield to logging trucks. There is no fuel available once you leave the state highways. Call in advance for road conditions during spring, fall, or when storms are expected. Allow 6 hours driving time if driving from the Boston area, 9 hours from the greater NYC area.

From the west via Greenville: Take I-95 north to exit 157 (old 39) at Newport, Route 7 north to Dexter, Route 23 north to Guilford, then Route 15 North to Greenville. At the traffic light in the center of Greenville, proceed north one block and turn right onto Pleasant Street. After 2 miles the road becomes gravel. Eleven miles from Greenville, stop and register at the Hedgehog checkpoint. Proceed 1.8 miles farther, turn right at the T intersection and continue on the KI road. Continue 3.5 miles and turn right onto the Chairback Mountain Road. Continue for 1.3 miles and turn right onto the Gorman Chairback Lodge and Cabins driveway, which will lead you directly to the facility.

From the east via Brownville: Approach the KI (Katahdin Ironworks) Road on Route 11 either southbound from Millinocket (26 miles) or northbound from Milo (12 miles). To get to Milo from the south, take I-95 north to exit 199 (old 53) at Old Town. Continue north on Route 16 to Milo, then take Route 11 north toward Brownville. **Note:** *Signage for the Katahdin Ironworks Historic Site (KIW) may be missing, so check your mileage.* Turn west onto the KI Road. The KI checkpoint is 6.3 miles from Route 11. Stop and register. From the gate drive 7.3 miles. Turn left on the Chairback Mountain Road. Continue for 1.3 miles and turn right onto the Gorman Chairback Lodge and Cabins driveway, which will lead you directly to the facility.

Winter Directions to Gorman Chairback: It is not possible to drive directly to Gorman Chairback Lodge and Cabins in the winter and access will be "ski-in" from the Winter Parking Lot. Ski-in access is 8.3 miles via the Trout Pond/Long Pond trail or 7.3 miles via the road/Gorman Lodge trail. Snowmobile transportation from the Winter Parking Lot to Gorman Chairback is available at extra cost. Advance reservation for the exact number of people requiring transportation is required and may be arranged with the AMC Reservations office. Personal snowmobiles cannot be accommodated at Gorman Chairback. When you arrive at the Winter Parking Lot, look for the gear sheds. You will need to drop off and tag your gear so it can be picked up and delivered to your destination.

Cabins: 4 private cabins (one ADA accessible) with private bath. Each includes a combination of queen, bunk beds, and futon. New, private cabins opened in 2011. 8 private shoreline cabins with shared bath sleeping 1 to 5 people, with combination of queen, full, and bunk beds. Each cabin has a woodstove and gas lamps. There is no running water in the old cabins; water jugs are provided for guests to take to their cabins. Nineteenth-century cabins, refurbished in 2010. Separate bunkhouse can accommodate 10 guests. Composting toilets, hot showers, sinks and sauna are available in the lodge. Linens provided include pillow, sheets, and towels. Please note linens are not provided in the bunkhouse. Please bring your own beach towels to use at the beach. Home cooked dinner, breakfast, and trail lunch included in lodging packages.

Prices: Rates vary. Check website.

Meals: Dinner served family style at 6 p.m. sharp, includes soup, salad, entrée, dessert. Breakfast served family style at 8 a.m. sharp. Lunch: made-to-order trail lunches are served after breakfast. Beer and wine available for purchase.

Activities: Fly-fishing for wild brook trout, canoeing, hiking, wildlife-watching; cross-country skiing and snowshoeing in winter.

Other: For AMC lodging guests, the KI Jo-Mary Forest gate fee is included in their reservation. Otherwise: May–October, gate fees are resident day pass, $7; non-resident day pass, $12; camping, $10. No pets. No Internet or cell phone service.

Season: January 1–March 15, May 14–October 25, December 28–December 31. Closed at other times.

The Travelin Maine(rs) Enjoy Winter Adventure

A group of mostly nonresidents were enjoying a spectacular L.L. Bean Discovery School adventure when we arrived at the Appalachian Mountain Club's Gorman Chairback Camps 13 miles east of Greenville. This is high-end comfort at reasonable prices, just the type of adventure that many of today's travelers seek. Good food, historic camps in the heart of the 100-mile wilderness. We rented cross-country skiing equipment from Northwoods Outfitters in Greenville before arriving at the camps on a Friday night in March. It was a weekend to savor and remember—until we return for a summer adventure!

Linda

When George said he'd like to stay at the Appalachian Mountain Club camps I was intrigued. When he went on to explain these are very comfortable camps, I was excited. But when he said people ski into and out of these camps, I was a bit panicked.

We used to cross country ski when the kids were young, mostly on Mount Vernon's snowmobile trails. Then thanks to Coach Steve DeAngelis and the Maranacook cross-country ski team, our kids, Josh and Hilary, learned how to ski. George kept up with them for a while (until they left him far behind). I, on the other hand, continued to shuffle along on my skis and soon felt like a grandma far before my time! I decided I liked snowshoeing much more and my skis gathered a decade of dust.

My old skis with the three-pinned bindings now stand out as antiques. I couldn't even locate my poles and ski boots. So George reserved appropriate equipment for me in Greenville at Northwoods Outfitters. I credit those top-of-the-line skis and boots with my success in skiing that weekend for sure! After such a mild winter, it was great to see the perfect winter scene at Gorman Chairback. The older sporting camps sit on the edge of Long Lake, while four new camps are located just in back of them.

The Discovery School participants, some who had never skied or snowshoed before, were in good hands. What a great way to have a winter adventure! Learn how to snowshoe and ski, visit a spectacularly beautiful area of the state, stay in comfortable camps, and have somebody cook for you for the weekend!

Our weekend was full of exercise. Knowing that I needed to practice skiing (so that I could actually make the six mile ski-out), we found the well-groomed trails just beautiful. We didn't break any speed records due to the breathtaking mountain views, and the fact George had to stop to examine every animal track, but it was so much fun. After enjoying our bagged lunch back at camp, we went snowshoeing.

Everyone had spent a busy day like that, and I don't think I've ever witnessed such thankful diners as those in the lodge that night. We indulged in a turkey dinner that will live in my memory for a long time. We were starving and the chef must have known it. Platters of turkey, potatoes, fresh green beans and carrots, and the best cornbread stuffing I've ever eaten.

After a hearty breakfast Sunday morning we struck out on the epic ski back to the winter parking lot. I was a bit worried that my knee wouldn't hold up but it did, and I remembered how much I loved being out on those snowy trails in the woods. It was spring skiing that day—warm and absolutely perfect. And though I certainly felt it the next day, I knew I'd welcome the chance to do it again.

George

I didn't think we'd get to breakfast on our first morning because the ground in front of the beautiful $2 million lodge was covered with colorful White-winged Crossbills, birds we hadn't seen all summer, and Linda insisted on watching and photographing them as my stomach grumbled. The food here is definitely worth waiting for. Served family style at breakfast and dinner, there was plenty for all. They pack lunches for you to enjoy wherever your daily adventure takes you.

Folks gather in front of a fire prior to meals—giving us a good chance to meet and visit with others including a nurse from Portland, L.L. Bean guides from Bath and Monson, a family with teenagers from Cape Cod, a senior citizen from Boston, a Maine couple with a camp nearby in Brownville (their second visit here in a month), and the very friendly staff. This place offers outdoor opportunities without regard to your experience or expertise.

As darkness settled in on Friday night, we drove the 13 miles from Greenville to the Gorman-Chairback winter parking lot (in the summer you can drive right to the camps). From there we were transported in a coach behind a snowmobile—a rather wild ride. They prefer that you ski in, but we were unable to arrive in time to do that.

On Saturday we skied above the lake in the morning, enjoying stunning views, and snowshoed along the enchanting Henderson Creek in the afternoon. We opted for one of the new camps that included indoor plumbing. The less expensive older camps are also comfortable, but you must trudge to the lodge for toilets and showers. Been there. Done that for many years. We're into pampering now.

In addition to the above, here's what I loved: the toasty warm cabin on our arrival—thanks to the fire the staff had started for us. The smell of the pine walls, my feet up while reading on the couch, beating Lin at cribbage, the view across the lake toward the mountains, the amazing breakfast frittata in a huge cast-iron fry pan, the old fishing photos on the walls (anglers really dressed up to fish in those days! And caught huge fish!).

On Sunday, we skied 6 miles to our Subaru (our longest ski ever), and then enjoyed the mud run the rest of the way to Greenville. The next day, almost a month early, AMC closed their camps because the roads were breaking up. It was a carefree in-the-woods weekend of relaxation, outdoor exercise, great meals, and a comfortable cabin—with just one problem. It went too quickly!

LITTLE LYFORD LODGE AND CABINS

I visited Little Lyford Camps in October of 2012 to catch native brook trout. But I need to go back to shoot grouse. John Boland, who retired that year as the Director of DIF and W's Fisheries and Wildlife Divisions, joined me for the angling adventure at AMC's Little Lyford Camps in the middle of AMC's 70,000 acre wilderness east of Greenville. The small trout ponds that are spread all over AMC's property are real treasures and well managed.

AMC has canoes stashed on all the ponds, and John and I picked out a pond at the foot of a mountain, hiked in, and enjoyed a memorable day of non-stop catching. Many of the trout bore their gorgeous fall spawning colors. Most were caught on or just under the surface, on floating line.

You might think that the camps of the Appalachian Mountain Club would be full of hikers, but this week, nearly everyone at Little Lyford was there to fish. Some had been fishing here for many years—although I didn't run into anyone who'd visited here the first year the camps were built: 1874. Understandable, really. I especially enjoyed meeting and visiting with Joe Cross, whose father Ruel was one of my all-time favorite legislators—back in the good old days when serving in and lobbying at the legislature was fun.

Every angler at the camps was eager to give us tips on where and how to fish, as was AMC's professional staff, and we appreciated that. John started his fisheries career in this region, so it was fun to hear his stories about some of these waters. Our cabin was rustic and comfortable, with an indoor faucet and woodstove, and an outhouse a short distance away. The camps also have a nice bathhouse and a very nice lodge where they serve exceptional meals. When AMC acquired the camps, I sharply criticized the group for eliminating opportunities to hunt with dogs. In fact, Pat Keliher, now Maine's Marine Resources Commissioner, was the first to alert me to this fact. Pat and some friends had planned to do some bird hunting out of Little Lyford Camps, but were informed that they could not bring their dogs. They canceled their trip.

In 2012, AMC reversed course and welcomed dogs to Little Lyford throughout the fall hunting season. This will be a fantastic place to hunt grouse and woodcock, away from the road hunters that dominate the sport in northern Maine. There are lots of side roads and trails where grouse hunters can enjoy this sport with their friends and dogs. I've gotta go back!

Cobb's Pierce Pond Camps

COBB'S PIERCE POND CAMPS IS A VERY TRADITIONAL SPORTING CAMP, remote, yet easily accessible. The last six miles are on a well-maintained gravel road, to a manned gate. The last bit of your trip will be by boat from the Lindsay Cove landing. This allows the camps to maintain the rustic, remote, wilderness experience for its guests—the same experience enjoyed there since the camps were built in 1904. The very friendly and hospitable Cobb family has owned and operated the camps since 1958.

Owners: Gary and Betty Cobb; PO Box 124, New Portland, ME 04961; (207) 628-2819 (summer), (207) 628-3612 (winter).

Directions: From North New Portland, take Long Falls Dam Road for 23.3 miles. Turn right onto gravel road, travel 2.5 miles to next intersection, turn right, go 1.2 miles, and turn left. Follow signs to the gate.

Description: 12 cabins, each accommodating 2–6 guests, with electricity (until 10 p.m.), screened porches, wood-burning heat, and complete bathroom. Includes full maid service.

Prices: $130/person/day, $240/couple/day, $770/person/week, $1,410/couple/week; children 3–12, $45, 13–16, $75. 10% discount for families during July and August.

Meals: All meals are served in the lodge.

Activities: Most guests fish; others kayak, canoe, swim, and hike.

Other: Dogs allowed for $20/day; boats and motors available for rent. No cell or Internet service. Guests may bring their own wine, beer, and alcohol.

Season: If the ice is out, they open on May 1. The last day of fishing is September 30, when they close.

PIERCE POND AND ME
—by David Peppard, retired Maine game warden

Thanks to Greg Drummond I was introduced to Pierce Pond in August 1979. Greg knew how much I liked to fish and hunt and because of that, he called several times prior to 1979 to tell me, "You need to come see this place and what it has to offer." So in August of 1979 I took the family to Cobb's Camps for my first trip to the area. Little did I know that the trip would lead to hundreds of trips over the next thirty years.

Upon arriving at the camps we were greeted by Greg and Pat, Floyd and Maudie, and Gary and Betty. I immediately knew that this place and the people needed to operate it would become a bigger part of my life. The next day Greg toured me around the three Pierce ponds and then it was off to Kilgore. It was a sunny, hot August day, a day I thought would not produce fish. I had a nice trout on that came off right at the surface and Greg landed and released a three-plus pound trout. After two or three hours we left Kilgore and hiked to Grass Pond.

Greg rowed me around while telling of fish he had boated there over the years. While talking I had a huge hit and a nice fish on for about thirty seconds. The hook wasn't set very well in the fish but the hook was set remarkably well in me! As we started out the trail I looked over my shoulder to the pond and said to myself, "I will be back."

The next four years I went to Pierce Pond for the last week of September fishing and later to help with ice cutting. During the September trip in 1983, Gary mentioned that I ought to think about getting my guide's license. He said that if I did, he could probably line me up with a sport or two. Having had my guide's license in the early 70s, I took his advice and renewed my license. In August of 1984 Gary called and asked if I was interested in guiding the last week of September. I said absolutely! And that was the start of an adventure that continues to this day.

I arrived at Cobb's eager to begin guiding. Gary advised that all my sport would need is for me to take him where he wanted to go. I would not have to give advice on how to fish, or what fly or lure to use. So, who is the sport," I asked? "Vic Staknis," responded Gary. I spent the week with Vic, who caught his share of fish. We fished the main ponds, Kilgore, Grass, and Pickerel. Conversation was minimal but what he taught me about fishing was very beneficial. I guided Vic many times after that and enjoyed every trip.

Over the next five years I guided a week in May, a week in June, and the last week of September. In 1987 Greg helped me build my laker and I vividly remember launching it in Lindsay Cove for the first time. There is sat on the water, glistening, beautiful, not a scratch. I motored across from Lindsay and pulled up to the main dock at Cobb's. Gary was standing there awaiting my arrival and walked over to check out the new craft. He remarked that it looked very nice and he supposed he could deal with the clear fiberglass instead of a painted green one.

Along came 1989 and little did I know my guiding career would dramatically change. Gary had advised me he had a new sport for me for the last week of September. That sport turned out to be Mike Scott. He showed up on the dock the first morning with an old 8½ foot fiberglass rod, a floating line that wouldn't float, and a little plastic box containing a dozen or so reject flies. The equipment had been supplied by a "friend."

On the first trip, Mike's fly fishing abilities were quite limited. However, over the years he has improved his equipment and technique. I have guided him every year since 1989, some years two or three trips a year. Over the years we have become really good friends and he has taught me a lot about fishing. I hope I've also taught him a thing or two. I have to add that Mike possesses unbelievable patience and enjoys a challenge.

I've watched him cast a sinking line all day long and not get a hit but at the end of the day, reeling in his line, he'll turn to me and say, "Great day!" I see many more trips in our future.

Since 2000 I have spent considerably more time guiding. I'm on the water most of May and June and the last week or ten days of September. Paul Miles and Don White are regulars and Paul's favorite saying, when with me, is "Protect the fish, hire a guide." Some really fun times are when you are with a large party like the Whitings and the Podkaminers.

It's fun and interesting to talk to different generations and discover what their outlook is on Pierce Pond, Cobb's Camps, and life in general. The Whitings are a great group. Tim Sr. and Anne are fairly low maintenance, especially Anne. Now when it comes to Bruce, Tim Jr., and Steve Whiting, that's when a referee is needed! Ha! I still need to find Anne a board trout to make up for the one she lost several years ago while I was guiding her. We talk about that fish every year.

I could go on and on with all kinds of stories—like when Bob Gibbs got hit in the head with my bow anchor—or when returning to camp one late afternoon and encountering 4 foot waves and swells, with Woody in the bow—or when Paul S. fell out of my boat while trying to dislodge the bow anchor in the thoroughfare on May 1—or when during the first week of May, fishing all day in a snowstorm on Grass Pond with Mike S.—or removing hooks from various people including myself.

2014 was my thirty-first year of guiding at Pierce Pond and I plan on guiding there as long as I am able—hopefully many more years.

Written with special thanks to Betty and Gary for giving me this opportunity to guide and be a part of Cobb's Pierce Pond Camps. It's a privilege and an honor—and also a lot of fun!

The Best Week of the Year
—by Liva Pierce (15 years old)

I have been going to Pierce Pond for fifteen years and I have no idea how to cast a line or load a rifle. Nor does my family, nor our friends, the Paternitis, who venture to the pond the same week in July.

For fifteen years we've been coming to Pierce Pond to experience this hunting and fishing camp as everything but a hunting and fishing camp. We use the boats not as vehicles for capturing that night's dinner, but as a leisurely mode of transportation that takes us from island to island. Once we arrive at our desired spot, we spend the rest of the day frolicking in as many ways as possible.

This may mean island exploration, reading, playing cards, or fort building. As soon as noon strikes (and usually earlier), we excitedly break open the cooler to find delectable sandwiches and heavenly cookies, for we are ravenous after a whole morning of play. Lunch is followed by more merrymaking both on water and on land, everything from Island Olympics and talent shows to malicious cookie thievery and ambitiously long swims until—to the children's dismay—cocktail hour emerges.

This holy time of day urges the adults into action and spurs the packing up and departure process. We ride home in our grand laker and arrive with just enough time to shower and maybe a sip of ginger ale before dinner. After dinner activities include, but are not limited to, baseball, manhunt, capture the flag, charades, and if we are lucky, a S'mores fest for all the kids in camp hosted by the legendary Fred himself. These jam-packed days are enough to put a person of any age to bed by 9 p.m.

And that's how I have spent one week every summer since I was so small that I couldn't swim without a floatie's assistance. No camping, no hunting, no fishing, just a blissful break from the real world for a short week once a year. We are aware that our preferences may seem blasphemous to other Pierce Ponders, but we would not have it any other way.

THE BIG RED BELL
—by Jeannie Merchant

Every traditional Maine sporting camp has a means to beckon their guests to the dining room for mealtime. One method some remote camps use is a striker on a steel musical triangle to produce varying sounds. Another method is the usage of bells of all shapes and sizes. The striking of the triangle or ringing of the bell confirms what your body has been telling you, that "It's time to eat!"

At Cobb's Pierce Pond Camps guests wait for the ringing of the Big Red Bell to head to the dining room. The Red Bell has been calling sports and guides to meals for many decades. A former school bell brought in from Martin Pond, it now sits in grandeur on the kitchen porch, never intending to move.

As a child, I remember my mother asking one of the children to "go ring the bell" which was always exciting. We would kick the heavy bell approximately four times to get the message across. Any more than four kicks would undoubtedly stir an irritated comment from the kitchen as it is very loud. To this day, the Big Red Bell stands ready and waiting for the mealtime ringing—three meals a day. That has been a constant in the daily routine of camp operation for decades and a memory for all guests who ever stayed there.

To my knowledge, the bell has only rung three times outside of its mealtime routine. It served as an alarm to call in my Dad or brother from the lake or perhaps a guest that practiced medicine. The first time was an emergency medical situation; the next was the announcement of a fire; and the third was in 1976 to celebrate our nation's bicentennial. Each occurrence was unique and stays in our memories for a very long time.

Just imagine—a remote sporting camp without a bell or triangle. Our society is now reliant on the technology of cell phones and text messaging for emergency communications. That is, unless you are a guest at Cobb's Pierce Pond Camps. There, the Big Red Bell reigns supreme.

Northern Outdoors

IF YOU ENJOY GREAT OUTDOOR ADVENTURES, WITH A CHANCE AT THE end of the day to return to a terrific meal in the lodge and a comfortable cabin, then you should head to the Forks where Northern Outdoors even offers its own popular microbrews.

Owners: Russell Walters, Jim Yearwood, Suzanne Hockmeyer; PO Box 100, West Forks PLT, ME 04985; www.northernout doors.com; (207) 663-4466, (800) 765-7238.

Directions: Route 201 to The Forks, on Old Canada Road—a National Scenic Byway. From the south, I-95 exit 133. From the north, I-95 exit 157.

Description: Many options including rooms in the lodge and a separate building, plus various sized cabins. All indoor lodging (except lodge rooms) have bathrooms and kitchens.

Prices: Wide range—see website for current prices.

Meals: Breakfast, lunch, and dinner available in the lounge and restaurant. Meal packages available for unguided hunts.

Activities: Focused on outdoor adventures including rafting, hunting, fishing, kayaking and canoeing, snowmobiling, cross-country skiing, and more.

Other: Cell and wifi available, pets accepted.

Season: Open year-round.

A GREAT STAY AND FISHING ADVENTURE
George

Actually, you don't have to leave the lodge for great adventures. They have a hot tub, pool, volleyball and basketball courts, indoor game and exercise rooms, and more, right on the premises. But the nearby Kennebec and Dead Rivers, and the vast forests offer outdoor action that will thrill you, including rafting trips with Northern Outdoors.

Owners Suzie Hockmeyer, Russell Walters, and Jim Yearwood are a great team—very experienced in the tourism business. I first rafted the Kennebec Gorge thirty-five years ago and Suzie was my guide. I guess I made it sound too exciting, because it took more than thirty years before I could convince Linda to try it!

This trip we got their cabin at the very top of the hill, nestled into the woods, cozy, cool, and comfortable. I was a bit concerned when I heard the name of the cabin: Widow Maker. But it turned out there was nothing to be worried about! Our cabin had a very comfortable bed (all rooms and cabins got new mattresses recently), a small kitchen and a full bath. They offer rooms in the lodge and a separate building, plus lots of various-sized cabins.

Best of all, you can walk from any of these to the bar/lounge and restaurant. They've been brewing their own beers for twenty years and recently began selling them in growlers—very popular with guests and local folks. All of their stout—a personal favorite—was headed to a Boston festival that weekend, so I stuck with their Magic Hole IPA and Sledhead Red, both very good. Linda enjoyed their Summer Ale.

Our fishing adventure on Saturday morning in the Kennebec Gorge, with Mike Pilsbury of Kennebec River Angler, was spectacular. We hit the river at 6 a.m. and caught landlocked salmon and brook trout for five hours, with a break for snacks on a beautiful sand bar, and still got back to Northern Outdoors for a delicious late lunch. It was a day we shall never forget. We have fished in the past with Mike's partner, Chris Russell, and these guys are the best.

Chef Seth Gavit arrived at Northern Outdoors a year ago, after cooking in some great restaurants in Portland and elsewhere, and he created a new pub menu with his own dips, sauces, and marinades. Russell and

Suzie joined us for dinner on Friday night, and I will be forever indebted to Russ for suggesting the chicken tenders, marinated in their Deer in the Headlight Lager, with Buffalo IPA sauce. Seth has mastered the art of a crunchy crust over moist and tender meat. It was super delicious.

My favorite entrée was similar, Beer battered fish (haddock) and chips. It was so good I stuck with it the next day for lunch, enjoying their fishwich, Deer in the Headlight beer battered haddock with the same amazing tartar sauce. And of course, more of their IPA. It went very well with their awesome fried pickles with a spicy aioli. We sat out on the deck, luxuriating in the sun, wishing we could stay longer. You will too.

Linda

We really couldn't believe that it had been four years since we last visited Northern Outdoors. In 2011, we tried to fit in everything including one of Northern's rafting trips. This time I saw the same joy on the faces of returning rafters that I had felt when we completed our trip down the Kennebec.

Our fishing guide Mike Pilsbury knows that river like the back of his hand. He maneuvered our raft expertly, almost as if he'd measured the distance between the rocks so we drifted through perfectly. Picture whitewater rapids in some spots and calm waters in other spots until they let the water go at about 10 a.m. from Wyman Dam for rafters. The water rises rapidly when that happens and the fishing techniques change too at that point. Luckily we'd had hours of great fishing before the water came down.

Mike is a blessedly patient man, and it seems that I gave him lots to do. Turns out I am a high maintenance fisherwoman. He untangled my lines, advised me which side and where I was to cast to, and retrieved things for me. He said he'd never seen a reel fall off the rod into the water before. He even had to reach way down into the river and get his shirt wet to retrieve that one! And when George requested a picture with one of the brook trout I caught, I was true entertainment for the whole boat. The poor fish popped out of my hands and landed in the boat three times! The beauty of that river and the ability to enjoy it on such a perfect day will remain in my memory as one of the highlights of my summer, I'm sure.

We were truly impressed with the new fare being served here. Seth, the new chef, has created incredible recipes, many using the beer created here. Suzie and Russell are both excited about the new menu and urged us to try some special appetizers and entrees.

The deep fried sliced jalapenos and the deep fried pickles were super! Russell insisted on the Boneless Crunchers—a version of chicken tenders. The chef marinates them in beer batter which holds in the moisture. The crust is crunchy perfection, and they come with a choice of eight sauces made here. I tried a bite the first night, then ordered them as my lunch the next day. Holy Moly, they were good! My two favorite sauces were Buffalo IPA and Bacon Maple Bourbon.

Since we'd had some appetizers, I went with a chipotle chicken Sandwich for dinner. Plates here are ample, and a giant brioche bun was filled with grilled chicken, mango salsa and chipotle mayo, mixed greens and tomato. The flavors ranged from sweet to mildly spicy in this great sandwich. And the sweet potato fries were as wonderful as I had remembered.

So were our cabin, the friendly staff, and the outdoor adventures. Enjoy your own adventure here soon!

Red River Camps

RED RIVER CAMPS ARE REMOTE, HISTORIC, COMFORTABLE, AND LO-
cated in a spectacular place favored by many hunters and anglers. Jen
Brophy serves as the president of The Maine Sporting Camp Association
and is committed to both her camps and all other traditional sporting
camps in our state.

Owner: Jennifer Brophy; PO Box 320, Portage, ME 04768; www
.redrivercamps.com, jen@redrivercamps.com; (207) 435-6000.

Directions: Red River is located on the north shore of Island
Pond (GPS coordinates: 46.955974, -68.842537) in the Deboullie Unit of Public Reserve Land (T15-R9 WELS). Access from
Portage to the east or St. Francis to the north is via gravel logging
road. Red River is behind the North Maine Woods gate, and gate
access fees must be paid prior to entering the woods. From the
south, take Route 11 north to the town of Portage Lake. Turn
left at Coffin's General Store and Dean's Motel onto West Road.
After a mile, turn left onto the woods road. Travel 4 miles (passing through the lumber yard) to the North Maine Woods Gate.
1 mile after the gate, turn right onto the Hewes Brook Road. Just
before Mile 13 on the Hewes Brook Road, follow the signs for
Red River and the Deboullie township; this will be a left-hand
turn. Continue following the signs for 8 miles to Red River. From
the east and north, take Route 161 from Fort Kent through St.

Francis toward Allagash. Turn left onto the woods road at Chamberlain's Store. Stop at the North Maine Woods gate and pay the access fee. After 8 miles, follow the Red River and Deboullie signs left onto the smaller dirt road. Follow the signs for another 8 miles to Red River.

Description: Red River Camps features a brand new main lodge, built in 2009, on the north shore of Island Pond. The lodge is surrounded by 8 hand-hewn log cabins on the mainland and 1 on its own private island in the middle of the pond. The island cabin was built in 1886, 7 mainland cabins were built between 1900 and 1957, and 1 mainland cabin was rebuilt in 2015. The cabins vary in size, with the smallest cabins sleeping 2 people each, and the largest sleeping 7 or 8. The cabins continue to undergo substantial renovations and improvements to make them comfortable and inviting, including new floors, refinished ceilings and trim, upgraded bathrooms, and new furniture. The lodge is powered by a solar array and battery bank. The cabins offer rustic charm with gaslights and woodstoves. Each cabin has its own bathroom with hot and cold running water, sink, shower, and toilet. They can also accommodate guests who need electricity in their cabins at night for medical necessities such as CPAP machines.

Prices: Red River offers two plans: the American plan and the housekeeping plan. The American plan costs $130/person/night, and includes a cabin private to your party, 3 meals per day, and use of our boats, canoes, kayaks, paddles, and PFDs. The rate also includes linens, towels, blankets, and pillows. The housekeeping plan costs $70/person/night, and includes a cabin private to your party that has its own kitchen facilities (range/oven, refrigerator, sink, and countertop space), the use of camp boats, canoes, kayaks, paddles, and PFDs. The rate also includes linens, towels, blankets, pillows, cookware, percolator, dinnerware, and silverware. The island cabin can be rented as a housekeeping cabin for $75/person/

night, or as an American plan cabin for the $130/person/night. For all plans, children under 16 are half price, children under 4 are free, and there is no charge for pets.

Meals: American plan meals are home cooked with as many fresh, local ingredients as possible. Breakfast at Red River is made to order and might include pancakes, french toast, eggs how you like them, bacon or sausage, homefries, or porridge, as well as fresh baked goods and toast on homemade bread. Lunch includes made-to-order sandwiches on homemade bread, fresh baked goods, and snacks. Lunches are packed in coolers so guests can eat them while they're out enjoying the township. Dinner at Red River is served family style with a rotating menu. Typical dinners include baked salmon or haddock, steak on the grill, roast beef, turkey with all the trimmings, ham, or pasta. Side dishes range from homemade garlic mashed potatoes to roasted maple butternut squash to caprese salad. The dessert menu ranges from Boston cream pie to raspberry cheesecake to strawberry shortcake with homemade whipped cream.

Activities: Fishing 17 nearby ponds, some with canoes available, hiking, swimming, hunting upland birds.

Other: No cell phone or Internet service. Pets are welcome, including dogs and cats.

Season: From late May through the end of October.

Unique in a Number of Ways
—by Bob Mallard, blogger, outdoor writer, www.bobmallard.com

As both a nonresident and resident fly fisherman, I have visited eight or so Maine sporting camps over the last two decades. In my more recent role as a fly fishing blogger, writer and author, I have visited another six or so. One of my favorites is Red River Camps in the Deboullie Region. This lodge is unique in a number of ways that just happen to align with what I am looking for in a fly fishing vacation spot.

While many sporting camps are located in the privately owned working forest, Red River Camps is located on publicly owned protected land—the Deboullie Public Reserved Lands. This 21,871-acre parcel of land encompasses eighteen lakes and ponds, four mountains—Black, Deboullie, Gardner and Whitman; and a 7,253-acre State Ecological Reserve. There are 12 miles of hiking trails and several small waterfalls in the area as well.

The Deboullie Public Reserved Lands are home to white-tail deer, moose, black bear, coyote, bobcat, rare Canada lynx and snowshoe hare. There are loons, small woodland ducks such as goldeneyes and buffle-heads, and eagles and osprey. There are stands of old-growth spruce and mature hardwoods.

As a strict fly fisherman, I do not have a lot of interest in large lakes. While admittedly beautiful, they do not offer me the fishing opportuni-ties that small ponds, streams and rivers do. Many sporting camps are lo-cated on large lakes that are best suited to trolling. And while surrounded by small ponds, streams and rivers; you have to leave the property to get to them.

Red River Camps is an exception. It is located on a small pond—Island Pond. Island Pond is a self-sustaining brook trout fishery. It has never been directly stocked—meaning that the brook trout are most likely genetically pure. At just 32 acres, it is perfect for fly fishing. And with an average depth of 14 feet, a maximum depth of 44 feet, and no competing species, it offers ideal habitat for brook trout.

The Deboullie Public Reserved Lands are also home to Black, Crater, Deboullie, Denny, Duck, Galilee, Gardner, Mud, Perch, Pushineer, Stink, Togue and Upper Ponds; North and South Little Black Ponds; and Fifth and Sixth Pelletier Lakes. They range in size from 4 to 388 acres. All but one—Mud Pond—are classified as a "Principal Brook Trout Fishery" by the state. Fifteen of these are self-sustaining fisheries. Of these, nine have never been stocked; and four have never been directly stocked and may—or may not—have received stocked fish from another source.

Black Pond, roughly a mile from the lodge, held the Maine state record for brook trout from 1979 to 1997.

Seven of the waters surrounding Red River Camps—Denny, Galilee, Island, North Little Black, Stink, South Little Black and Upper Ponds—are restricted to fly fishing only. Two others—Black and Crater Ponds—are restricted to artificial lures only. Three—Black, South Little Black and Crater Ponds—have a 1-fish, 18-inch minimum length limit. Another—Stink Pond—has a slot limit that prohibits the harvest of fish over 12 inches.

Of greater interest to me, is the fact that four of the waters near Red River Camps—Black, Deboullie, Gardner and Pushiner Ponds—are home to rare adfluvial Arctic char. All of these waters are within walking distance of the lodge, and represent roughly one-third of the remaining native Arctic char waters in the Contiguous United States. Formerly known as blueback trout, these are by far the rarest salmonid east of the Mississippi.

Red River Camps is set up ideally for the fly fisherman. To be able to step out of your cabin and onto a quality fly fishing–only wild brook trout pond is a real bonus. It is also a great place for those traveling with non-fly fishers. The lodge and cabins are clean, comfortable and well equipped. The food is home-cooked food and plentiful. The staff is helpful and personable. And the area is one of the most beautiful in Maine. Best of all, Red River Camps offers guests the opportunity to catch a "bucket list" species—rare Arctic char.

Rockwood Cottages

Stunning lakeside views, comfortable cabins, wonderful friendly hosts, and guests who have been returning every summer for decades tell you all you need to know about Rockwood Cottages.

Owners: Ron and Bonnie Searles; PO Box 176, Rockwood, ME 04478; www.mooseheadlakelodging.com; (207) 534-7725.

Directions: Route 15 in Rockwood, just north of Greenville.

Description: 2-bedroom housekeeping cottages, each with kitchen and bathroom, located on the shore of Moosehead Lake with direct view of Mt. Kineo. Cottages were built in the 1950s and have been well maintained. BBQ area with picnic tables by the water. Permanent docks.

Prices: $51/day

Meals: Fully equipped kitchens in each cottage.

Activities: Fishing, boating, canoeing, kayaking, hiking, biking, birding, moose watching, nature photography.

Other: Some cell service and Internet service. Pets accepted.

Season: May 1 to November 30.

A Place Where Guests Return Year After Year
George

Ron Searles is my cousin and you could not ask for a nicer couple than Ron and Bonnie to serve as your hosts. And you don't have to take my word for this. Just read the stories below from long-time guests. As Bonnie says, "We are so blessed! After doing this for thirty-one years, about 75 percent of our guests have become our friends and repeat guests." Their location on the edge of Moosehead Lake looking right at Mt. Kineo is stunning, and their cottages are comfortable, clean, and up-to-date. If you can't relax here, you can't relax anywhere!

I know some of their longtime guests, including one southern Maine couple who come several times a year, sometimes to fish, sometimes to simply relax. The cottages are cozy and comfortable, with everything you need for a great vacation.

Sit yourself down in one of the comfortable chairs or benches lining the shore, early one beautiful and quiet morning, staring across Moosehead Lake at the stunning Mount Kineo, and you may want to sit there all day. Ron and Bonnie are unusual hosts, spending lots of time with their guests and thoroughly enjoying those experiences. As their brochure notes, "The only thing we overlook is Moosehead Lake."

Nearly every night, Ron piles the wood into a large outdoor grill and starts the fire, inviting guests to cook their dinners on the grill and take them back to their cottages or join the group eating together on the lakeside picnic tables. Here, guests get to know each other, and now, many return the same week each year, in order to spend time with the friends they made at these wonderful gatherings.

I delivered a talk on Maine sporting camps at Forest Heritage Days in Greenville last August, and Linda and I stayed with Ron and Bonnie that night. We thoroughly enjoyed the cookout and getting to visit with other guests. It was so much fun, I got to the talk a bit late!

Ron and Bonnie enjoy taking their guests around the lake in their pontoon boat. We spent a great morning, with other guests, boating all around Mount Kineo with its amazing cliffs, while Ron and Bonnie shared stories with us. Fun!

Their brochure explains the experience here better than I can: "Where inspiration meets adventure." And speaking of adventure, there is a surprising number of fun things to do in this area. In addition to being on the edge of Maine's bountiful north woods, Greenville is only about a twenty minute ride away, where Linda and I enjoyed a tour of the historical museum. You will want to take a ride on the steamship, too, enjoy the local restaurants, and check out the guided trips—including moose watching—offered by Mike Boutin at Northwoods Outfitters.

Just don't overbook yourself. Those lakeside chairs are the place to spend your vacation!

Our Moosehead Experience
—by Harold Porter, Sanford

My wife Gloria's grandparents had always spent their vacations in the Moosehead area and she grew up hearing stories about the Moosehead area, especially Rockwood. When we were married that is where we decided to spend our vacations.

In March of 2004 we were disappointed to learn that the camp we had reserved in Rockwood for many years was closing. We drove immediately to Rockwood to ty to find another place for our annual two-week vacations there. After looking at several places, we stopped at Rockwood Cottages and looked at their camps. Yes! It was just what we were looking for.

Ron and Bonnie were very welcoming, showed us around, and we told them we'd think about it. We drove out one end of the driveway, up the road a short distance to the other entrance to the camps, drove back in and reserved a camp for two weeks. It's a beautiful spot where we enjoy fishing, watching the nearby nesting eagles, riding the back roads, and most of all, the many wonderful friends we have made here over the years. We all reserved the same two weeks and it's like a family reunion.

Ron and Bonnie are wonderful hosts and see to your every need. We have been with them for 11 years now and hope for many more to come.

A Honeymoon That Continues Every Year!
—by Mary and Jim Smart

My husband Jim and I were married June 9, 1996. We had decided to honeymoon at Moosehead Lake, Maine, since we both loved the outdoors and moose watching. We had to bring my step-daughter back to Cape Code after our wedding so we spent our wedding night in Hyannis and left the next morning for Maine.

The next night we found ourselves in Waterville, Maine, for the night. We found a brochure for the Moosehead Lake Region and saw an ad for a resort on Moosehead Lake. It looked like a very nice place so we called and booked a cabin for our stay. When we arrived the next day what we found didn't live up to what the brochure had promised so we got our deposit refunded and left.

Now what? It's late in the afternoon and here we are miles from nowhere and no place to stay; on our honeymoon, no less. We started to drive back toward Greenville and we saw the vacancy sign at Rockwood Cottages and pulled in. We found the sign that said "office," knocked and Bonnie answered the door. She welcomed us in and had us sit at the kitchen table. We explained our predicament and asked if they could accommodate us for three nights. Bonnie confirmed they had a cabin available and led the way to give us a tour. She showed us the cabin and the docks and gave us the lay of the land, so to speak.

Needless to say, we were absolutely thrilled! The next evening we went for a ride to look for moose. Bonnie and Ron had given us directions to several places. When we returned after dark we noticed that the porch light had been turned on for us. What a homey touch, we said to each other. When we walked in we found a vase with lilacs and an ice bucket, wrapped in aluminum foil, with a bottle of sparkling wine. Jim and I were so touched by these simple gestures. We finished out our honeymoon and had already decided we were coming back.

A year later we returned to Rockwood Cottages to celebrate our first anniversary. Again we went out in the evening to look for moose and upon our return found the same aluminum foil wrapped bucket with a bottle of sparkling wine and an anniversary card!

We have been married for nineteen years and continue our tradition of returning to Rockwood Cottages each year. Bonnie and Ron and their family have become part of our family. Over the years we have shifted our vacation from June to July and now consider the others who also spend the same weeks with us at Rockwood Cottages as family. There is no other place on earth that we'd rather be!

Every Year Here
—by Pam Kavanaugh

Where can you go for a daily walk and see deer grazing in the grass or the most beautiful sunsets at night? Moosehead Lake in Rockwood, Maine, is the answer. For the past thirty years I have spent my summer vacation at Rockwood Cottages with my family. Every year I count the weeks waiting to return to my little "piece of heaven on earth" (I have forty-six weeks and five days to go).

My time spent at Rockwood Cottages includes daily walks in the early morning, reading a collection of books sitting on the dock by the lake or on the screened porch of the cabin, dinner at the BBQ pit with family and friends and listening to the haunting cries of the loons. A night ride on a pontoon boat across the lake at sunset is spectacular! There are no words that can adequately describe it.

What makes the entire vacation even more special is spending time with the owners of Rockwood Cottages, Ron and Bonnie Searles. Over the past thirty years they have become a part of my extended family. They make every guest feel important and welcomed. Their hospitality makes this vacation spot the very best! Who needs Disney World when you have Rockwood Cottages on Moosehead Lake!

Twin Pines Camps at the
New England Outdoor Center

To TRADITIONAL SPORTING CAMPS ADD ENVIRONMENTALLY FRIENDLY houses and the best restaurant in this region and you have the New England Outdoor Center. The stunning view across Millinocket Lake to Mount Katahdin, and the many outdoor adventures available, make this one of our favorite places.

Owner: Matt Polstein; Manager: Shorey Ewing; www.neoc.com, info@neoc.com; (207) 723-5438, (800) 766-7238.

Directions: (GPS coordinates: 45.726778, -68.81912) From Millinocket, take Bates Street—heading towards Baxter State Park and drive for 8 miles. Bates Street turns into the Lake road. After 8 miles you will see signs indicating a right hand turn for "Twin Pine Cabins" and "The River Driver's Restaurant." Take the right-hand turn onto Black Cat Road. Follow Black Cat Road for 1 mile until you see signs for "check in." Note for guests traveling via I-95, Millinocket is exit 244. Millinocket is the nearest local town—8 miles. Main roads are paved; Black Cat Road is a well maintained dirt road.

Description: 20 lakeside cabins that sleep from 4 to 14 people. All cabins are fully winterized; 15 are either new or completely renovated. The other 5 are in very good condition and with upgrades scheduled in 2015. All cabins have private bathrooms; 10 have radiant heat floors. All cabins come complete with full linens, including sheets, blankets, and towels. All cabins have kitchens, gas or electric stove and gas heating. Some have a secondary source of heating including gas fireplaces or woodstoves. Kitchens have plates, cookware, cutlery, coffee pots.

Many of the cabins are located lakeside on Millinocket Lake, some have views of Katahdin, Maine's highest Mountain. Others are on the Cove and have views onto the forest surrounding the property and the lake.

Prices: Cabins start at $245/night. Hunters Special Rates available and off-season rates available in November, December, and April.

Meals: Meal packages can be purchased for one to three meals a day (breakfast, lunch, and dinner). Award-winning River Driver's Restaurant is on site and is open 364 days a year. It is open for dinner every day and for breakfast and lunch January to April and June to October. Parties staying other months can have breakfast and lunch provided on request.

Activities: Conferences, weddings, rafting, hiking, biking, fishing, hunting, hiking, snowshoeing, snowmobiling—all outdoor activities. Next door to Baxter State Park.

Other: Only requirement is a minimum of 2 nights stay on the weekend in winter, January through March. All other times no minimum requirement. Cell phone service available in many locations on the property, but not all; coverage also depends on service provider. All cabins have wifi. Pets are accepted. NEOC offers a number of guided experiences, including overnight camping and guided canoe trips on the East branch of the Penobscot. They provide all the equipment and the guide (usually the owner, Matt Polstein, runs these trips). They also offer overnight camping trips on Millinocket lake, at points accessible by boat only, guided hiking up Katahdin and in the area for individuals and groups, and hunting and fishing guides.

Season: Open year-round. Busiest times of the year are January–March and mid-June through mid-September.

A Winter Adventure
George

Matt Polstein is the perfect example of what it takes to succeed these days in the sporting camp business. Matt has renovated most of the old cabins that were part of Twin Pine Camps, constructed new cabins and luxurious three-bedroom houses, added a superb restaurant, and partnered with conservation groups to protect surrounding lands and with outdoor recreation groups to add experiences to the traditional pursuits of hunting and fishing.

For example, as rafting, one of his principal businesses, declined, he expanded into birding, biking, and other outdoor activities. And he added "floating" the West Branch of the Penobscot River, a half day trip, for those who are less adventurous and don't want to devote an entire day to white-water rafting. Passive activities like moose watching are also featured in the summer and early fall.

When we were there on a winter outing, it was clear that the New England Outdoor Center is a major destination for snowmobilers. While Matt rents snowmobiles, many of his guests arrive with huge trailers full of them. Some bring two for each member of their party, in case one breaks down!

Of course, it doesn't hurt that NEOC sits on the shore of Millinocket Lake, just 8 miles on a paved road from the town of Millinocket, with gorgeous views of Mount Katahdin and access to the entire North Woods, and just minutes from one of my favorite rivers, the West Branch of the Penobscot, with fabulous fishing, canoeing, kayaking, and rafting.

I've visited great lodges in Montana, Alaska, and Quebec on fishing adventures, and Twin Pines ranks right up there with the best. And oh yeah, the food here is worthy of the Portland dining scene, but it comes with better scenery!

In 2012, Linda and I stayed in one of Matt's new environmentally friendly houses (he insists they're cabins, but they are huge), so this time we asked for one of the original Twin Pine cabins. All of the cabins, old and new, have full kitchens and lots of beds. The largest cabin sleeps fourteen people. Little Mud cabin was down on the lake with stunning views of Katahdin. Well, there would have been one if it wasn't snowing most of the time we were there!

We actually drove up to Millinocket in a blizzard, and that was adventure enough for that day, so even before we settled into our camp, we decamped in the River Driver's Restaurant for lunch. Matt moved his popular restaurant from east of Millinocket to Twin Pines a few years ago. I loved it in the old location, but here, it's an impressive two-story building with conference and celebration spaces and huge windows offering views of the lake and Mount Katahdin.

As impressive as the location and view are, the food is even better. After that drive, I was ready for a beer and was delighted to find one of my favorites, Allagash Black, on the menu. It went very well with my pulled pork sandwich. The fries are large and crispy, and I actually couldn't eat all of them, you get so many.

As much as I enjoyed my sandwich, I had to admit Linda's blackened cajun chicken breast was even better. It was very spicy. At one point, she exclaimed, "My mouth is on fire—in a good way!" When I asked her what would be a bad way, she said, "That time you ate the hot cherry pepper." Well, yes, but that was a mistake!

We settled into our cabin for the afternoon, glad to be inside while the wind-whipped snow flashed past our windows, until we bundled up for the short walk to the restaurant for dinner. Before ordering, I walked around, taking photos and admiring the artwork and other decorations.

I have to admit, I'm in a rut here. I love their crab cakes appetizer, so I convinced Linda to share that. And they were delicious with fresh herbs, lemon zest, seared in butter, and covered by a peppered limoncello remoulade. I've never forgotten the crab-stuffed haddock I had here in 2012, so I was ecstatic to see it's still on the menu. And it's still fantastic, topped with a lobster claw and delicious lemon caper cream sauce.

The crispy carrots were a tasty surprise. When Lin asked if I knew why I loved them, I had to admit I did not. "They are glazed in honey and cooked in butter," she explained. No wonder I loved them! We both fondly remembered the chocolate torte dessert and shared that. It was so good. We lingered in the very busy restaurant until 9:30 p.m., enjoying the wonderful dinner, feeling blessed. And eleven hours later, we were back for breakfast!

But after that Linda insisted on some exercise, so we put on our snowshoes and hiked Matt's ski/snowshoe trail up on the ridge. The woods were far less windy and we enjoyed a nice snowshoe for about an hour before packing up and heading home. If our own north woods camp wasn't nearby, we'd spend a lot of time at Twin Pines.

Linda

We've been looking forward to visiting Twin Pines Camps for some time now. On a February break three years ago we found out what a gem this place is. At the time we stayed in one of the new "green" guesthouses, an ultra-modern space that can accommodate a dozen people. But because there were only two of us we wanted to stay in one of the older cabins this trip.

Twin Pines has been updating some of their older cabins and Little Mud, the cabin we stayed in, had just been remodeled. They have installed new interior walls and half walls to enclose sleeping spaces. This camp had two full beds and one set of bunks, so six could sleep here. New cabinets were filled with everything you'd need to cook with, from dishes and silverware for six to a coffeemaker, microwave, and toaster.

Matt told us they had built four new smaller "green" cabins on the lakeshore that were similar to the larger ones we'd stayed in. We took a peek at one of these and it was truly beautiful. This is not roughing it to be sure . . . two full queen beds, flat screen TV, a modern kitchen, and a nice living space with comfortable seating. These would be perfect for families or two couples.

The weather this trip wasn't as cooperative as last time, but even with snow and whipping winds people were having an outdoor winter experience. This is the home base of the New England Outdoor Center (NEOC).

Trails for skiing, snowshoeing, and snowmobiling are well kept and easily accessible, and I even got George to go snowshoeing despite the incredible winds and blowing snow. The trails were beautiful and it was very pleasant in the woods out of the wind. He even admitted that it was great once we got out there. An hour of exercise in winter beauty really can help with cabin fever.

River Driver's Restaurant is the place to eat up here. Their food is consistently great. For lunch I loved the Twin Pine sandwich—cajun blackened chicken, bacon, Swiss, tomato and jalapeno ranch dressing. The cajun spices were cooled by the dressing and accented with the salty bacon. I enjoyed every bite. This would be my "go to" sandwich if I lived closer.

During our evening meal we sat in the more private section, which has a lovely feel. One entire wall of wine in a custom made rack, which is as pretty as a sculpture. Copper topped tables, soft lighting, and windows facing Katahdin add to the ambiance here.

I ordered one of the evening specials—Steak Caprese. An expertly cooked sirloin was topped with basil and mozzarella, and served with mashed potato and glazed carrots (caramelized and yummy). The servings here are generous, so I enjoyed it just as much as leftovers a few days later.

We agreed to split their chocolate flourless torte, which was decadent and delicious. Served with vanilla bean ice cream and a chocolate drizzle, this one had a gooey filling and a crunchy chocolate crust. It was "over the moon" good!

And to round out the dining experience, we enjoyed breakfast here before we headed home. My NEOC Egg Scramble held spinach, mushrooms and Swiss cheese. It is made with three eggs, and they couldn't really cut it down to two as I requested, so it was an enormous breakfast. When our server delivered this she said, "You probably won't need lunch!" And I certainly didn't, but it was great reheated the next day. I'd be remiss if I didn't mention the amazing three potato home fries. The combination of sweet, red, and white potatoes is as pretty as it is delicious.

The Twin Pines Camps are prime accommodations in any season. It's a short drive to Baxter State Park and all the outdoor experiences the park offers spring through fall. If you want a "lake and woods vacation," this is a sure bet, and NEOC's whitewater rafting or leisurely float trips are great. Wintertime enthusiasts come here for snowmobiling adventures. As we were leaving they told us they were expecting a group of ten snowmobilers and another group of twenty-two coming for the weekend!

Tim Pond Camps

TIM POND CAMPS IS THE OLDEST CONTINUOUSLY OPERATED SPORTING camp in New England, hosting guests since the mid-1800s. The pond harbors lots of wild native brook trout, and the gated, controlled access road assures that remote wilderness experience many of us seek.

Owners: Harvey and Betty Calden; PO Box 22 Eustis, ME 04936; www.timpond.com; (207) 243-2947.

Directions: 9 miles of dirt woods roads on the Tim Pond Road in Eustis off route 27. Gated access and the only camps on the entire pond.

Description: 11 log cabins, hot and cold water, private bathrooms. They all have woodstoves for heat and vary in size sleeping 2–6 people each. All overlook the pond.

Prices: Fishing rates: May–September, $ 215/person/night, children 12 and under half price, children 5 and under free; July and August reservations 10% discount; fly-fishing school: $525 includes school, cabin, meals, use of a boat and motor. Upland game: $135/person/night; deer hunting: $750/person/week (Sunday to Sunday) includes cabin and meals.

Meals: Main dining lodge on top of hill, three full meals per day. American plan only.

Activities: Fly fishing, hiking, bird watching, moose watching, mountain bike riding, canoeing, bird hunting, deer hunting.

Other: Cell phones but limited Internet service; pets allowed,

Season: Open May–September for fishing—fishing always good—for native brook trout; the pond has never been stocked. Two weeks in October for bird hunting (grouse and woodcock). Two weeks in November for deer hunting.

From Maine to Labrador—
My Harvey and Betty Calden Experience

Harvey and Betty Calden are veteran sporting camp owners who offer the very best in hospitality and outdoor experiences, focused on hunting and fishing. Tim Pond Camps was always Betty's project while Harvey focused on their camps in northern Quebec and Labrador. I took my son Josh, when he was 16, to Harvey's Little Minipi Camp in Labrador and we had a phenomenal experience, catching huge brook trout.

I did have an opportunity years ago to stay at Tim Pond Camps, and discovered Betty's wonderful food and hospitality. Sitting on the porch of my rustic cabin, I tried to imagine those three Indian trappers, Tim, Jim, and Lutton, when they arrived in this area in the 1830s to work for a logging operation. Tim took an interest in the mile-long pond and brought people there to enjoy the exceptional brook trout fishing. And just like that, it became Tim Pond.

By 1847, Tim Pond was a major hunting and fishing destination with its own sporting camp. In 1964, when Wayne Hussey, who had owned the camps since 1945, died, there was talk of turning the camps into a membership-only club. Fortunately for all of us, that didn't happen.

And in 1981, the Caldens purchased the camps, which are still the only ones on the remote pond that contains some of Maine's very special wild and native brook trout. I worked for more than a decade, as the director of the Sportsman's Alliance of Maine, with SAM's Fishing Initiative Committee, on legislation to recognize and protect our native brook trout.

I am proud to say we were able to convince the legislature to name the brook trout our state's heritage fish, and protect them, initially, in more than 300 ponds that had never been stocked. Today, nearly 500 native brook trout ponds are on the protected list, including Tim Pond, and Maine has 97 percent of the nation's remaining brook trout waters.

I have never forgotten the photo of F.E. Stanley and his son, Raymond, with a record brook trout taken in Tim Pond that is hanging in the lodge. F.E. Stanley and his brother F.O. invented the Stanley Steamer automobile, and we have a museum dedicated to the family and its inventions in Kingfield. That's enroute to Tim Pond, so you can check it out!

TIM POND CAMPS—SUBURB OF EUSTIS
—by Glenn Hodgkins, Hallowell

I have fond memories of Tim Pond and Tim Pond camps from different parts of my life, beginning in the late 1970's on fishing trips with my dad and continuing to this day. My dad's main leisure activities have always been fishing, hunting, and exploring remote corners of Maine. These interests naturally led to finding old Maine fishing camps.

We've tried several fishing camps in Maine over the years, but our favorite and the one we still come back to forty years later, is Tim Pond near Eustis. These sporting camps, which have been in operation since the mid-1800s, are the only buildings on the pond. The woods and low mountains around the large pond are a perfect and peaceful setting for a classic sporting camp.

On my first trip to Tim Pond in the late 70's both my dad and I were very much into fishing, though most of my experience was trolling for salmon and togue and casting for bass, on Sebago Lake. Fly fishing was new for me, and I liked it from the beginning. I don't recall having any trouble catching our limit and brook trout for breakfast was a new treat. I didn't appreciate it at the time, but Tim Pond has never been stocked, so we were catching all native fish.

My most vivid childhood memories, however, were the setting and the wildlife, rather than the fish. One morning we were out fishing early in the fog with bull-moose bellows echoing around the lake. I've never heard that since. Later in the day when the fog cleared, we saw the big bull along with a cow and calf. The foliage that year was the most spectacular that I've ever seen, with blazing reds and orange from the pond up the sides of the mountains.

I've always liked old cabins, perhaps because of experiencing them from a young age. I like the old wood, the uneven painted-wood floors, the rustic electricity and plumbing features, and the stone fireplaces. It takes you back to a simpler time of cribbage and family. These days it's a great vacation from a busy life filled with computers and all kinds of electronic distractions. I don't know how old the Tim Pond cabins are, but most of them feel like they are more than 100 years old. In the 1970s we cooked our own food on the woodstoves.

The old wooden Rangeley boats also seemed like they were more than 100 years old. Many of the newer boats at Tim Pond are based on molds of the old boats. Back in the 1970s we rowed them to our favorite fishing spots, or let the wind slowly push us across the pond. I don't recall if motors weren't available; we preferred rowing, or may have been too cheap to rent a motor. These days most everyone uses the small outboard motors to get to their favorite spots.

The second major life stage of Tim Pond trips was with my wife Sara and our kids; Anna was 6 and Ben was 3. I had a few more distractions at this point, but still did manage some fishing with my dad. I also introduced fly fishing to Anna. Ben was a little young for fishing, but he did enjoy casting a 2-foot long rod with a 4-inch long hard rubber figurine of SpongeBob (with no hook). He didn't realize for a couple of years that a hook was an important part of catching fish. Regardless, he had a lot of fun and could cast that figurine a good 75 feet though.

The kids really liked all the local wildlife around the camps and around the pond. The snowshoe hares weren't that shy and are a popular kid animal. Maybe these snowshoe hares are descendants of the hares that started cropping the grass around the camps in the 1800s. There certainly isn't any other lawn-type areas anywhere nearby. Moose of course are a big crowd pleaser and a large exotic animal for kids.

One year when the kids were small we loaded up a couple of boats with family and friends and hightailed it across the lake to get a good look at a moose feeding along the far shore. This (unbeknownst to kids of course) followed a long period of binocular scanning of the shores to try to assure a moose on the trip. We had both sets of grandparents together with the kids one year and Sara's Hoosier parents very much enjoyed the place. There's certainly nothing like it anywhere near the flat corn and soybean farms of northern Indiana.

For the last decade, my mom, Ruth, and dad, Norm, have made an annual trip with friends to Tim Pond. They make the annual pilgrimage from the western mountains of Maine. It's their regular late summer/ early fall vacation. We celebrated their fiftieth wedding anniversary there with lobsters in the lodge. My dad has shown the fly-fishing ropes to several non-fisherman friends. My mom very much enjoys playing games with friends in the lodge and reading on the cabin porch. My dad faithfully goes fishing morning and evening, regardless of the weather, or whether others are that dedicated. It's a big treat to have hearty meals cooked for you and always wonderful to talk with friends and family around a big table in the lodge.

I have been joining my parents' group the last few years and enjoy several activities and non-activities. There's a certain timelessness to fishing with my dad on the same pond for forty years, and a great comfort to me that very little has changed there. I have to admit that fishing hasn't been a high priority for me in recent years. A current passion of mine is birding and I find myself distracted by interesting raptors, ducks, and song birds as I'm casting a fly. I like to paddle the pond in one of the newer kayaks and photograph the loons, Goldeneye, Waxwings, Cooper's Hawks, and many others. I still like to go out fishing at Tim Pond and having a good pan-fried brook trout for breakfast though.

Hewes Brook Lodge

HEWES BROOK LODGE IS NESTLED IN THE NORTH WOODS ON THE BANK of the 24-mile long Fish River. It is a four season all-inclusive focused on hunting of deer, bear, moose, coyote, and grouse, or just plain getting away from it all.

Owner: Phil Daggett; 33 Great Meadow Lane, Fairfield, ME 04937; www.HewesBrookLodge.com; (207) 453-7036, (207) 313-3616.

Directions: T14 R7, in the North Maine Woods, with gate fees (but the lodge provides guest passes at the gate). Well-maintained gravel road. See website for detailed directions and GPS coordinates.

Description: On Fish River. The first camp was built in 1888. Phil is the 5th generation owner and guide. 4 bathrooms and 1 has an 8-person hot tub. 9 private bedrooms, 2 bunkrooms. Large lodge with over 10,000 square feet of space.

Prices: Private room $165/person/night or $250/couples/night. Bunk room $150/person/night.

Meals: American plan, three meals/day.

Activities: Family vacations and reunions, weddings, canoeing, fishing, hunting, snowmobiling.

Other: Cell phone but no Internet service.

Season: Year-round.

There Was No Grousing about the Great Food and Lodging at Hewes Brook Lodge

"Do you have a radio?" the guest asked Dana Daggett, owner Phil Daggett's brother. "I'm having trouble sleeping here. It's too quiet."

Yes, it's quiet at Hewes Brook Lodge in Portage. As we enjoyed morning coffee in one of the lodge's beautiful historic rooms one morning, watching the Fish River slide by, Dana tells me about the time he was sitting outside with a guest on a bench that his grandfather made. Dana said, "Listen to that?" The guest looked at him curiously. "I don't hear a thing," he said. "Yes, that's what it can be like here," replied Dana.

For years, my friends Jim and Jenness Robbins, Steve and Donnie Lucas, Pete Williams and I have hunted wild pheasants each fall in North Dakota. But in 2015, we decided to break out of that routine and hunt grouse in Maine's north woods. Jim selected Hewes Brook Lodge for our fall adventure, after visiting there during the previous winter while snowmobiling in the area.

It turned out to be a great choice. Well, except for the grouse. But first, let me tell you about why I loved Hewes Brook Lodge. Start with its history, displayed on every wall with things like the Daggetts' grandfather's snowshoe. You would love the story that goes with the snowshoe. I encouraged the Daggetts to walk through the lodge and video tape themselves telling those wonderful stories of the mounts, art work, and especially the historic items. Phil, Dana, and their younger sister Sue, are the fifth generation here. They have so many great memories of growing up at the lodge and their stories kept me entertained every evening.

The meals here are remarkable. All of the Daggetts are great cooks. One night, Sue made their mother's old fashioned caramel custard. Sue called it "very basic" but it was soooo tasty. Their mother only made it for special occasions. I told them every time I'm here, it needs to be considered a special occasion! And then they tantalized me with a story about their mother's brownie pudding, which she called "poor man's pudding."

The only complaint I had about the food was there was too much of it. After returning from a day of hunting, they'd have a table full of appetizers, followed by a huge dinner. Luckily, we walked a lot each day.

The old log siding, inside pine boards and floors, very comfortable rooms, amazing food, Fish River flowing past, and three million acres in the North Maine Woods right outside the door—well, it's all spectacular, and I haven't mentioned the wonderful hospitality of the Daggetts. I loved listening to them in the morning, preparing breakfast together, laughing and laughing.

They have managed to link the modern—including hall lights that snap on when you step out of your room at night, powered by a solar unit—to the historic, including journals from the twenties and furniture made by generations of Daggetts, including Phil who made the gorgeous dining room table at his work shop in Skowhegan.

Enjoying an old brochure for their grandfather's camp, Chrystal Springs Camps on Portage Lake, I read: "The fishing for landlocked salmon, trout and togue in these waters can seldom be excelled. Salmon average in size from 2 to 5 pounds, and square tailed trout about the same. The togue run larger up to 12 pounds and even 20 pounders have been caught by lucky anglers."

And while bear hunting is a very important economic boost for camps in this area, I noted in the brochure, "No bag limit on bear. Bear are numerous in this section, owing to the fact that there is no bounty on them. Bears are still numerous here, but now we're making money from the hunt, not paying hunters to shoot them!"

And here's something else that has changed here. The brochure noted, "These camps are easily reached by canoe or team." Today a good gravel road takes you right to the lodge.

And I just have to tell you something more about the food here. I liked Dana's story of a guest, as he sat down to his first meal of the season here and told them, "Last year I gained 10 pounds here. But I fixed that problem this year."

"What did you do?" asked Dana. And the guest reported, "I didn't weigh myself before I came!"

A snow storm in this area the previous May wiped out grouse broods, so the birds were few and far between. Each of us got a bird or two every day, but as we traveled the roads, appreciating our access to all that private land, admiring the stunning beauty of the fall foliage, seeing moose, deer, and even a bobcat, and walking old logging roads and trails with the dog working hard to find birds for us. Well, it was a wonderful, relaxing, restorative trip.

Phil said, our last morning there as we enjoyed stories by the fire, awaiting their typical huge breakfast, "Like that song 'Hotel California' says, you check in here but you can't ever check out." Don't I wish.

Snowmobiling the Back Country
—by Corey Lathrop

I've been an avid snowmobiler since age four and until 2010 was pretty sure I'd seen everything you could see in Maine on a snowmobile, ridden every trail, stayed everyplace you could stay and of course had the best meals you could find by sled. Then one day Phil Daggett walks into my office and starts asking me about a truck he's seen in the parking lot (my truck) and two hours later we're still talking sledding and the my introduction to Hewes Brook Lodge begins.

Hard to believe, but in 2010 back country sledding in Maine was not like it is now, just five years later, and Hewes Brook Lodge was not known to many Maine sledders. You could not find it easily on the trail system. Phil had started marketing the lodge for winter usage and it was not long before we started working the GPS routes and tracks to destinations like the trains in the Allagash—100 miles each way from HBL to the trains without using the trail system.

In 2015, we guided backcountry trips to the trains, Libby Camps, Allagash Falls, Deboullie Mountain, and many more. The back country rides are a great opportunity to see Maine as most people have never seen it. The frozen beauty is breathtaking.

The lodge is "A Bit of Paradise" as the sign says. The accommodations are top notch. And I know you cannot find this setting duplicated any place in Maine in the winter. The meals and food are beyond description. Every group that comes makes the same comment when the call comes from the kitchen that dinner is ready, "What? Dinner, already, again?! We're still packed full of ribs, shrimp, bacon wrapped scallops, homemade fries, onion rings, and the lodge beverage of choice—Crown Royal." The family is incredible. Phil, Dana, Susan, Mom, Carol, Candy, Sandy, and all the staff are just awesome Maine people.

Our family loves HBL and we can't wait for August 22 as our son is getting married at the lodge. It'll be a special place for years to come.

More Camps

Allagash Sporting Camps

Mike Paquette is a Maine guide whose Allagash Sporting Camps focus on hunting, fishing, snowmobiling, canoing, and other traditional outdoor activities, both guided and unguided.

Owner: Mike Paquette; 145 Inn Road, Allagash, ME 04774; www.allagashsportingcamp.com, mike@allagashsportingcamp.com; (207) 398-3555.

Directions: Paved road, 145 Inn Road, Town of Allagash. Transporation is provided from Allagash or the Presque Isle airport.

Description: The lodge sleeps 6, and 2 camps sleep 4 each. Camps were rebuilt in 1976, with new bathrooms and kitchens added in 2012.

Prices: Varied depending on activity. For example, large groups of snowmobilers are charged $45/night with children under 12 free. Deer hunters pay $850/week, bear hunters $1,500/week, and partridge hunters $450/week.

Meals: Can be prepared by guests in the camps, and meals are also served in the lodge.

Activities: Hunting, fishing, snowmobiling, family, scout, church group trips, Allagash River canoe trips.

Other: Free use of canoes and kayaks and a sunfish boat and boats available for rent. Cell phone and Internet service is available. Pets are welcome. Personal care devices that draw lots of power are not. Guests must bring their own towels.

Season: Year-round.

Attean Lake Lodge

The Holden family has been welcoming guests to Attean Lake Lodge since 1900. Today the second and third generation Holdens own and operate the resort, located on an island with stunning views and fifteen comfortable log cabins and great meals.

Owner: Brad Holden; PO Box 457, Jackman, ME 04945; www. atteanlodge.com, info@atteanlodge.com; (207) 668-3792.

Directions: Three miles from Jackman to the boat landing on Attean Road.

Description: Island location on Attean Lake. All 15 cottages have full baths and accommodate 2 to 6 guests. The main Lodge was built in 1991.

Prices: Before July 11 and after August 22, $290 daily or $1,850 weekly for 2 adults, $100 daily or $725 for third adult, $80 daily or $425 weekly for children 6–11, and $40 daily or $160 for children under 6. July 11–August 22, $365 daily or $2,250 weekly for 2 adults, $150 daily or $975 weekly for third adult, $100 daily or $550 weekly for children 6–11, and $50 daily or $225 weekly for children under 6. Includes all meals.

Meals: Breakfast and dinner served in the lodge. Box lunches provided for all. No cooking in cottages.

Activities: Fishing, hiking, swimming.

Season: Summer only. July and August are busiest months.

BALD MOUNTAIN CAMPS

BALD MOUNTAIN CAMPS ARE THE OLDEST CAMPS OPERATING IN THE western part of the state and have been renovated in recent years, adding comfort without diminishing the historic character of the camps. The lodge/restaurant is stunningly beautiful, and serves the public for dinners that draw rave reviews.

Owners: Steve, Fernlyn, and Tyler Philbrick; 125 Bald Mountain Road, Oquossoc, ME 04964; www.baldmountaincamps.com; (207) 864-3671; Facebook.

Directions: Route 4 through the town of Rangeley into the village of Oquossoc; take a left onto Bald Mountain Road. Camps are ¾ mile on the right.

Description: Log cabins located on the shore of Mooselookmeguntic Lake that were established in 1897 and renovated from the ground up. They offer year-round lodging. Cabins have woodstoves or fireplaces along with monitor heaters, full linen service, direct TV, and covered porches with rocking chairs.

Prices: Varies by season and cabin, starting at $145/night in off-season.

Meals: Restaurant is open to the public for dinner. Breakfast and lunch available during peak season.

Activities: Fishing, hunting, boating, hiking, snowmobiling, and other outdoor fun.

Other: Minimum 3-day stay in summer, 2-night the rest of the year. Internet and cell phone service. Pets accepted.

Season: Year-round; closed the month of April.

Surrounded by Great Outdoor Adventures
George

What would you hope to find at a favorite sporting camp? Maybe historic camps of varying sizes, all restored for your comfort without losing the original features? Perhaps a deck with lots of rocking chairs, overlooking a beautiful lake with mountains beyond? How about a beach, with plenty of room for the kids to frolic? Would you enjoy a fantastic restaurant right on the grounds?

I'll bet you would enjoy hundreds of thousands of acres of conservation lands, with terrific hiking trails, within a few minutes ride of the camp. Of course, if you are me, you'd look for one of Maine's best places to hunt and fish.

Well, Bald Mountain Camps in Oquossoc has all of this and more. Linda and I were particularly fascinated by our visit to the Rangeley Outdoor Sporting Heritage Museum, just a mile up the road from the camps. It's filled with amazing historical items from this region's famous hunting and fishing past, and manager Bill Pierce is as friendly and engaging a host as you'll ever find.

Steve Philbrick spent a lot of time at Bald Mountain Camps when his grandparents owned them, and later purchased the camps from his grandparents. Now Steve's son Tyler has joined them on the management team. They rebuilt the lodge first, adding space for events, celebrations, and conferences, and then reconstructed all the cabins. The restaurant/lodge is particularly beautiful, with lots of mounts spread throughout the three rooms. Linda and I both particularly loved the bobcats at the top of one of the rafters.

We had only a short one-night stay on a night when highly-regarded chef Brian Anderson was off and the restaurant was not open for dinner, but Steve, who cooked here for more than twenty years, stepped up to prepare a wonderful meal for us. We particularly appreciated Amanda, our server, who came in just to serve us that evening. She's got a wonderful story too, having moved here after working in Massachusetts for many years, simply because she loved her trips to the Rangeley region as a kid. She met the mother of Sue Anderson, Brian's wife who handles reservations and other details for the camps, at the local laundry and that led to Amanda's job here.

We enjoyed a stunning sunset from our table overlooking the lake. My BBQ ribs were perfectly cooked with a very tasty maple BBQ sauce, and I also really enjoyed the corn salsa. Portion size is huge, so I got to enjoy some of the ribs the next day for lunch at home. The menu is extensive and I really need to return to try the Caribbean Fish Tacos. Several of our friends told us that Chef Bryan is very creative and they are right. The restaurant here has developed a great reputation.

Linda

We had stayed at Bald Mountain Camps more than ten years ago so the details of these camps were a sketchy memory. It was a cloudy day with showers when we headed out on our recent trip there. But when we arrived the clouds parted and the clear beauty of the grounds and lake sparkled in the sunshine.

While George was busy taking pictures I strolled down to the dock, planted myself in one of the chairs I found there, and enjoyed the peaceful surroundings. As I sat there overlooking the many boats owned by the camp and the mountains in the distance I thought: It doesn't get any better than this.

This pattern continued during my stay here. I took a lot of relaxation time in rocking chairs on the outside porch of our camp. I thoroughly enjoyed early morning with that outstanding view of the water. The birds were very active in the trees by the camp and the quiet beauty is reason enough to visit here.

But the spectacular lodge, open for public dining, is something you must experience. The two large dining rooms have log walls and the sporting tradition is a clear theme. There's even a full sized canoe suspended from the ceiling. Our window table was so close to the water I could have thrown a stone into the lake.

Steve cooked a delicious meal for us. I started with a nice garden salad and ended with an entree of rib eye steak, baked potato and brussels sprouts. The rib eye was massive.

On the regular menu I noticed a good variety of appetizers, four nice salads, and several choices of entrees. Offerings included fillet and ribs, duck, pasta and burgers as well as many nice fish and seafood options. Choose the "American plan" if you want meals provided during your stay or dine here as you wish during your stay. The restaurant is open to the public year-round and is a popular destination for snowmobilers.

Bald Mountain Camps also has a great indoor and outdoor facility for special events, including weddings. And it's not that long a drive if you want to come up here for dinner some night. The ride up is especially nice in the fall with stunning views of the forests and mountains. We drove up from Farmington through Rangeley, then home from Oquossoc through Mexico across the Highlands. Absolutely spectacular.

BEAR CREEK LODGE

JOHN SCHMIDT IS A MAINE GUIDE WHOSE LODGE FOCUSES ON GUIDED and unguided hunting and fishing trips. Much of his business comes from bear hunters.

Owner: John Schmidt; 77 Bear Creek Lane, Island Falls, ME 04747; www.bearcreeklodge.net, bearcreek@fairpoint.net; (207) 463-2662.

Directions: At Chrystal Road off Route 2. West 3 miles on Route 2. 5 gates but no fees.

Description: All lodge and cabins with bathrooms and showers. Private rooms for couples.

Prices: Varies by season, from $595 for fishing to $2,195 for hunting bear with hounds. Hunting prices include guides.

> **Meals:** Provided.
>
> **Activities:** Hunting and fishing.
>
> **Season:** Year-round.

My Bear Creek Experiences
—by Shelby Hartin

Registered Maine Master Guide John Schmidt has been leading hunters through the northern Maine woods for thirty-seven years. His business allows him to share his love for the outdoors with others from around the country, but it took him a while to realize that guiding hunts was what he was meant to do.

Born and raised on a farm in Michigan, and after a stint in the military, Schmidt worked as a mechanical engineer, quickly figuring out that desk work was not for him. In 1964, he took his first trip to Maine. It took one visit to decide it was the state where he wanted to spend the rest of his life. He got that chance when his uncle Harold decided to move to Maine and start a business. John followed, ready to take on the challenge.

John was introduced to bear hunting by his uncle and describes his first bear hunt as dull. He dropped a bear with one clean shot. "I thought, jeez, this is no fun!" he told me. But because he loves spending time outdoors, with like-minded people, he started his own business, Bear Creek Lodge.

Bear Creek, located between Pleasant and Mattawamkeag Lakes, offers all outdoor experiences, not just bear hunting. But bear hunting is the primary focus. John describes a typical day in the life of a Maine bear hunting guide this way.

"It's a lot of work; you don't just walk out in the woods and start shootin'," he said. He stresses safety and caution when hunting bear, and emphasizes the importance of patience and persistence. "Nothing is guaranteed when you go into the woods. I always tell them you gotta work at it," John says. When asked what his constant advice is for his hunters, John says he always tells them that they should, "hunt each day like it's the last five minutes of Saturday."

The black bear helped John build his life. Instead of sitting at a desk and longing to step into the woods, his business lets him enjoy the outdoors every day. When asked if he'd change anything about his way of life, he responded simply, "I wouldn't trade it for the world."

Bear Spring Camps

Bear Spring Camps was established in 1910 by George D. and Alice R. Mosher. The couple moved to Rome, Maine, from Derby, Connecticut, with their two sons, Durwood and Bertram. Originally the property was a farm but by building six cottages and converting a wood shed into a dining area, they were soon ready to rent to families traveling from Boston and New York by train. In those days guests were picked up at the Belgrade Depot and transported back to camp. In 1911 Bertram married the girl next door, Irma Richardson, and they began to run the family business. As their family grew so did the number of cottages. By 1946 when their only son, Bertram G. Jr., married Marguerite Tobin there were twenty-one cottages. Bert and Marguerite added eleven more cottages, installed indoor plumbing, and expanded the dining area. They continued to run the camps until Bert's death in 1987 at which time his youngest daughter, Peggy, and her husband, Ron Churchill, took over. Today the camp continues to operate in the same simple manner as it did in 1910 with lakefront cottages, home cooked meals in the Main House, and families traveling from away to find a few days of old fashioned rest by the lakeside.

Owners: Ron and Peg Churchill; 60 Jamaica Point Road, Rome, ME 04963; www.bearspringcamps.com; (207) 397-2341.

Directions: On Great Pond in the Belgrade Lakes Region (just north of Augusta).

Description: Accommodates an average of 130 persons with 32 1- to 4-bedroom cottages.

Prices: Range from $750 a week to $3,450, depending on season and size of cottage.

Meals: 3 meals a day served in the dining room of the Main House.

Activities: Fish, swim, hike, kayak, sail.

Other: Motor boats, canoes, and kayaks available for rent. No pets. Cell phone and Internet service.

Season: Mid-May to October 1.

BEAVER COVE CAMPS

GUESTS HAVE BEEN ENJOYING THIS LOCATION, LOCATED ON THE EAST shore of Moosehead Lake, since 1905. The camps are only a ten minute drive from Greenville with easy access to shops, services and restaurants.

Owner: Marilyn Goodwin; PO Box 1233, Greenville, ME 04441; www.beavercovecamps.com, info@beavercovecamps.com; (207) 695-3717.

Directions: Nearest town: Beaver Cove, 6 miles north of Greenville. Lily Bay Road toward Kokadjo. 6.5 miles north, blinking light, sign on left (don't turn at Beaver Cove Marina sign!). Paved and gravel roads.

Description: 6 rustic yet modernized camps ranging in age from 30 to 111 years, all with indoor plumbing and fully equipped kitchens, outdoor fire pits, and picnic tables. Four have lake view and all have access to Moosehead Lake via the camp's boat launch. All of the camps have been updated within the past 5 years.

Prices: Cabin rentals start at $110/night, with each addition person $25/day or $150/week.

Meals: Not provided.

Other: Pets are welcome in all cabins with a $10/pet/night fee. Boat launch fee of $10. Canoe/kayak/ice shack rentals.

Activities: Ice fishing, snowmobiling, skiing, hiking, wildlife viewing, ATVing, hunting, fishing, boating, leaf peeping, birding.

Season: Year-round.

Boulet's Sporting Camps

Boulet's is a very traditional sporting camp in a remote section of the state, open only for the fall hunting seasons.

Owner: Joshua Bisque; PO Box 291, Millinocket, ME 04462; www.bouletsportingcamps.com, boulet2camps@aol.com; (207) 723-8800.

Directions: T4 R15 Township, Russell Stream, off North Maine Woods 490 Road. Nearest town: Millinocket, 72 miles. North Maine Woods gate fees.

Description: Mix of camps, apartments, and rooms. Indoor plumbing. Originally a logging camp.

Prices: Range from $77 to $88/day with meals and $27 to $40/day without meals. Sometimes you can rent by the day, other times a full week's rental is required.

Meals: Buffet style meals are available.

Activies: This is mostly a hunting camp.

Season: September through November only.

Hunting Camp
—by Guy Randlett, Maine guide, www.mainetrophymoose.com

It's 3:45 a.m., a cool, clear fall morning. The only noise is that of a bull moose grunting down by the Russell Stream. The silhouettes of tall pointed spruces surrounding Boulet's Sporting Camps in remote T4 R15 are framing a wildly black sky that seemingly could not possibly contain even one more star. I am at one of my favorite places on earth.

Built as a logging camp in the 1960s, purchased in the '90s by the Busque family of Millinocket, Boulet's Sporting Camps is a great place to stay for hunters that want great food and service right in the middle of wildlife action in the remote part of Maine north of the Golden Road. I have enjoyed hunting from many commercial sporting camps in Maine and Canada. For a serious hunter, Boulet's is at the top.

Be forewarned: BSC is open only for hunting season starting with a couple weeks of bear hunting, and ending with deer season. In between JD Busque and his crew are ably making life easier for moose hunters and bird hunters. The cabins are clean, warm, and dry, and have modern heat and plumbing.

The food, prepared and served in traditional logging camp fashion, is outstanding. Each table always has a jug of real maple syrup produced at the Busque family's sugar house. Frankly, the moose and deer hunting, while excellent, are secondary to me. The real draw are the food and atmosphere created in the dining lodge. Everyone there has "the right attitude."

You won't be confronted by anybody that harbors anti-hunting or anti-logging sentiments. You can openly enjoy and discuss the hunting and trapping displays that adorn the walls. BSC is neither fancy nor cute. It is not a place for someone who just wants to hang around camp all day. There exist no distractions such as live TV, hot tubs, or pool tables. No ice-makers or room service. Don't show up in your Forester or Rav 4, the invisible "bow wave" alone of a logging truck will blow you off the side. I have brought first-timers there often who look at me with fear and loathing upon arrival. One of my first impressions was "Oh, this must be where Clint Eastwood filmed *High Plains Drifter*." (minus the arid mountains and plus the spruce trees). All the better, and by the way those doubting first-timers always love the place long before departure.

Hunters can stay there "American plan" (all meals included) or bring their own food and prepare meals in their cabin. Boulet's Sporting Camps meals are all hot and delicious, at breakfast and when you return from a long day's hunt. Don't even consider the do it yourself option; that's my advice.

9:30 p.m.: Both the blueberry pie and the cranberry crumble (made from fresh berries harvested nearby) are settled into my stomach. The dishes and dinner commotion are done. I stand just outside enjoying the air before I hit the sack. Inside I can hear muffled conversation and an occasional laugh. When the generator goes off at 10 p.m., I will already be sleeping soundly, refreshed and fulfilled by another day of hunting from Boulet's Sporting Camp.

BUCKHORN SPORTING CAMPS
LOCATED ON AN ISLAND, THESE CAMPS DRAW LOTS OF REPEAT VISITORS who enjoy everything here from the stunning views of Mount Katahdin to fishing to getting married!

Owner: Grey Pellegrini; www.buckhorncamps.com; (508) 400-6274.

Directions: Jo-Mary Island in the middle of Jo-Mary Lake, Indian Purchase T4.

Description: Fully equipped cabins that sleep 5 to 6, with kitchen, bathroom and hot and cold running water.

Prices: Yearly and seasonal rentals are available from $250 to $550 per month, depending on cabin and length of rental.

Meals: Only during moose hunt.

Activities: Hunting and fishing, special events including weddings.

Other: Gate fees depending on your route. One week minimum rental. Long-term and season rentals. Some cell phone but no Internet service.

Season: Ice out to ice in.

Love at First Sight
—by Anne Clark

I remember the first time I arrived at the boat landing on Middle Jo Mary Lake and how beautiful it was. The lake was still with a clear reflection of the shore line everywhere I looked. We loaded the boat and headed across towards Buckhorn Sporting Camps. The view of Mt. Katahdin was breathtaking. As we turned toward Jo Mary Island I could see the cabins. It was love at first sight.

Since that time I have been fortunate to return every year and share the experience with family and friends. We have enjoyed summer fun as well as snowmobiling in the winter. Each visit has brought a new adventure. One summer day Katahdin Air Service flew into Buchorn's Sea Plane Base and picked us up and we flew off to the Allagash, over the lost locomotives, around Mt. Katahdin and down the West Branch of the Penobscot back to camp. It was an amazing experience.

Buckhorn Sporting Camps sits between Middle Jo Mary and Lower Jo Mary lakes. A thirty minute boat trip on Lower Jo Mary Lake and you arrive at the first of two natural white sand beaches where we have enjoyed picnics and swimming. The Appalachian trail borders the second sand beach which connects to a spur trail that leads to the top of Padawadjo Ridge where there is an amazing view of the entire Jo Mary area. I have had the opportunity to talk to hikers who come to enjoy the great pleasure of the lake before continuing on to Mt. Katahdin.

The history of Buckhorn Sporting Camps goes back over 100 years to 1897. Remnants of logging equipment are present as well as old wooden boats used many years ago. There are pictures of men and women in the early 1900s with lines strung full of fish and men tying their float planes to the docks. People have come and gone over the years but the beauty and charm still remain. I have enjoyed all the people I have met at Buckhorn, especially the children. Many of them are now adults who return with their young families. Let this be the next generation to continue the tradition and preserve the history of Buckhorn Sporting Camps.

Bulldog Camps

The first time I called Dick Mosher, a master guide for his entire life, to ask him to write a story about Bulldog Camps, I spent over an hour captivated by Dick's stories. Clearly, this is a place that has generated lifelong memories for many guides and guests for a very long time.

Owner: Darren Savage; PO Box 152, Jackman, ME 04945; www.bulldogcamp.com; (207) 243-2853.

Directions: Ten miles from Route 201 on a well-graded gravel road, about 23 miles from Jackman and West Forks.

Description: Turn-of-the-century log cabins with full kitchens and bathrooms with showers.

Prices: $45/night (housekeeping), $85/night (American plan), $100/night (fishing package). Weekly rates available.

Meals: All meals are served in the lodge, for American plan customers.

Activities: Fishing, hunting, ATV riding, hiking, swimming.

Other: Cell phone but no Internet. Pets allowed. Customers must bring sleeping bags and towels.

Season: May 1–December 1.

Great Memories at Bulldog Camps
—by Dick Mosher, longtime guide

Bulldog Camps at Enchanted Pond brings back many memories for me at 81 years of age—all good. Even though I have spent my whole life in the Maine backwoods, and as a native Mainer and master guide for fifty-four years, when asked about experiences at Bulldog Camps, I think back to 1952 when my best friend Gil Gilpatric and I graduated from high school in Fairfield.

Gil and I have been together as youngsters and spent our adult lives guiding and hunting, so it was only natural that as a graduation present to ourselves we headed to the woods. Gil had flown with an older friend into Enchanted Pond earlier and had fishing off the sandbar on the southwest end of the pond. He'd had a great time catching trout with worms and bobbers.

We could not fly so decided to hike in on an old logging trail that had been used in the early 1900s. The trail at that time went from Mile 4 on the Hardscabble Road to the northeast end of Enchanted Pond. This was about an 8 mile hike and I remember seeing Grace Pond on the way in.

We arrived at Enchanted at what is now Bulldog Camps. At that time the camps were abandoned. However, we were greeted there by an old timer and his German Shepherd dog. They were keeping an eye on the camps for the owners and said game wardens flew in occasionally to check on him and drop off supplies. He had a signal system if he needed help.

He offered us one of the cabins to stay in, but we declined as Gil and his friend had caught all their fish off the Sandbar at the south end of the pond. So off we went around the north end of the pond, wading across the inlet stream with our clothes over our heads to keep them dry. Then down the west side of the pond climbing over a rock slide and under alder bushes, until we finally got to the sandbar with our light pack, blankets, and fish poles.

We ate fish and canned beans and slept in our home-made lean-to for three days. We had hiked 10 miles to get there. Today it seems impossible, but for us it was the trip of a lifetime that set up my love for the best place in the state.

Bulldog Camps is now a premier traditional sporting camp which maintains a strong support of Maine culture for Mainers, and as I have learned through years of guiding people from all over the world, a place of equal value to them who join us for this age-old traditional experience.

My wife Judy and I were married at Bulldog Camps in 1986 and so were our daughter Jesse and her husband Andrew in 2014. Judy and I, with family and friends, have fished and hunted bear, moose, birds, coyotes, and rabbits from the camps. We have also enjoyed ATVing, bicycling, horseback riding, and relaxing in Mother Nature's beautiful wilderness, and these days, it's good that we don't have to hike 10 miles to do it!

CANALSIDE CABINS

CANALSIDE CABINS, LOCATED IN GRAND LAKE STREAM, HAS SIX TRAditional Maine Sporting Camp Cabins that have been catering to vacationing fishermen, hunters, and families since the early 1900s. The camps are open year-round.

Owners: John and Mary Arcaro; 31 Canal Street, Grand Lake Stream, ME 04668; www.canalsidecabins.com; (207) 796-2796; Facebook.

Directions: Located in the village of Grand Lake Stream, on a paved road. GPS coordinates: 45 degrees 10.835N by 67 degrees 46.560W.

Description: 6 housekeeping cabins located overlooking Grand Lake Stream, about 200 yards to West Grand Lake. All of the cabins have hot and cold running water, showers, bathtubs and toilets. All of the cabins have propane heat and screened in porches. They were licensed in 1922. Constant improvements, all cabins are winterized and open all year.

Prices: $45/person/night. 2-person minimum and 2-night stay on weekends.

Meals: No meals; guests are able to cook in the cabins.

Activities: Fishing, fly-fishing the stream for landlocked Atlantic salmon and brook trout. Trolling West Grand Lake for landlocked Atlantic salmon and lake trout (touge). Smallmouth bass fishing in the many lakes around. Ice-fishing the St. Croix watershed. Hunting big and small game, woodcock, grouse, waterfowl, and turkey.

Other: Cell phone service (sometimes) and Internet service. Pets allowed. Guests must bring their own towels. December to end of April guests must bring sleeping bags.

Season: Open all year, May, June, and October for fly-fishing and trolling for salmon. June, July, and August for bass and white perch fishing. August and September bear hunting over bait. October and November hunting. February and March ice fishing. January is our slowest month.

CASTLE ISLAND CAMPS

LOCATED ON A TWO-ACRE ISLAND, BUT WITH ROAD ACCESS, THIS IS A unique place with twelve water-front cabins only a few feet from the lake (two are actually over the water!). The Belgrade Lakes is a historic and popular tourist destination, and Castle Island gets plenty of vacationing families, but they also cater to anglers eager to fish these storied waters.

Owners: John and Rhonda Rice; PO Box 251, Belgrade Lakes, ME 04918; www.castleislandcamps.com; (207) 495-3312.

Directions: Located on Long Pond in Belgrade, just 20 minutes from the capital, on a paved road off Route 27.

Description: Family owned and operated since opening in 1929, this two-acre island is home to 12 waterfront cabins, a main lodge, and a recreation building. Cabins are no more than a few feet from the water and 2 are actually over the water. All of the cabins have been recently refurbished with new pine walls, flooring, showers, updated electrical, and other improvements. Cabins are heated, have private bathrooms with showers, and include a small refrigerator. Daily housekeeping includes linens and towels.

Prices: Single adult (16 and older) $92/day; couples $170/day; children 2 and under $40/day, 3–6 $50/day, 7–15 $75/day.

Meals: American plan, 3 meals/day. Set menus each meal, but dietary requests can be met.

Activities: Most guests come here to fish. The lake is home to large and smallmouth bass, crappie, northern pike, salmon, brown trout, and white perch. In the summer months, guests enjoy hiking, biking, swimming, and water sports.

Other: Fishing boats available for rent. Free use of canoes and kayaks. Minimum stay of three days. Cell service and limited Internet. No pets.

Season: May 1 to mid-September

CEDAR MILL FARM AND CABINS
CEDAR MILL HAS FOUR CABINS, FOCUSED ON HUNTING, BUT THEY DO get families on vacation and some snowmobilers and ATV riders.

Owners: Michael and Teresa Stasiowski; 354 Brighton Road, Athens, ME 04912; www.cedarmillfarmandcabins.com; (207) 654-2195; Facebook.

Directions: The nearest town is Skowhegan. Main lodge is on a paved road, while cabins are on a gravel road.

Description: Four cabins constructed between 2004 and 2006. Cabins have gaslights and heat. The two newer cabins are wired for electricity by generator, but guests must bring their own generator. Each cabin has either an outhouse or portable toilet. 1 cabin sleeps 4 with two sets of bunk beds and the other 3. $6.95 box-lunch, $13.95 supper.

Meals: Guest can cook for themselves in the cabins, where there is a stove and sink, or choose to have meals in the main lodge.

Activities: Most guests rabbit hunt. Secondary to that is bear hunting, with some deer, turkey, and coyote hunting. Fishing. ATV and snowmobile trails are accessible from the camps. Kennels are available for dogs, without charge.

Other: Cell phone and Internet service. Pets allowed, but cannot be left in cabins unattended or allowed on the beds.

Season: Year-round.

CEDAR RIDGE OUTFITTERS

I CAN'T GIVE YOU A BETTER SUMMARY OF WHAT YOU WILL FIND HERE than this one from longtime customer Joe Hectus, who also wrote the story for this lodge. Here's what Joe told me: "I have stayed with outfitters in Alaska, British Columbia, Alabama, Wyoming, New Mexico, and elsewhere. Ron and Lynda Hamilton, the owners of Cedar Ridge, would give L.L. Bean a run for their money when it comes to customer service! I have been fortunate to have mostly very good experiences with outfitters but Ron and Lynda provide a superior experience. I am sure that skill as a cook, manager and a lot of experience has a lot to do with it but having an attitude that they want to provide the best experience for each guest takes them over the top."

Owners: Ron and Lynda Hamilton; PO Box 744, Jackman, ME 04945; www.cedarridgeoutfitters.com, cedarridge42@gmail.com; (207) 668-4169.

Directions: For a GPS search, punch in 36 Attean Road, Jackman Maine 04945. Cedar Ridge Outfitters is located on the outskirts of Jackman and just 15 miles from the border of Quebec.

A 4-hour drive from Kittery (Kittery sits on the border of Maine and New Hampshire, off route 95). Take exit 133 off 95 just after last Waterville exit. (Waterville is approx 2½ hrs from Kittery.) Then take 201 north to Jackman/ Moose River Region (approximately 1½ hour from this exit to Jackman). You will see a big Moose River sign entering town. You will pass Mountainview Timeshares and Jackman Trading Post on the right. At the bottom of the hill, turn left onto Attean Road. Go ½ mile, Cedar Ridge Outfitters is on the left. Take note when driving up 201 and watch carefully for moose. They can weigh as much as 1,500 hundred pounds, which is like hitting a brick wall. Their hair is dark brown/black and is very hard to see in the dark. No access fees required.

Description: Located just 1½ miles from the center of town, but far enough out of town to be peaceful and secluded. 7 cozy 2 and 3 bedroom cabins with full size kitchens, bathrooms, oil heat, air conditioning, ceramic tile, carpeted floors, and TVs with satellite. Cabins all have front porches with gas grills for barbecuing and porch furniture for enjoying the outdoors without leaving your cabin. Free wifi, long-distance calling, and satellite TV in all cabins. Bathrooms have all the towels you'll need for your stay.

Prices: Vary according to the cabin. Example: Deer shack/ Buckstop—These small cozy cabins have 2 bedrooms, 1 bathroom, a small full size kitchen and living room. Bedroom 1: queen sized bed; Bedroom 2: 2 twin/bunks; Rate: 2 guests/night minimum, $90/night. Additional guests are $45/person/night. Moose Wallow—This large stand-alone cabin has 3 bedrooms, 1 large bathroom, a large full-sized kitchen/dining, and living room. Will sleep 12 total with couples/9 singles; Bedroom 1: 2 full size beds/bunks; Bedroom 2: 4 twins beds/bunks; Bedroom

3: 2 twins beds/bunks and 1 full size bed; Rate: 6 guests/
night minimum, $270/night. Additional guests are $45/person/
night.

Meals: All meals are home cooked in a newly remodeled kitchen,
using fresh, high quality ingredients for each meal. There is a
family atmosphere in the main lodge and guests are served in the
newly expanded dining room where they can meet other guests
and the Cedar Ridge staff. On remote hunts, guests are served a
similar menu adapted for outdoor cooking by the guides.

Activities: Hunting and fishing. Guides available.

Other: Cell phone and Internet service available. Pets accepted.

Season: Year-round.

My Bull Moose Hunt
—by Joe Hectus

My wife, Mike (Mary Michael) and I started planning our trip to Maine
in June 2014 when I drew a coveted Maine Bull Moose tag during the
annual lottery. I considered myself lucky since 2014 was only my four-
teenth consecutive year applying for a Maine Bull Moose tag and the
number of tags available had been reduced twenty-five percent by Maine
Fish and Game in 2014.

I booked my week hunt with Cedar Ridge Outfitters in June and
contacted Ron Hamilton a couple of times prior to our arrival in Jackman
on October 12. Ron was always accommodating and answered all of my
questions. In addition, my guide, Chuck Theriault, contacted me approximately two weeks prior to my hunt to introduce himself. Chuck was very
discreet asking questions about my experience and physical limitations.
This was very important to tailor the hunt to my ability and to assure
success. Very good planning on the part of Cedar Ridge Outfitters!

My wife and I arrived in Jackman on Sunday, October 12. We met Ron, Lynda, and Chuck. At dinner, we also met other guests who were at the lodge to do some fall trout and salmon fishing.

Sunday dinner introduced us to what was a week of gourmet meals served at dinner, breakfast and lunch in the beautiful main lodge. Ron and Lynda prepare all meals using the best of ingredients. Dinners included turkey with fresh fall vegetables and homemade cranberry sauce, pork loin with fresh vegetables, prime rib with salad and baked potato as well as a fantastic meatloaf one evening. Breakfast included fresh baked cinnamon rolls and bread each day along with eggs and bacon or blueberry pancakes with maple syrup. My wife and I very much enjoyed each meal served in the main lodge by Ron and Lynda as well as the conversation with our hosts and other guests. I don't want to forget the fresh baked desserts as they were so good that I'm sure we added a few pounds during our stay.

My hunt started on Monday morning, October 13, with a wake up at 3:30 a.m. I met Chuck at the Main lodge at 4 a.m. for a hearty breakfast and then we were off to the north of Jackman to start our hunt. Chuck did his homework by working with Billy, another Cedar Ridge guide. We entered the woods by navigating a small stream which mitigates our scent and masks any noise we might make.

Chuck started calling when we arrived at our destination and he immediately got a response from a bull moose. We also encountered a cow and young bull when Chuck was calling. The cow angrily responded to Chuck's calling as she did not want us on her turf! This encounter lasted several minutes and was an experience worth coming to Maine for. In a short time, we had the mature bull moose within sight again and the hunt was over.

Chuck had successfully guided me during the first couple of hours on opening day. We both knew our opportunity would be on the morning of opening day since the weather would warm to the mid-seventies by noon and remain in the mid-sixties at night and the mid-seventies during the day for the remainder of the week. The moose would find a cool place to rest during the remainder of the week until cooler temperatures arrived. The warm weather resulted in the poorest moose harvest since moose hunting was re-established about twenty years ago.

Ron and his grandson Brent were on the scene within a half hour helping with the chore of getting the moose to the Maine check station and then to the butcher. The next day Ron invited me to hunt ruffed grouse with him and his bird dog. We had a great day with the dog but were unsuccessful because of the heat. The next day Ron took me to New Frontier Taxidermy in Solon, Maine. The trip was over an hour's drive each way.

I have hunted and fished with outfitters from Alaska to New Brunswick and from Wyoming to Alabama and have never had owners who were more accommodating than Ron and Lynda Hamilton at Cedar Ridge Outfitters. Their customer service may exceed the superior service at L.L. Bean. My guide, Chuck Theriault, was a master of his profession as well as an extremely enjoyable person to hunt with. My wife and I thoroughly enjoyed our stay at Cedar Ridge Outfitters and we are looking forward to our next visit with Ron, Lynda, Brent, Chuck and Billy. We left Maine with new friends in Jackman!

CHANDLER LAKE CAMPS
OVER 100 YEARS OLD, THESE ARE THE ONLY CAMPS ON A REMOTE North Maine Woods lake.

Owners: Jason and Sheralyn Bouchard; PO Box 27, Ashland, ME 04732; www.chandlerlakecamps.com; (207) 290-1424.

Directions: Leaving Ashland you enter the North Maine Woods, travel to 6-mile gate where access fees apply and turn left on to the Pinkham Road. Travel to mile 27 and turn left onto the Craigville Road. 3 miles to the lodge; follow the signs. Industrial forest, gravel roads, and gate fees apply.

Description: Original cabins were built in 1902, only camps on Chandler Lake. Cabins with baths, modernized with generator, solar, and other amenities. Traditional Maine sporting camp with a few modern conveniences.

Prices: $168/person all-inclusive at Chandler Lake Camps. $200/person at 4th Musquacook Lodge, all inclusive, only additional charge is the state lodging tax of 8%.

Meals: 3 meals each day. Home cooked with only the best quality. Prime rib, roast pork tenderloin, lobster/steak and roast lamb to name a few.

Activities: Fishing: spring trolling and fly fishing for native brook trout. Upland hunting with and without dogs. Deer/moose hunting. Relaxing family vacations. Automated grouse walk, hunting preserve activities with chukars and quail. Dog training on wild and pen raised birds.

Other: Phone and wifi if needed. Pets allowed.

Season: May–December. Fishing: May–July 25 and September 15–October 1. Upland hunting: October 1–November 15.

Musings of Chandler Lake Camps
—by Fred Beck

The Chandler Lake Camps have existed for over 100 years. The camps started out as a sporting camp later to be sold to a private family from New York State known as the Hart family. The Harts were the longest continuous owners of the camp. It was during their ownership tenure that I have my first recollections of the camps.

As a young lad in the 1950s I spent every summer at Portage Lake at my family's camps. During those years the Hart family spent most of their summers at Chandler Lake. The only way to get supplies in to them was by floatplane. In those days there were a number of flying services based at Portage, most notable being Coffin's flying Service. The Coffin family also owned the general Store in Portage. As a youngster I had a great love of flying and spent many idle hours hanging out at the seaplane base.

I knew all the pilots and quite often, if they were going on a supply flight to one of the many sporting camps in the area and had room, they would invite me to go along. That was how I first visited the camps at Chandler Lake. I recall making a number of such trips to Chandler over a period of several years. Mrs. Hart would always have a fresh cookie or piece of pie and a glass of milk for us after we had unloaded the airplane. I can remember, even at the tender age of ten or eleven years, being struck by the raw beauty of the area and the view of Chandler Mountain from the front porch. I would often daydream about what it would be like to spend a whole summer there. Little did I know what would be in store for me many years later.

More than fifty years went by before I again returned to Chandler Lake. I had met Jason Bouchard, the current owner, while flying in and out of the Lincoln Airport for the Civil Air Patrol. Having a lot in common we struck up a friendship and one day Jason invited me to fly up to Chandler Lake to see the camps he had recently purchased. I thought, could this be the same camps I remembered from my childhood? Sure enough it was. But my how it had changed.

The camps had been abandoned for many, many years and were in a sad state of disrepair. Jason's goal was to bring the camps back to life and operate it as a commercial sporting camp once again. I recall thinking at the time what an uphill battle he was facing and better him than me. Again little did I know what was in store for me.

In 2004 a year or so after our visit to Chandler I retired from a long career in the forest industry in Maine. That fall Jason said he was having a few hunters at camp for the first time and asked if I might be willing to go up and do the cooking for them as well as some guiding. And so it started. The following spring he asked if I could come up for a week or so to help out with some carpentry projects. Nearly five years later I retired again. My childhood daydreams of what it would be like to spend a whole summer at Chandler Lake were answered. I had spent nearly five full seasons at camp.

Today the Chandler Lake camps are a very low key but first class sporting camp operation. They cater to only a few guests at a time and that means that they receive the full attention of the owners and staff.

The food, which is a key part of any sporting camp operation, is second to none. I am very proud to be able to say that I had a small part in making the camps what they are today and I still enjoy visiting there when time permits to enjoy the more genteel sports of hunting and fishing while someone else wields the chain saw and axe.

CHESUNCOOK LAKE HOUSE AND CABINS

THE LAKE HOUSE IS A SMALL WILDERNESS LODGE, BUILT AS A FARM-house/boarding house in 1864 at Chesuncook Village, to supply logging operations in Northern Maine's Wilderness. It is now on the Federal Historical Register. The Lake House is located 50 miles north of the Moosehead Lake Region and 60 miles west of Millinocket, situated in the center of the last recognized wilderness area in the East. The Lake House has been featured by numerous magazines as a "very unique and special place" (*Yankee*, *Down East*, *Boston Globe*, *New York Times*, and others.). *Yankee Magazine* selected the Chesuncook Lake House as the "Editors Pick of Outstanding Places in New England."

Owners: David and Luisa Surprenant; Hc 76 Box 656 Greenville, ME 04441; greatnorthernvacations.com, greatnorthernvacations@gmail.com, chesuncook@hughes.net.

Directions: Located at the north end of Chesuncook Lake, 2 hours from either Greenville or Millinocket on dirt road; follow Golden Road to mile 50 then 14 miles on Pine Stream Road. GPS coordinates do not work. Located behind NMW gates subject to land access fees.

Description: Main house has 4 bedrooms with queen beds with two shared baths; built in 1864, fully renovated.

3 housekeeping cabins with 2 bedrooms, full kitchen and bath, sleep 6–8 each built in 2002. Downstairs has living room and dining room all with original tin walls and ceilings. House was originally a boarding house for The Great Northern loggers.

Prices: $150/person/night includes all meals in the main house, use of canoes and kayaks. Cabins are $200/night for up to 4 people, additional persons $50 each. Cabins require 2-night minimum.

Meals: Three meals daily for American plan guests. Cabins have full kitchens. All meals served family style, packed lunch available on request. Typical suppers include turkey, ham, pot roast or guest requests.

Activities: Winter—snowmobiling, summer—canoeing, family vacation.

Season: January–March and May–November.

CHET'S CAMPS

LOCATED DOWN EAST IN AN AREA HISTORICALLY FAMOUS FOR ITS FISH-ing and hunting, Chet's Camps continue to draw sportsmen and women for great outoor adventures, including Erin Merrill, one of Maine's best outdoor writers and a leader of programs for outdoor women.

Owners: Sue and Al Laplante; 140 Chet's Camps Road, Grand Lake Stream, ME 04668; www.chetscamps.com; (207) 796-5557.

Directions: On a .7-mile gravel road just off the Grand Lake Stream/Milford Road between Princeton and Grand Lake Stream.

Description: 5 lake-front cabins with docks on Big Lake. Fully equipped, linens and towels, showers, and heat.

Prices: Cabins $55/person/night (2 or more), $75/individual in a cabin, $135/family/night. Group rates available.

Meals: $20 cabin dining, $15 picnic lunch, $20 shore lunch, $25 lobster lunch.

> **Activities:** Fishing, boating, canoing, kayaking, hiking, hunting, birding, wildlife watching, geocaching.
>
> **Other:** Canoes and kayaks free for guests, boat rentals.
>
> **Season:** Ice out mid-April to mid-October.

Running Away to Chet's Camps
—by Erin Merrill, outdoor writer and blogger, www.andastrongcupof coffee.com

The most amazing thing happens when you turn off of the pavement and head towards Chet's Camps in Grand Lakes Stream. The world slips way and you are surrounded by beautiful waters, incredible hosts and world renowned fishing.

Chet's Camps were built in the early 1940s and since their construction, they have served as seasonal camps for those who are eager to get away from everyday life and relax in the outdoors. The four cabins range in size but all have incredible views of the Big Lake and come equipped with everything you could possibly need; a shower, coffee pot, comfortable relaxing chairs and couches, and from the front windows you can watch loons swim by, hear osprey calling and watch them catch fish as well as catch some of the most breathtaking sunrises.

In 2002, Chet's Camps were bought by Sue and Al Leplante, two Maine guides with a passion for the outdoors. Both former teachers, Sue and Al work to promote the outdoors and are passionate about the outdoor issues that impact Maine and Grand Lakes Stream. More than once I have been invited to come into their home and sit down for great conversation about past hunts, latest catches and the need to preserve and protect Maine's beautiful lands and incredible hunting and fishing resources. Once you arrive at camp, there is no need to look further for a local guide to help give you the inside scoop of where the best activities are. Sue and Al can help to customize your trip in a number of ways, from guided fishing, ATV trips, back country canoe and kayak expeditions, to GPS and geocaching instruction, fly fishing instruction, and river expeditions.

That is what drew me to this hidden gem in Grand Lakes Stream. I spent my first Mother's Day with a fly rod in my hand on the Big Lake with Al. We were looking for some of the lake's best known catches; salmon, small mouth bass, togue, perch and pickerel but all I caught was a small salmon that I had to throw back. While we were trolling around the lake I had the opportunity to talk to Al about the rich fishing and Native American history of the area, the bear, grouse and deer hunting and the excellent hiking trails that have been established by the Downeast Lakes Lake Trust, for hikers of every kind. Al taught me how to cast and what proper fly casting form looked like. He was more than happy to take the time out of his day to teach me how to tie a clinch knot to secure my lock and answered all of my questions, no matter how small they may have seemed.

The first year that my family went to Chet's Camps, we had our dog and 11 month old son. Sue emailed me a few times prior to our arrival to make sure that I had everything taken care of or if I needed things like a Pack 'n' Play and highchair. The cabin was packed with infant necessities and ready for us when we got there. There is nothing better for a new mom than to know that things as simple as a high chair were waiting at camp so that we didn't have to pack ours into an already filled car. The second year that we headed back, Sue did the same thing and made sure the cabin was as family friendly as it could be. Chocolate chip cookies, a basket of kids books and a stuffed loon were wonderful surprises that my son could enjoy when we were not playing on the docks, kayaking or fishing.

In addition to the fishing, we used the available kayaks and paddled around the Big Lake and up the stream. The minute that we said we may want to go, Sue had them ready down by the water with lifejackets and paddled waiting. Our son was able to enjoy his first kayak trip as we paddled around, watching the loons and seeing the turtles sunbathing out on the rocks. It was a perfect way to get outdoors as a family.

After only two years of going to Chet's Camps, my family and I already have great memories. It is the place where we can relax and watch the Maine outdoors around us. I hope that as we continue this yearly tradition, my son can begin to create his own fond memories of our time there on the Big Lake.

For anyone who wants to get away, go fishing or hunting and who enjoys the Grand Lakes Stream area, Chet's Camps is a must.

Crooked Tree Lodge

Crooked Tree specializes in bear hunts over bait and with hounds. They also host moose hunters. In 2013, the lodge hosted the national Crossroads TV show on both a bait and hound hunt. A full episode was produced and aired in the spring of 2014 on the Pursuit Channel, gaining Crooked Tree Lodge National Recognition on the big screen.

Owners: Denny and Stephanie Davis; PO Box 203, Portage, ME 04768; www.crookedtreelodge.com; (207) 435-6413.

Directions: In Portage, paved road from Presque Isle, then gravel from Huntingon. North Maine Woods gate fees.

Description: Log cabins set up motel style, with bathrooms and showers.

Prices: Call for prices.

Meals: All meals provided.

Activities: Bear hunting over bait or with hounds, moose hunting, fishing.

Other: Minimum 6-day stay. Arrive Saturday and leave the following Sunday.

Season: Opens last week in August; open all September and October, plus moose hunting week in November.

Debsconeag Lake Wilderness Camps

Chewonki's rental cabins on Fourth Debsconeag Lake are situated in the heart of Maine's North Woods on an exquisite chain of lakes and ponds that are permanently protected as an ecological reserve. The cabins on Fourth Debsconeag Lake date back to the early 1900s and have all of the charm and beauty one would expect. This is a great setting for a family getaway or a family reunion.

Owners: Chewonki Foundation; 485 Chewonki Neck Road, Wiscasset, ME 04578; Greg Shute, outdoor programs director; www.chewonki.org/vacations/vacations, debsconeag.asp; (207) 460-5226 (summer), (207) 882-7323 (winter); Facebook.

Directions: T1 Raa on Fourth Debsconeag Lake, 22 miles in on the Jo Mary Road from Route 11. North Maine Woods access fees.

Description: Camps are the only structures on Fourth Debsconeag Lake and date from the turn of the 20th century, but updated in 1996, 2206, and 2008 including new composting bathroom facility and shower house. Enlarged and renovated lodge. Eight yurts added in 2007 and 2008.

Prices: Cabin and yurt rentals range from $50 to $200 per night depending on number of guests.

Meals: Kitchens in cabins including refrigerators. Full meals can be arranged for organized groups.

Activities: Hiking, fishing, swimming, birding, canoeing, kayaking.

Other: 2-night minimum, no cell or Internet service, pets allowed. Youth programs offered during some summer weeks.

Season: May through October.

Chewonki's Camps
—by Anne Leslie

At dawn, sun floods Fourth Debsconeag (DEBS-con-eeg) Lake below the granite cliffs that rise steeply above the northern shore. From our cabin in the Fourth Debsconeag Lake Wilderness Camps, the sight beckons. We begin the day with a swim in the deep, clear water. After breakfast and conversation over a map of the Nahmakanta Reserve around us, we set forth in canoes.

From the far shore, we hike a mile and a half to the Appalachian Trail for an expedition up Nesuntabunt Mountain. We return to Fourth Debsconeag in time to pick blueberries on top of the cliffs. As twilight falls, we put a streamer fly on the end of our line in hopes of bringing a lake or brook trout back to camp. After dinner, the swirl of stars and the call of loons remind us that we are only visitors in this breathtaking territory.

So it's been on Fourth Debsconeag Lake for more than a century. "This site is as pristine and idyllic as one can find in Maine," says Greg Shute, director of outdoor programs at Chewonki, a Maine guide, and a frequent visitor. "It's easy to imagine the Wabanaki feeling a similar appreciation for this beautiful spot a thousand years ago."

An equally enthusiastic visitor established Pleasant Point Camps for hunters and fishermen on Fourth Debsconeag in 1901. Nearly a century later, Mardi and Cliff George took ownership, carefully revitalized the buildings and site, and ran a successful sporting camp business. In 2007, retirement prompted them to sell to the Chewonki Foundation, a non-profit environmental education organization based in Wiscasset, Maine.

Chewonki renamed the property Debsconeag Lake Wilderness Camps and gave it a dual purpose. In summer and winter, Chewonki uses it for educational programs; in spring, late summer, and fall, the camps are available to rent. Chewonki added eight yurts to the seven existing cabins, enlarged the main lodge, added composting toilets, and installed a solar array to provide most of the energy. Simple kitchens, hot and cold running water, showers, and woodstoves keep things comfortable. Canoes are available for guests.

For those seeking a wilderness adventure or a peaceful getaway, "Fourth Debsconeag is absolutely magical," says Betta Stothart, who has stayed at the camps several times and whose daughter participated in a Chewonki program there. "It feels a thousand miles away from busy modern life."

"We're the only place on the lake and the only place that will *ever* be on the lake," Greg Shute says. And the lake sits in an ecological reserve of more than 11,000 acres within the 45,000-acre Nahmakanta Reserve, which in turn is skirted by hundreds of thousands more acres of conserved land. There's excellent access to countless trails and waterways.

In the summer, when Chewonki students are at the camps, through-hikers might hear the joyful cheer, "Debsconeag Lake, awake, awake!" In the spring, late summer, and fall, you'll hear only birdsong, wind in the trees, water eddying around your paddle, or your footsteps reaching for the trail ahead.

EAGLE LAKE SPORTING CAMPS

A TRADITIONAL SPORTING CAMP WITH FIFTEEN LOG CAMPS FACING Eagle Lake, open spring through fall.

Owner: Alvin Theriault; PO Box 249, Eagle Lake, ME 04739; www.eaglelakesportingcamps.com; (207) 444-5108, Gloria Theriault, manager; Facebook.

Directions: 20 miles by privately maintained gravel road from either State Route 161 or State Route 11 south of Eagle Lake Village. 35 miles west of Caribou. 7 miles by boat from Eagle Lake Village.

Description: 15 log cabins face the lake, constructed from large logs and modernized in 2001. Each cabin has a full bathroom with antique soaking tub and shower or a modern shower stall. Propane heaters. The Guide House has laundry facilities and additional bathrooms. Maid service.

Prices: Rates range from $135/person/night during the low season to $175/person/night during the busy fall season. An 18% resort fee is applied.

Meals: Three meals/day, with wine list, in Roosevelt Dining Room that seats 30. Rough Rider Tavern is a bar with a large fieldstone fireplace, pool table, and game room. The restaurant and lounge are open to the public by advance reservation.

Activities: Fishing, birding, boating, canoeing, hiking; shooting sports—skeet, pistol, and rifle ranges.

Other: Minimum stay 2 days. Cell phone and Internet service. Pets allowed.

Other: 4WD vehicle recommended during wet conditions in spring and fall.

Season: Spring through fall.

Food and Friendship
—by Tom Crowley, Lincolnville Beach, with Jack Garofalo, New Orleans, LA

A few days at the Eagle Lake Sporting Camps in northern Maine will heal the body and mind as the experience takes you back in time to when excellence in service, food, and friendship were standards kept in high regard. Whether you go there to hunt, fish, meditate or just mellow out you will manage to end the day by a pristine, quiet lake where eagles and falcons soar overhead and the sunrise illuminates a beaver's wake approaching a favorite grass bed.

My first visit there enabled me to enjoy the company of my friend and brother-in-law of over forty years as we fished the lake and nearby tributaries for brook trout hiding behind beaver dams by day and savored gourmet meals and a nice bourbon by the lakeside fire as the sun went down. Climbing into bed at midnight back at our 100 year old log cabin with birch bark wall covering and gas lighting, we traveled back in time to the days when Teddy Roosevelt and his pals walked these grounds. We will go back again and again, bringing our spouses, children, and grandchildren to share and extend the experience.

Eagle Lodge and Camps
Twenty mile long Eagle Lake is one of the famous Fish River chain of lakes that stretches, in northern Maine, 60 miles through beau-

tiful forest almost to the Canadian border, surpassing in primeval beauty and grandeur many of the better known woodlands and lakes of Maine. Established in 1889, the camps are located on a peninsula 7 miles up the Lake from Eagle Lake Village at the outlet of Square Lake thoroughfare and in the midst of a 23,000 acre wilderness reserve. They are on a high knoll among beautiful white birches, facing the lake in a southwesterly direction. The view is magnificent; lake and forest blend; ridge upon ridge looms up, until finally Three Brooks Mountain caps in the distance.

Owners: Justin and Loraine Morse; 600 Folsom Pond Road, Lincoln, ME 04457; www.eaglelodgemaine.com; (207) 794-2181; Facebook.

Directions: Exit 227 off Route 95, on a dirt road, no access fees, in Lincoln.

Description: 5 cabins and a main lodge, located directly on Folsom Pond, 500 acres of water from dock. About 100 years old; lodge updated in 2012/2013 for a beautiful view of the lake. All cabins have bathrooms with toilets and shower. All fully furnished cabins.

Prices: Housekeeping plan (you cook) $140/night or $900 for the week, American plan (we cook) $125/person per night, includes cabin, breakfast, and dinner in the lodge, packed lunch. 3-night minimum stay.

Meals: Breakfast and dinner in the lodge, lunch packed to go for meal plan. All cabins have fully furnished and fully equipped kitchens for those that want to cook for themselves. Meal plan dinners include lobster/steamers, steak, chicken, pork, ham, turkey, lasagna, chicken parmesan. All dinners include potato/rice, vegetable, homemade bread/roll, and desserts. Desserts include homemade apple pie, blueberry pie, chocolate cream pie, graham cracker pie, choclate cake, cranberry bars, peanut butter cake, and more. Breakfast includes casseroles, pancakes, french toast, and eggs. All breakfast have bacon/ham/sausage, home fries and fruit.

Activities: Most guests fish, canoe, swim, rent boats, and take day trips to Baxter and Acadia National Park. Some hunt in the fall.

Other: Free use of canoes and kayaks.

Season: May–October. Cell phone service but no Internet. Pets allowed.

EAGLE MOUNTAIN GUIDE SERVICE—WILDERNESS LODGE

A TRUE SPORTSMAN'S LODGE FOCUSED ON GREAT HUNTING AND FISHING experiences, including those of Robin Follette, a wonderful full-time writer and leader of Maine's community of sporting women.

Owners: Matt and Lisa Whitegiver; 48 Bunker Drive, Otis, ME 04605; www.eaglemountainguideservice.com; (207) 537-5282.

Directions: The lodge is right at mile marker 246 on Route 9 (the Airline). Beddington is 10 miles west and Wesley is 10 miles east.

Description: In the remotest section of the Airline, the lodge was built in 1963, just 2 miles from the Machias River. It is off the grid and run by a generator. The lodge has 10 rooms (7 doubles and 3 singles), each with a full bath.

Prices: See website.

Meals: Three meals/day.

Activities: Hunting bear, moose, deer, grouse; fishing (brook trout and smallmouth bass).

Season: Spring to late fall.

Hollywood in Wesley, Maine
—by Robin Follette, outdoor writer, www.robinfollette.com

Traveling on Route 9, also known as the Airline, you might not notice the town of Wesley until you reach an icon called Wilderness Lodge. Built in the 1960s, the locals tell a tale of the lodge once having been owned by Jackie Gleason, though there's nothing to support the claim. Wilderness Lodge was the first building in what was supposed to be a getaway for the big names in Hollywood. The Rat Pack did visit but plans fell through and the lodge became what it's best known for today, a sportsman's lodge.

Currently owned by Matt and Lisa Whitegiver, Wilderness Lodge has ten rooms. Seven are doubles and three are singles, and each room is equipped with its own full bath. There's no waiting in line here. Lisa built much of the furniture including tables, side tables, and bed frames, some of it using white birch trees. Bear, deer and moose mounts decorate the walls and help set the warm feel of the lodge. A small bar, dining area and great room give guests plenty of space to move around outside of their rooms.

The feel of the lodge is rustic from the moment you pull into the parking lot. Located on a wilderness highway, the lodge is the only building for miles. There are no neighbors other than the bear, moose, deer, and smaller wild game. You are surrounded by thousands of acres of forest, blueberry barrens, and water. Off the grid, power is supplied by a generator; the nearest power line is more than 2 miles away.

Family style meals are served at Wilderness Lodge. Lisa runs the kitchen with the help of one cook. The food is delicious and there's plenty of it so active outdoors folks never leave the table hungry.

Hunting seasons at Wilderness Lodge cover bear, moose and deer. Matt is a Master Maine Guide. Downeast Maine is well-known for the large number of big Maine black bears. They offer three and six day hunts over bait. Wilderness Lodge has thirty-five proven bait sites spread across a 50 mile area, giving baits enough distance in between to keep the bears spread out. There is a limit of thirteen bear hunters per week to allow full attention and bear hunting education to every bear hunter. Hunters are picked up and brought back to the lodge before bears are retrieved so that everyone is back to enjoy a full supper.

Wilderness Lodge sits on the border of Wildlife Management Districts 19 and 28, and offers hunts in 11, 18, 19, 26, 27 and 28. You don't have to go farther north for a trophy moose. You may choose between a fully guided or semi-guided hunt depending on your experience and equipment. Your guide works one-on-one with the hunter and sub-permittee to find the moose and set up to call the moose to you.

The area around the lodge is as well-known for its big bucks as it is its moose. Tree stands and blinds sit in established deer trails that have proven themselves for decades. Your guide will work with you to create the hunt that best suits you if sitting is not your favored method of hunting whitetails.

Lakes and streams around Wilderness Lodge provide excellent fresh water fishing. You may stay at the lodge as your base and walk to or make a short drive to top-notch trout and bass fishing. You'll find excellent fishing within 15 miles of the lodge.

There are hundreds of miles of connecting ATV trails surrounding Wilderness Lodge. You may leave on the trail that runs through the parking lot to connect to other trails, ride all day, and return to the parking lot without ever needing to trailer your ATVs.

The lodge is an excellent place to spend a few days hiking and bird walking. Maintained roads allow you to drive beyond your comfortable hiking distance. American bald eagles, Eastern wild turkeys, osprey, owls, gulls and a large number of songbirds are found on roads and trails behind the lodge. You can stop at the top of a hill and watch birds of prey riding the updraft far above your head. The blueberry barrens give a clear view of the sky for miles.

The lodge is a forty-five-minute drive from the border crossing to New Brunswick, Canada. You can travel to Eastport to whale watch, drive to Lubec to be the first in the nation to see the sunrise, or head north toward Grand Lake Stream and Baxter State Park. If you'd like to spend the day at the beach you'll find Roque Bluffs an easy drive.

Wilderness Lodge offers something for everyone who loves the outdoors. It's also available for conferences and workshops that are a day, a weekend or longer.

Echo Lake Lodge and Cottages

Since 1937, guests have been enjoying Echo Lake Lodge and Cottages, focused on family vacations and outdoor adventures. The lodge and cottages share over 600 feet of lake frontage on beautiful Echo Lake, and are located just 15 miles northwest from Maine's capital city of Augusta and I-95, at the end of a quiet, wooded road.

Owners: James and Evelyn Feagin; PO Box 495, Kents Hill, ME 04349; www.echolakecottages.com; (207) 931-8531.

Directions: 230 Echo Lake Road, one mile down gravel road from Route 17 in Fayette.

Description: Built in 1937, the largest building was completely rebuilt in 2014. Main lodge with 8 rooms, 5½ bathrooms, commercial kitchen, dining room that seats 48, living room, and game room. 9 cottages sleep 2, 4, or 5 with private baths and kitchenettes. 8 are on the waterfront.

Prices: Daily and weekly rates, varying by season. Group rates for the lodge: $600/night, $3,700/week; rooms $81/night including breakfast. Cottages range from $100 to $125/night or $600 to $700/week.

Meals: Available for cottage renters for $7.65/person (only when lodge has no group rental).

Activities: Summer activities including fishing, swimming, boating, hiking, nature walks. Hunting and winter sports. Family reunions and weddings.

Other: Cell phone and Internet service. Dogs allowed for $8/night or $50 per stay for week or longer.

Season: Opens May 1 and closes around the end of February (depending on when mud season arrives).

FISH RIVER LODGE

MANAGER TENLEY BENNETT HAS BEEN ONE OF MY FAVORITE OUTDOORS women for a long time. She moved with her husband to northern Maine to pursue her outdoor passions and has served on many key hunting and fishing groups and committees. I thought the message (opposite) I received from Miranda was so wonderful that I just had to share it with you.

Owner: MaryLu Medina; 444 River Road, Arundel, ME 04046; www.FishRiverLodge.com; (207) 468-8841.

Manager: Tenley Bennett, crowFlies@roadrunner.com.

Directions: About 1½ miles off Route 11 on Eagle Lake in the town of Eagle Lake. Stay on Route 11 to Eagle Lake. In the village, go right at the first store on the right, Eagle Lake Grocery. The lodge is 1½ miles from the store at the end of the road. 5-hour drive from Portland.

Description: A traditional sporting camp, with a log lodge and rustic cabins with private bathrooms and showers, kitchens with gas range and refrigerator, bedrooms with double beds and single bunks. Some cabins have multiple bedrooms or a private bunkroom.

Prices: Summer cabin rates: $550 to $750/week or $110–$175/night. Fall cabin rates: $750/week or $175/night. Spring fishing package: cabin for 4 days and 3 nights, all meals, free boats, 1-day guide service—$800/person double occupancy. Family "summer camp experience": cabin for 4 to 6 guests for 7 days and nights, Thursday night dinner in lodge, canoeing—map and compass—tree identification instructions, fishing, free canoe—$1,600 for family of 4–6. Allagash River trip packages. Hunting and trapping packages. Lots of customized packages including a guided photo safari.

Meals: Three meals/day available for $400/person/week or $60/person/day.

Activities: Fishing, swimming, wildlife watching, paddling, hunting all species, ATV riding.

Other: Guests may bring their own wine, beer, and alcohol. No cell phone service but it is available 1½ miles up the road in town. Internet service in the lodge. Pets allowed.

Season: Spring through fall.

A Message from Miranda

I just wanted to take a minute to recognize my favorite Maine sporting camp—really, my favorite Maine vacation spot of all time. I have made many memories at Fish River Lodge. I may seem biased as my Mom, Tenley Bennett, manages the lodge. However, I also know the back story on how Fish River Lodge came to be and what passion and life my Mom brought to the little camps on the lake.

We grew up in a fishing community on the coast, so I never knew of "the County." I grew up hunting with my Mom but always in the mid-coast area. We never really explored "the County." While I was in high school my Mom decided to try for her Master Maine Guide license. It was a dream she had for years. And it was a dream that became a reality.

She worked behind a computer for years to pay the bills, but was never satisfied. After gaining her guide's license she started to do some bear baiting and hunts on weekends out in the Eustis area. I was busy being a teenager so I didn't get to experience much of this with her. I wish I had!

A couple years passed and her desire to leave it all behind took hold. She took a leap of faith many would never have the courage to do, leaving her job of twenty years, her retirement, and her benefits, to move all the way up to Eagle Lake to renovate and bring to life the derelict little cabins now called Fish River Lodge. We all thought she was nuts and she was! The amount of work ahead of her was tremendous. She had to revamp this place with very little money, and turn it into a thriving business. Well . . . she has done just that! There were many bumps in the road but Mom and her husband Wayne Bennett pulled off what might have seemed impossible at the time.

Fish River Lodge dates back to the early 1900s and was a big sporting camp in its heyday. What I love is that my Mom and her husband brought that back and in a tough economy. The camps are being used today as they were intended to be used back in the day.

I now have two daughters and they have kind of grown up there. We spend our summers there fishing, moose watching, swimming, hiking, cooking out, bird watching . . . the list doesn't end! The amount of beauty the land up there has! There is never a lack of something to do. I love Eagle Lake and I love Fish River Lodge. I was even married there down on the beach.

There is the main lodge where meals are served with a deck that overlooks the lake. A lakefront with the best private beach around. Boats and canoes to rent. Seven cabins of different sizes. Every season there is something different offered.

My mom and Wayne guide very successful moose and bear hunts in late summer through the end of fall. The fall bird hunting is incredible too. In the winter months you can enjoy the best snowmobiling trails the state has to offer, ice fishing, a muskie fishing derby, the CanAm 250 sled dog race! In the spring comes the fishing, with especially great early season angling. I'm not much of a fisherman but my husband has spent many hours fishing that lake.

The summer up there is a great time for families and kids to get away and swim and hike and look for moose and grill outdoors and do things they never get to do back home. I have met so many families from all over the country who visit there. It makes me very proud to know what Fish River Lodge has become. It was given a second chance because of my mom who had a dream and saw it through amidst some great barriers. For all those reasons and more, I choose Fish River Lodge as my favorite sporting camp in Maine. Thanks for listening!—Miranda Brannigan

FOX CARLTON POND SPORTING CAMPS
FOX CARLTON POND IS A PRIVATE 5 ACRE TROUT POND LOCATED ON 63 acres. The property runs beside 3,800 feet of Sandy River waterfront,

and guests come to fish, get married, enjoy a reunion, or participate in company outings.

Owners: Jon and Annette Pound; PO Box 103, 35 Fox Carlton Pond Road, Phillips, ME 04966; www.foxcarltonpond.com; (207) 639-2538.

Directions: 3.7 miles off Route 4 in Phillips. Take Route 142 towards Salem, turn left onto Reeds Mills Road, take a left on Toothaker Pond Road. Camps are first driveway on left. Gate fee of $5 per guest.

Description: 4 camps, 1 guest room, 5 RV sites. Some cabins have full kitchens, one has kitchenette, others have mini-fridge, microwave, and coffee pot. Lodge is new, cabins have been remodeled; cabins and guest room have private bathrooms.

Prices: Cabin prices range from $100 to $149/night. Guest rooms $149/night. RV sites $50/night.

Meals: Not provided.

Activities: Fishing, mountain climbing and biking, fall foliage viewing, ATV riding, weddings, fly fishing school June 6.

Other: Camps have a private 5-acre fly fishing catch and release trout pond along with 3,800 feet on the Sandy River. 2-night minimum stay. Orvis fly fishing shop on site. Canoes, kayaks, paddleboats, fishing rods, and waders available for rent. Limited cell phone and Internet service.

Season: May 15–November 1.

Frost Pond Camps

Frost Pond Camps is a remote, yet very accessible, sporting camp surrounded by numerous waterways and forests. The camps are close to Maine's magnificent Baxter State Park and Mount Katahdin, and near a lot of great fishing spots including the West Branch of the Penobscot River, one of my favorite places to fish.

Owners: Maureen Raynes and Gene Thompson; P.O. Box 622, Millinocket, ME 04462; www.frostpondcamps.com, info@frost pondcamps.com; (207) 852-4700.

Directions: 35 miles from Millinocket. If you are heading north on I-95 take exit 244 and turn left. Go to the end of route 157 and turn right, following the signs towards Baxter State Park. At the Northwoods Trading Post and Ambejejus Lake, cross over to the "Golden" road, which is on your left and runs parallel to the state road. If you miss this turn, then a short distance up the road there is a sign to Allagash and Greenville, where you may cross over to the left to get on the Golden road. Continue in the same direction but do not follow the signs to Baxter State Park from this point on. Look for signs to Frost Pond Camps and Ripogenus Dam after about 20 miles. Take the right, at the height of the land, onto the unpaved road. Continue until you see the house up on the hill directly in front of you; bear right down over the hill and across the dam. Continue to Frost Pond Camps. You can expect to arrive in about an hour from Millinocket. Many GPS units will not bring you to camp.

Description: 4 of the cabins are equipped with gaslights, full kitchens including sinks, refrigerators, and dishes and pots and pans to cook and eat with, and all bedding. The fifth cabin has all of the above, but has electric lights off an inverter rather than gaslights. Indoor plumbing with hot and cold running water, flush toilet, and a shower.

Woodstoves provide heat in all of the cabins during the colder months. 2 of the cabins have been changed to a bunkhouse style cabin, so bring all of your gear, just like you were going camping. You will still be in a cabin with a woodstove for heat, but bring everything else. Beds and mattresses are in each of these 2 cabins. Water is provided in 5-gallon containers from a nearby tap; each cabin has its own clean and private outhouse. There are coin-operated hot showers available at the office area. All housekeeping cabins contain blankets, fresh bed linens, bath towels, hot pads, dish linens, and a complete supply of cooking and eating utensils.

6 cabins are spaciously scattered among the trees and lawn of the camp yard, gently sloping to the water's edge. There is 1 large isolated log cabin overlooking the pond a short distance away. The cabins accommodate 2 to 8 people.

Prices: Two-night minimum on all stays except in the bunkhouse cabins. The rates are for the spring and summer season. October 1–April 30 there is a 15% additional charge due to the increased operation costs that time of year. (Showers are not operating after October 1 unless the weather permits).

Children under the age of 15 are $15/child/night in the cabins after minimum is met.

Minimum Rate per Cabin (when booked under the special rates policy); "Special" (pre-paid, non-refundable reservation)

Small cabin	$102 for 1 or 2 people; each additional person $51
Medium cabin	$102 for 1 or 2 people; each additional person $51
Large log cabin	$153 for 1 to 3 people; each additional person $51
Cabin with plumbing	$178 for 1 to 3 people; each additional person $51
Large bunkhouse	$125/night for up to 6 people; each additional person $15
Large bunkhouse 3+ nights	$100/night for up to 6 people; each additional person $15

Small bunkhouse	$60/night for up to 2 people; each additional person $15
Small bunkhouse 3+ nights	$50/night for up to 2 people; each additional person $15

Minimum Rate per Cabin (when booked under regular rates policy)

Small cabin	$148/night for 1 or 2 people; each additional person $74
Medium cabin	$148/night for 1 or 2 people; each additional person $74
Large log cabin	$ 222/night for 1 or 2 people; each additional person $74
Cabin with plumbing	$247/night for 1 or 2 people; each additional person $74

Meals: Provided (3/day); kitchens available in camps.

Activities: Canoeing/kayaking, bird and moose watching, hiking in Baxter State Park and Mt Katahdin, Maine's highest peak. Fishing for coldwater species, salmon, trout, togue. Scenic float plane trips. White water adventure on the Penobscot.

Other: Each of the housekeeping cabins comes with a canoe to use on Frost Pond. Additional canoes and kayaks for rent if needed. No cell phone or Internet service. Pets allowed.

Season: Year-round.

15 Years and Counting
—by Bruce and Sharon Palombo, Bridgewater, MA.

For more than fifteen years, my wife and I have made the annual two week pilgrimage to Frost Pond Camps, a naturalist's, outdoorsperson's or sporting enthusiast's paradise located a mere 30 miles northwest of Millinocket, Maine.

A small, private, family owned and operated campground with cabins and campsites located on the wooded shores of pristine Frost Pond, the peaceful environment offers the opportunity for campers to enjoy the quiet beauty of the Maine woods. While the potential activities afforded by the location are many, the focal point (for us) is the silence of the woods, broken only by the ever present haunting, mournful wail of the loons and the night time hoot of barred owls, raspy croak of bull frogs or distant howl of coyotes.

Wildlife abounds in the area, affording opportunities to see pileated woodpeckers, kingfishers, moose and bear tracks on hikes on the many gravel roads and trails in the area. Partridge, hare and the occasional moose may be seen, particularly if one ventures forth around dusk.

The fishing at Frost Pond is outstanding, offering abundant opportunities for both stocked and natural brook trout and splake. Fly fishermen, spin, and bait fishermen generally all enjoy high rates of success, frequently catching their limit. The clean water also allows for a myriad of swimming and recreational activities. The helpful, hospitable husband and wife proprietors of Frost Pond Camps, both Registered Maine Guides, can offer not only exceptional advice, but also provide campers or day visitors with options to rent motor boats or canoes for fishing, or kayaks for scenic paddling. Moreover, the pond itself provides water access for car top boats during the day.

The silence of the night, wonderfully tainted by the sweet scent of campfire wood smoke, can be occasionally broken by the subdued distant chug of a small outboard motor as an early morning fisherman wends his/her way across the lake to a preferred fishing hole.

All of the campsites are clean and private, as are the outhouses located close by each campsite. For those less adventurous, however, heated cabins with indoor cooking facilities are available. Clean showers and drinking water are also available for all campers.

A multitude of sightseeing adventures await any camper willing to make a short drive from Frost Pond Camps: The West Branch of the Penobscot River, Chesuncook Lake and the unique, quaint and remote Chesuncook Village, the Allegash Wilderness and Waterway, Mt. Katahdin and Baxter State Park (with the Appalachian Trail) are all within a forty-five minute drive. To access the Golden Road from Frost Pond, one must cross the Ripogenus Dam, a sight worthy of one's perusal en route. The West Branch of the Penobscot provides a renowned salmon fishery which is an attraction to fly fishermen from all over the northeastern US. Its huge flowage and multiple class rapids also provide thrilling rafting opportunities for those who wish to opt for river adventure.

A camping experience at Frost Pond Camps will provide recollections sure to warm the coldest weather that our winters can provide. My wife and I excitedly anticipate our next visit with proprietors Maureen and Gene Thompson, who have provided us with so many indelibly etched wonderful memories of unexcelled camping!

GRAND LAKE LODGE

I LOVE THE WAY THE WHEATONS DESCRIBE THEIR LODGE: "WE HAVE owned Grand Lake Lodge in Grand Lake Stream since 2003. 2014 will be our 11th season. Chris grew up in the village of Grand Lake Stream and works as a fishing guide, canoe builder and carpenter. Our daughter Ali is seven years old and is in the second grade. She enjoys helping her dad with the boats on the docks and playing with the kids who come to the lodge. We live in Grand Lake Stream year round. Lindsay also works at the elementary school on the local reservation."

Owners: Chris and Lindsay Wheaton; 86 Canal Street, Grand Lake Stream, ME 04668; www.grandlakelodgemaine.com; (207) 796-5584.

Directions: 86 Canal Street, Grand Lake Stream.

Description: 6 housekeeping cabins on the shore of West Grand Lake. All cabins have bathrooms, kitchens, propane heat, and screened-in porches.

Prices: $45/person/night, $50 for single occupancy, July and August weekly rates $500–$725 depending on size of camp.

Meals: All camps have kitchens.

Activities: Fish the lakes, flyfish the stream, hunt, hike, nature watch.

Other: Cell phone and Internet service, pets allowed.

Season: Spring ice out to October 20.

GRAY GHOST CAMPS

THESE CAMPS OPENED IN THE 1950S TO SERVE ANGLERS, BUT NOW HOST many families for their outdoor adventures.

Owners: Steven and Amy Lane; PO Box 35, 161 Jackman Road, Rockwood, ME 04478; www.grayghostcamps.com; (207) 534-7362 home/office, (207) 943-3815 cell/text; Facebook.

Directions: GPS coordinates: N45° 40' 25"/W69° 47' 23". By water, Gray Ghost Camps is located on the Lower Moose River, midway between Brassua and Moosehead Lakes, about 1½ miles from each. By road, off of paved Route 6/15 in Unorganized Territory of Rockwood. The villages of Greenville and Jackman are each 25 miles from camp. By motorized trail, Gray Ghost Camps is 1 mile from the intersection of Route 66 and ITS 88. No fee.

Description: Originally built in the 1950s as fishing camps, Gray Ghost has been improved over the years to provide comfortable, modern accommodations in Maine's Northwoods. Located directly on the Moose River, 12 waterfront cabins offer private baths, full modern kitchens, living rooms with leather sofas, and flat-screen TV, DVD and wifi. Choose screened porch or open waterfront deck, woodstove or automatic heat, wood or mountain views. There is a different cabin for every taste.

Prices: Nightly rates begin at $40/adult/night, $20/child grades K–12. Weekly rates begin at $240 for 7 nights, $120/child. 2-night minimum.

Meals: Fully equipped kitchens in every camp.

Activities: Guests at Gray Ghost come to rejuvenate at the end of a day spent in Maine's vast Moosehead Lake Region. Whether fishing, boating, paddling, hiking, skiing, or snowmobiling, there is a new adventure to be had every day of every season.

Other: Free use of kayaks, canoes, standup paddleboards, water trampoline. Cell phone and Internet service. Pets allowed.

Season: Year-round.

Great Adventures and Memories Are Created Here
—by Jim Smith

Anyone who has experienced an outdoor sojourn in Maine is either aware of or has experienced the adventure of "Going to Camp." One of Maine's citizen comedians has a skit titled "UpTa Camp" that, in one context or another, will evoke memories of the experience of staying at a Maine Sporting Camp. Thanks, Bob Marley, I still visualize you entering the stage on a boat eliciting full-belly laughter from the audience.

I have personally stayed at several sporting camps throughout Maine and have enjoyed every one of them. There is one sporting camp, however, that for me and my family has been the source of many of our most memorable outdoor experiences for more than thirty-five years. That sporting camp is Gray Ghost Camps in Rockwood, Maine.

While my primary focus is fly fishing when staying at Gray Ghost, my wife and I with our two daughters have very special family memories of Gray Ghost Camps. These memories when retold not only include the narrative of the event, they always include a lead-in such as, "Remember when we were at Gray Ghost and we … !"

While fishing with me, my oldest daughter caught her first piece of driftwood and a yellow perch in Brassua Lake. Our Golden Retriever loved to swim in the Moose River with our daughters. Why is it that such cold water is not an issue for young kids or dogs? My wife and daughters always loved to get into truck-sized inner tubes, a canoe or kayaks, and float or paddle around in front of Gray Ghost in the Moose River. They also did more than one inner-tube float trip down the Moose River from Brassua Lake dam with a final exit at Gray Ghost camps.

In many such instances I would be fly fishing in the Moose River as they floated by me screaming with delight. On many occasions we packed a lunch and headed out for a hike along the shore of the Moose River or along the many trails that exist throughout the region.

I recommend a trip to Mount Kineo and a hike along the shore of Moosehead Lake. You can also hike up the trail to the top of Kineo for a view of Moosehead Lake that is unsurpassed. There are many places to stop and have a nice shore lunch with friends and family.

These are memories that will always bring a smile to my face and tears of joy to my eyes. Steve and Amy, the owners and caretakers of Gray Ghost Camps, will be happy to recommend many options for adventure. You can rent a boat for fishing, a sailboat or a pontoon boat to cruise Moosehead Lake from Gray Ghost Camps. Or arrange a fishing trip with a local guide on Moosehead Lake, the Moose River or the East Outlet of the Kennebec River.

If fishing is your interest, the Maine Guide Fly Shop in Greenville is a great starting place. Dan and Penny will be happy to arrange a float trip in a Drift Boat or recommend flies and places to fish. Steve (of Gray Ghost) also guides customers on Moosehead Lake.

Gray Ghost is a place where a stay will most certainly result in guests meeting and getting to know each other. There's nothing like an evening at Gray Ghost sitting around a fire in the stone fire pit on the shore of the Moose River, where guests share the adventures of the day and reflect on how their escapades are indelibly burned into their respective memory banks.

As I write this I am literally taking time away from packing for my annual week-long May fishing trip in the Moosehead Lake region. And yes, I am staying at Gray Ghost Camps. So see you soon, Steve and Amy, and my dear friends Tom and Carol. And to the many other people who are both regulars and first-time guests at Gray Ghost Camps, I will enjoy seeing you again or meeting you for the first time. I cannot wait to create some new memories.

The Gray Ghost is not only one of the best flies to fish in the Moosehead region of Maine—Gray Ghost Camps is one of the best sporting camps to be found anywhere in Maine.

HARRISON'S PIERCE POND CAMPS

HARRISON'S TRADITIONAL SPORTING CAMPS ARE SET ON REMOTE PIERCE Pond, scattered with natural forested islands and surrounded by the hillsides of western Maine. Built of peeled round logs in 1934, the camps are just a quarter-mile from the Appalachian Trail and draw a lot of hikers who want to take a break in this beautiful place.

Owner: Tim Harrison; PO Box 315, Bingham, ME 04920; www.piercepondcamps.com; (207) 672-3625, (207) 612-8184.

Directions: Off unimproved gravel Bowtown Road in northwest corner of Carrying Place Township on Pierce Pond Stream. Nearest town is Bingham, about 20 miles from the camps. Detailed directions on website.

Description: Old log lodge and nine traditional log cabins overlooking Pierce Pond Stream, just 1,300 feet southeast of Pierce Pond. Facilities include the generator-powered main lodge and bathhouses. The main lodge (108 feet x 36 feet) contains a spacious recreation and living room as well as dining room overlooking the stream and waterfalls.

The clean, comfortable, furnished cabins are 14 feet x 16 feet inside. Each has a porch facing the water. The individual private bathhouses with shower and toilet facilities are heated and have plenty of hot and cold water; towels and soap provided.

Prices: Not provided.

Meals: American plan 3 meals/day.

Activities: Primarily fishing; also a stop for AT hikers.

Other: No cell phone or Internet service. Dogs allowed. Bring your own alcohol.

Season: May–October (closed after Columbus Day).

Indian Rock Camps

Another Grand Lake Stream traditional lodge with historic log cabins, located in one of the top fishing destinations in Maine.

Owners: Ken and Jo-Anne Cannell; 15 Church Street, Grand Lake Stream, ME 04668; www.indianrockcamps.com; (800) 498-2821, (207) 796-2822.

Directions: Princeton is the nearest town. On a paved road off Route 1. Turn left onto Grand Lake Stream Road and go 10 miles. The camps are located on Church Street in the village.

Description: Traditional lodge (over 130 years old) with 5 historic log cabins with complete housekeeping needs, hot showers, 4 to 5 beds, screen porches.

Prices: $45/person/night for housekeeping but no meals. $125/person/night for American plan meals. Also open to the public by reservation for meals.

Meals: American plan, 3/meals/day, at times convenient to guests.

Activities: Hiking, fishing, swimming, birding, boating, canoeing (the camps have a private dock on the lake), ATV riding, lots of activities for families and children (including a craft cabin for rainy days).

Other: Dogs allowed, for small fee, but must be on leashes and cannot stay in cabin all day alone. Internet in cabins and TVs (but only available for DVDs and CDs).

Season: Closed one week in August to host "Camp Clearwaters" for young adults with cancer.

KENNEBAGO RIVER KAMPS

CAMP OWNER REGGIE HAMMOND WAS AN AWARD-WINNING MAINE game warden who retired in 2014. These are fishing camps, located in an area of the state that offers spectacular fishing for native brook trout and landlocked salmon.

Owner: Reggie Hammond; PO Box 677, Rangeley, ME 04970; www.krkamps.com; (207) 864-2402.

Directions: On the Kennebago River between Big and Little Kennebago Lakes. Free gated access 20 miles north of Rangeley.

Description: 3 housekeeping cabins with electricity, hot/cold water, all on the river.

Prices: Depends on number of people in the cabin. Generally $600 to $750/week for a cabin.

Meals: Kitchens in all cabins.

Activities: Fly fishing, hiking, bird and deer hunting.

Other: No cell or Internet service. Pets allowed. 2 night minimum stay, with preference given for week-long stays.

Season: Mid-May to end of November.

Lake Parlin Lodge and Cabins

Located in the heart of the western Maine mountains, Lake Parlin Lodge is rich in history, developed in the 1920s as a wilderness retreat and stop over on the Old Canada Road (now Route 201). The beautiful lakefront lodge includes a seasonal restaurant with guest rooms, and they also have newly constructed lakeside cabins.

Owners: Joe and Liz Kruse; 42 Brians Way, Norridgewock, ME 04957; www.lakeparlinlodge.com; (207) 668-9060.

Directions: 6003 Main Street, Route 201, Parlin Pond Township. Ten miles south of Jackman directly on Route 201.

Description: Main lodge with full restaurant and bar as well as 4 lodge guest rooms. Also 6 lakefront cabins that are all new within the past few years that have full kitchens with stoves, fridges, and microwave ovens. Flat screen TVs with propane fireplaces in every cabin as well as radiant heat in the bathrooms. Across the road and off the lake, there is a mini-lodge. It is a 5-bedroom, 5-bath house that is rented to bigger groups.

Prices: All accommodations are sold as a unit. Lodge rooms are $120 and sleep 3–5 people. 1-bedroom cabin that sleeps 2 starts at $150 and goes up to a 2-bedroom cabin with a loft that sleeps 6 for $250. Mini-lodge is $350 up to 6 people and $450 up to 10. All cabins have full linens, TV, full kitchen, fireplace, canoes and kayaks that are free to use, and free wifi. Minimum stay of 2 nights in cabins and 3 nights in mini-lodge.

Activities: Snowmobiling, fishing, hunting, whitewater rafting, kayaking/canoeing, swimming, hiking, biking, ATVing, and just plain relaxing around the firepit.

Other: Cell phone and Internet service. Crated dogs allowed during bird season.

Season: A seasonal operation. Restaurant/bar is open January–March catering to snowmobilers at this time, their busiest season. Closed in April and reopened in May–December for lodging. Main lodge rented during the summer/fall for weddings and special events.

THE LAKESIDE COUNTRY INN AND CABINS

THE LAKESIDE IS LOCATED ON LEWY LAKE IN PRINCETON, A LOCATION that gives guests access to over 75 miles of shoreline to fish and explore, while also offering convenience to shopping and sightseeing of many local attractions.

Owners: Gary and Jen Dubovick; PO Box 36, Princeton, ME 04668; www.thelakeside.org, info@thelakeside.org; (207) 796-2324.

Directions: 14 Rolfe Street, Princeton.

Description: 5 lakefront cabins (4) 2-bedroom, (1) single-bedroom with full bath, full kitchen, cable TV, and full linens. Some with screen porches. Six lodge rooms (2 with private bath, 4 with shared bath). All rooms have cable TV.

Prices: Visit website for most up-to-date rates, specials, and discounts.

Meals: Cabins are set up for housekeeping but American plan is available. American plan includes breakfast and dinner served family style in the lodge with box lunch cooler and maid services. Home cooking with accommodations for special dietary needs.

Activities: Fishing (primary), canoeing, kayaking, hunting, ATV-ing, hiking, bird watching, golfing.

Other: No minimum for lodge room. Cabins have 3-day minimum. Cell phone and Internet available. Pets allowed only in cabins.

Season: Open May–October.

LAKEWOOD CAMPS

LAKEWOOD CAMPS ARE HISTORIC, REMOTE, AND A SHORT WALK TO ONE of my favorite places to fish in Maine, the Rapid River, known for its large native brook trout.

Owners: Whit and Maureen Carter; PO Box 331, Andover ME 04216; www.lakewoodcamps.com; (207) 243-2959.

Directions: Middle Dam, Lower Richardson Lake, headwaters of the Rapid River. Lakewood provides lake boat travel to the camps. This trip is included in the price of guest stay.

Description: Lakewood was founded in 1853 on the west shore of Lower Richardson Lake. 12 cabins with potable water, hot water, living rooms, private porches, private baths. Cabins accommodate between 2 and 6 guests and all have water front views of the lake. Exclusive access to the Rapid River.

Prices: $170/person/night, service charge of 15%, Maine sales tax of 8%. Includes transportation to and from the camp by boat, private cabin, daily housekeeping service, ice service, firewood, and three full meals in lodge; access to canoes and kayaks. Traditional American plan. Two-night minimum.

Meals: Traditional home cooked meals, upscale entrees, and local organic summer vegetables and salads. Everything is cooked from scratch on the premises.

Activities: Primary activity is wade fishing the Rapid River. Kayaking, canoeing, swimming, nature hiking and viewing, lake boats, and picnic sites available. During October and November, grouse and deer hunting.

Other: Cell phone but no Internet service. Pets allowed.

Season: May–November.

THE LAST RESORT

A RUSTIC PLACE THAT WILL TAKE YOU BACK IN TIME, FOCUSED ON THE traditional activities of hunting and fishing. The Caseys told me they "screen our guests for a good fit."

Owners: Tim and Ellen Casey; PO Box 777, Jackman, ME 04945; www.lastresortmaine.com, caseys@lastresortmaine.com; (207) 668-5091.

Directions: Northwestern shore of Long Pond in Jackman, 6 miles of gravel road, seasonal access only.

Description: 8 log cabins, central shower house, outhouses, limited generator-powered electricity, 4 wilderness tent sites. Camps started in 1902, most rebuilt in 1950s.

Prices: Vary by season, averaging $25/person/night.

Meals: Modified meal plan for November deer hunters; packed lunch and full dinners.

Activities: Fishing, family vacations, bird and deer hunting, hiking, canoeing, kayaking, wildlife photography.

Other: Cell phone but no Internet service. Pets accepted except mid-July to mid-August.

Season: May–November.

This Is Not How You Want to Enjoy the Lake!
—by Stan Keach

Setting is one of the first things you want to know about a sporting camp, especially if you're particularly interested in "getting away from it all." In my book, the Last Resort earns a lot of points for setting. The nearest town, Jackman (not much of an urban center, by any means), is a good twenty minutes away, and The Last Resort has all the elements of a lovely Maine wild country spot—mountains, water, trees, and wildlife. Unless you're in the main lodge yard, or out on the lake, you may be near ten or twelve buildings, but you won't be able to see more than one or two at a time; the rest are hidden by the trees.

In late September 1999, Liz and I and our 11-year-old daughter Carrie headed up to The Last Resort in Jackman for an impromptu fall outing. We wanted to celebrate the conclusion of Liz's long ordeal with radiation treatment and chemotherapy, and our optimistic attitude toward a cancer-free future. The trip was hastily planned, and we made plenty of mistakes. We opened the minivan doors and threw in a couple of bags of clothes, some groceries (which we'd supplement at the Jackman grocery store), a few books (one or two each for Liz and me, and about twelve for Carrie, who was a voracious reader).

"Did you call the kennel?" I asked Liz. "Oh, let's just take Barley. He won't be any trouble. Besides, there isn't time to go by the kennel and still get to Jackman in time to get some groceries," she responded. "Oh fine!" I capitulated. Barley, a small and unimposing beagle-terrier type, was to figure prominently in our adventures.

The Last Resort is a charming, rustic wilderness sporting camp on appropriately-named Long Lake (9-miles long, about a mile wide). Although it's only 7 miles from downtown Jackman, it took about forty minutes to cover those 7 miles on the rough, rutted road. Today, the road is much improved and can be covered in around twenty minutes. We'd stayed there a for a weekend a couple years before with Liz's sister and her family, and we'd had a wonderful time canoeing, moose watching, fishing, and playing games with Carrie and her two cousins. It's quiet, peaceful, and there are always great opportunities to see wildlife in a beautiful and wild Maine setting.

As soon as we'd unpacked the car and neatened up the cabin a bit (our cabin was called The Ledge, and it sits on a rocky prominence 12 feet above the water's edge), we embarked in a 14-foot-canoe to paddle across the lake to look for moose and to just enjoy the scenery and being outdoors. The air was chilly, and we were sure the water would be, too, but we didn't plan to go in, so that wouldn't be a problem. Barley had been in a canoe before and was generally comfortable with the experience.

We paddled over to the far shore, and down a short way into the serpentine meandering of the Moose River outlet. Rounding a corner, we surprised a loon, who made a big fuss, which almost made us drop our paddles since we were at least as surprised as the loon. Not wanting to bother the loon, we headed back to the lake proper, and decided to head back over to camp. "I'm getting really hungry," I said, and Liz and Carrie concurred. "I'm not used to this," Liz added. "I'm feeling pooped."

Liz has always been a tough and physically fit woman, but six months of chemo and radiation had taken its toll on her stamina. Four or five minutes later, we were about a quarter of the way across the lake when a brood of ducks swimming on the starboard side caught Barley's attention. He put his front paws up on the gunwhale, and started cheerfully barking at them. I'm a pretty big guy, and with Liz, Carrie, and me plus a 30-pound dog, in a 14-foot canoe, we were already riding just a little low in the water. "Try to get Barley to sit down," I said to Carrie, "or he's gonna tip the gunwhales down to the water line!" Too late.

The starboard gunwhale dipped just a bit below the water line, and that was it. We went over so suddenly that I don't think I even finished that last sentence. My first impression was this water's not all that cold, but I immediately reversed that assessment. It was cold. I quickly looked for heads. Liz's popped up first. "Where's Carrie?" we blurted simultaneously. Up she came. "Carrie, are you all right?" I asked. "I'm cold!" she sobbed—upset, but not frantic, which I felt relieved about, under the circumstances. "Liz! Are you okay?" "I think so." Carrie asked frantically, "Where's Barley?" We all turned our head this way and that. No Barley. He was the only one without a PFD. "Barley!" Carrie cried. "Barley!" I thought I heard something under the canoe, and, lifting the edge up, I discovered Barley, treading water under the canoe. Liz grabbed his collar and pulled him out of there.

The water was pretty cold, and I figured we could be in danger of getting hypothermic, and I was also afraid Liz's condition might be severely compromised by her recent bout with cancer and the treatment thereof. Was she therefore at risk of a heart attack or who-knows-what? I didn't know. "We've got to swim for shore as fast as we can. Start swimming, Carrie!" "But I'm cold!" "Just swim. Worry about being cold later." Obediently, she did just that, and so did Liz and I, me pushing the canoe as I went.

Ten or twelve minutes later, we were spotted by someone near the camp dock, and the spotter immediately got into a motored boat and headed toward us. By that time, though, we were almost back to shore. The guy in the boat reached us just in time to help us get the canoe emptied out, as Barley, onshore, cheerfully shook himself dry; he danced around a bit, and then looked up at us as if to ask, "Where's supper?" We all agreed that we seemed to be okay—breathing normally, just shivering a little—and so Liz hurried up to our cabin to get dry clothes on her and Carrie, while I paddled the canoe over to the main dock, about 100 yards from where we came ashore.

Supper was American chop suey, and, as always after a cold, wet, and maybe a little scary adventure, it seemed like the best meal any of us had ever partaken of. Warm and dry and well fed, we all felt great and were able to laugh at our misadventure.

Tim and Ellen Carey bought the The Last Resort and its 70 acres of spruce, pine, birch and cedar woods and half mile of shoreline in 1987 and have lived there from April through deer hunting season ever since. The camp is laid out in a bowl effect, with the lodge, a large cabin with cathedral ceiling, dominating the dock area. Eight rustic cabins, well-hidden in the trees, are scattered along the shore. The cabins sleep from two to five people, have outdoor picnic tables and fire pits; screened in porches; fully equipped kitchens with gas lamps, gas heaters, gas refrigerators and ranges. Additionally, there is generator-powered evening electricity for lighting (dusk to 10 p.m., and nearby outhouses. State-approved spring water is available at faucets near the cabins.

There are also four primitive tenting sites, a small grassy playground, hiking and ATV trails, rough roads, and plenty of shoreline. There are three centrally located shower rooms with hot water. Beautiful, meandering Churchill Stream is only a five-to-ten minute walk away down a wooded trail, and provides excellent brook trout fishing. Long Lake itself boasts brook trout, salmon, white perch, chub, and recently smallmouth bass. The area is home to plenty of wildlife including deer, moose, bear, eagles, ospreys, herons, and otters; there have even been reports of mountain lions in the area. The resort itself is loaded with hummingbirds, lured by flower gardens and feeders.

The cove provides excellent swimming, with shallow water—a comfort to parents of young children. The Last Resort is an excellent choice for mountain bikers and photographers, too. Fifteen years ago, The Last Resort was a spectacular moose watching setting; Ellen reports seeing up to nineteen moose at one time during daylight hours! In recent years, sightings have decreased, and most of the sightings have been at dawn or dusk. Still, we know that moose and other wildlife abound. The fishing and deer hunting are good. There's plenty of peace and quiet and plenty of opportunity for outdoors adventures. The owners are nice people. I'm planning to go back for a wilderness vacation soon, but this time I think I'll leave the dog at home.

LONG LAKE CAMPS

LONG LAKE CAMPS ARE ON A PRIVATE 40 ACRE PENINSULA (ROLFE Point) surrounded entirely by woods and water. Long Lake is part of a huge watershed which includes Long Lake, Big Lake, Lewey Lake, West Grand Lake, Grand Lake Stream, the Grand Falls Flowage and the St. Croix River, top destinations for anglers.

Owner: Steve Whitman; PO Box 817, Princeton, ME 04668; www.longlakecamps.com; (207) 796-2051.

Directions: Camp is located in Princeton, on a gravel road about 1.2 miles off West Street, which is off Route 1.

Description: The camp is on Long Lake, which is connected to Big Lake, Lewey Lake, and Grand Falls Flowage. The camp was built in 1945–48 and consists of 12 cabins on the water. They have a recreation hall, dining lodge, full tackle shop, and guest laundry. Many improvements have been made since the owners purchased the camps in 2004, including new water and sewage systems, additions and renovation to the cabins, several new buildings, new docking facilities, and other amenities including swings and swimming areas for children. All cabins have full kitchens and bathrooms. Most cabins have private docks with power available. They also have a boat launch for guests.

Prices: Lodging only, approximately $55/person/night depending on size of cabin. American plan $140/person/night.

Meals: Can be done in cabins or via American plan with 3/meals/day (breakfast and dinner with cold packed lunches).

Activities: Primary activity is smallmouth bass fishing. Land-locked salmon and white perch also available. Swimming and family activities. Recreation hall available for rainy days.

Other: Cell phone and Internet service. Pets allowed. Motor boats available for rent.

Season: May through the end of September.

LOON LODGE MAINE

THE COOLEYS HAVE OWNED THE LODGE, INITIALLY OPENED IN 1985, since 2009, diving right into bear hunting their first week there. Mike Yencha, who built the camps with his wife Linda, wrote this great story of what it takes to build a sporting camp from the ground up. The Yenchas now own a lodge in Alaska but still return to Maine every year.

Owners: Fay and Leslie Cooley; PO Box 404, Millinocket, ME 04462 (May–November), PO Box 254, Bethel, ME 04217 (December–April); www.loonlodgemaine.com; (207) 745-8168.

Directions: About 86 miles from Greenville and 75 miles from Millinocket, 48 miles on gravel road from Millinocket. Golden Road to Telos Road, left at Chamberlain parking lot on the Grand Marche Road, then left on the Ledge Pit Road, then 7.5 miles on the left.

Description: The lodge was built in 1985 on Round Pond, T7 R14. Four cabins and a lodge for meals and gathering and a shower house. Cabins have outhouses, but there is an indoor toilet in the shower house.

Prices: American plan $100/person/night or $525/person/week (seven nights). Semi-American plan with just the evening meal $75/person/night or $445/person/week. Housekeeping $50/person/night or $300/person/week.

Meals: American plan 3/meals/day, semi-American plan dinners only. Or all cabins have kitchens.

Activities: Fishing, hunting (grouse, deer, moose, bear), wildlife viewing, canoeing, kayaking, day trips to see the locomotives in the Allagash, remote muskie fishing on the St. John River.

Other: Internet but no cell phone service. Pets accepted.

Season: May 1–first week of December. Open in February for Allagash Lake ice fishing.

The Founders' Story
—by Mike Yencha

Loon Lodge is unique in the fact that it is not as old and historic as many of the great sporting camps of Maine. The creation of Loon Lodge came from the desire of a young couple from Pennsylvania who wanted to move to Maine to live the outdoor lifestyle of sporting camp owners. When we first started looking for a place to set down roots in 1983, we took the natural approach and checked the real estate listings for existing lodges that were for sale. Unfortunately, the lodges that were for sale were well beyond the funds we had to purchase them.

At the time we started looking I was twenty-two years old and Linda was twenty, so you could say we didn't have a lot of life experience at that point or a lot of money. Disappointed but not deterred, we started looking for property for sale to build a lodge but land that was for sale was not in ideal locations and far from the "remote" setting we were looking for. Still undeterred we were told that sometimes the big logging companies will lease land to people. We began the long process of calling different companies like Great Northern, Scott, and Boise Cascade, only to be turned down and told they are not doing leases any longer.

Each time we were turned down we asked for suggestions as to who might consider doing a lease for us. Finally someone suggested a company called Seven Islands out of Bangor. We called them and they said that they would consider a lease for a commercial sporting camp on their lands. After getting so many rejections over the past months we took this as a definite yes.

They asked if we could come to their office to meet with them in Bangor. We drove up from Pennsylvania excited that we were finally getting somewhere. At the meeting I believe that the people from Seven Islands were surprised and maybe put off by our age. I think they were a little worried about leasing land to two people so young and inexperienced— something we managed to overcome after time.

Looking over their maps we showed them the area we were interested in and they were very receptive to having a sporting camp in the remote Allagash Lake area. We drove back to Pennsylvania and about a week later I came back up with my brother to look over potential building site locations. We flew into the area using Folsom's Air Service out of Greenville. After spending a week paddling around the area and looking over many locations we settled on a remote spot on the west side of Loon Lake, hence the name Loon Lodge.

Little did we know of the push back we would get from Great Northern Paper and the head Fisheries and Wildlife Department biologist out of Greenville. Clearly Great Northern did not want us there and the head biologist put in a statement to the Land Use Regulation Commission (LURC) voicing his opposition to the building permit application we put it.

After the aggravation of trying to work with these two organizations we decided to choose another location in the area that would not draw as much opposition—after great expense moving in supplies and equipment, preparing for what we thought would be a sure approval of our development application. So that is how we ended up on Round Pond in T7 R14 near the carry trail to Allagash Lake. After the fact it was probably a better location for us because it provided much better access to more woods and waters of the Allagash region.

It took over a year, from the time we first spoke to Seven Islands, to when we secured a building permit for Loon Lodge. We were finally ready to get started! It was October 1984. If we were going to be able to start taking in guests in the spring of 1985, we needed to get started, fast! I spent two months alone living in a tent while clearing the land, building our first cabin and outhouse, and clearing a driveway to access the camps from the nearest road. I spent two and a half days clearing a driveway that was about two hundred feet long so that the local logging company could come in and gravel it for us. This gave me access to bring in building supplies by vehicle. Up to that point I carried in supplies by boat from the nearest road access.

I built our first cabin in those two months so that we would have one cabin to rent out the following spring when "hopefully" our first guests would arrive. I finished up the cabin, outhouse, a storage shed and the driveway and parking area Thanksgiving week.

That winter was one of our biggest tests. How do you book fishermen and hunters, with no pictures, no history and no experience? We did several outdoor shows and ran magazine ads hoping to drum up business. Remarkably we succeeded! Not a lot at first, but enough to say we were here to stay and we were not giving up!

Also over the winter we needed to figure a way for us to house ourselves while we rented out our one and only cabin. We purchased a small Scotty Sierro Camper. I couldn't even stand up in the little thing. Linda, myself and our black lab Fred would be sharing that little space for the next two months while we built our second cabin.

Spring of 1985 Loon Lodge officially opened! Our first guests, a couple from Pennsylvania, came up for spring fishing in mid-May. Fortunately I was not guiding yet so this gave Linda and me time to start building. We built our second cabin in two months and moved into it while still renting out our first cabin.

What a relief to get out of that little camper. While I am sure it was perfect for weekend camping trips and maybe even a weeklong campout, it was not comfortable living out of it for two months. With only a two burner stove I craved something cooked in an oven. The dampness of spring didn't help either, and Linda developed bursitis in her shoulder. But we survived it and were happy to finally move into a cabin, our black lab too!

You would think getting the second cabin done we could relax a little and settle in to the lifestyle. No such luck. Mid-summer 1985 we had another huge building project before us. We had booked both cabins for the month of November for deer season and these people paid for the American plan (with meals). So how do you feed deer hunters in November when you only have two cabins? You build a lodge! No pressure here right?

While I cut down spruce trees on the site and cleared the land, Linda went to work peeling logs, 120 of them! The poor girl had a pair of jeans and sweat shirt that could stand by themselves from all the sap on them when she was done with this daunting task. Plus let me point out that we had no running water for showers or baths. Shortly after beginning this project our one and only generator broke (beyond repair). So needless to say we had to improvise. That is where the chainsaw became a very valuable tool. Every board, log, sheet of plywood needed to be cut with the chainsaw. After all the site prep work and log peeling, we began building the 40-foot by 20-foot two-story lodge on August 1.

Linda and I went to work building the lodge. Linda's parents took their vacation and came up to Maine from Pennsylvania to give us a helping hand. We'd only been married two years, and I am sure they wanted to see where I took their daughter away to. Not much of a vacation for them, either, because they spent two weeks working alongside of us trying to carve Loon Lodge out of the wilderness. I still remember the first time they drove in from Greenville following our pickup over the 90 miles of logging roads in a small Chevy Citation. A Canadian logging truck came flying up behind them laying on the air horn nearly giving my mother-in-law a heart attack! I am sure they were not impressed about where I had hauled their daughter off to but they never showed it and over the years they came back to help us many times along with my mother who always spent her vacations helping us out.

It took us right up to the week before deer season but we finished the log lodge and we moved in and prepared for our deer hunters. The start of Loon Lodge was quite a challenge for us but we survived the first season and had formed the beginnings of the lodge's history.

Over the years Linda and I built as we could afford to. Each year we would pick out a project and, just as we did our first year, we would book people for a cabin or a project that didn't even exist yet. Over the next twenty-five years that we owned Loon Lodge we built five cabins, two outpost cabins, a central showerhouse, additions onto our lodge and several other structures.

We built a summer business (July and August) in the sporting camp business when most lodges stayed empty because the fishing was slow and the hunting had not begun yet. We did this by purchasing kayaks and sailboats, putting up a volleyball and basketball area, and promoting hiking in the area. We ran special summer rates to bring people in. One of the things we did which we like to claim credit for is offering a modified or semi-American meal plan. At the time many lodges were either full American or Housekeeping. We started doing a lodging with dinner plan and it really took off. Shortly afterward we started seeing other lodges offering the same plan.

After twenty-five years of building and running Loon Lodge we felt our success would allow us to sell the lodge. It had gotten to the point where we had more then we could handle. We still love the lifestyle and we miss Loon Lodge at times, but it was time to hand the reins over to new owners.

Maine Huts and Trails

Huts and Trails is a unique concept, offering the opportunity to hike from one lodge to another, or locate in one for the duration of your trip. They sponsor many special events. Linda and I enjoyed a weekend birding adventure here and loved it. Here's our story.

Executive Director: Charlie Woodworth; Maine Huts and Trails, 496 Main Street, Unit C, Kingfield, ME 04947; www.mainehuts .org; (207) 265-2400; Facebook.

Directions: Stratton Brook Hut: Located in Carrabassett Valley. Accessed from the Stratton Brook Trailhead located just north of the Sugarloaf Access road on Route 27 in Carrabassett Valley. Distance from Trailhead to hut is 3 miles.

Poplar Falls Hut: Located in Carrabassett Valley. Accessed from the Airport Trailhead located off Route 27 in Carrabassett Valley on the northern end of the town airport. Distance from Trailhead to hut is 3.2 miles.

Flagstaff Lake Hut: Located in Dead River Township. Accessed from the Long Falls Dam Road/Flagstaff trailhead located off the Long Falls Dam Road in North New Portland. Distance from trailhead to hut is 1.8 miles.

Grand Falls Hut: Located in West Forks. Accessed from the Big Eddy Trailhead located off the Long Falls Dam Road in North New Portland, or from the West Forks Trailhead in West Forks. Distance from Trailhead to hut from Big Eddy Trailhead is 7.8 miles; from West Forks Trailhead is 14.4 miles.

Description: Maine Huts and Trails consists of four "huts," which are off-the-grid eco lodges, all designed by local architect John Orcutt. Each well appointed hut has a comfortable seating area with leather couches, stone fireplaces, and a well-curated collection of locally made art. These self-sufficient huts all have spectacular backcountry views, with three of the four located on, or in close proximity to, lakes, rivers, or waterfalls. Accommodations include shared and private bunkhouses. The bathrooms offer clean composting toilet systems and warm showers. A true luxury after a day of adventure.

Prices: For up-to-date rates, check their website.

Meals: The hut staff prepares a hearty, healthy dinner each night, made from locally sourced and organic ingredients whenever possible, including a good beer and wine selection with a focus on local microbrews. Breakfast is full service, with options such as eggs, pancakes, and bacon. Lighter fare like yogurt and granola are also available. Guests are given a healthy bagged lunch for the trail, and special dietary restrictions and food allergies are easily accommodated with notification at the time of reservation.

Activities: In the winter months, guests enjoy Nordic skiing on the groomed trail system, which is used by both skate and classic Nordic skiers. Snowshoeing, winter hiking, and fat-tire biking are also enjoyed during these months. Summer is a beautiful time of year to visit Maine Huts and Trails, as Carrabassett Valley is becoming a true four-season destination. Guests of the system can enjoy mountain biking on trails that have been designed for all ages and ability levels. Paddling on Flagstaff Lake or the Dead River is also a great way to experience the western Maine region. Other adventurers can enjoy fishing of all kinds, leaf peeping, and hiking while completing the hut-to-hut experience.

Other: Reservations are required. Huts and Trails is a nonprofit organization. Individual memberships cost $50/year and family memberships $75. No cell phone or Internet service. No pets. All guests must be able to hike, ski, or snowshoe to the huts from a trailhead. No motorized access. From April–early July, the huts are "self-service", with the guests preparing their own meals in the lodge.

Season: Year-round.

High Adventure Featuring Comfort and Great Food
Linda

Okay, I was clueless about the Maine Huts and Trails system before this adventure. When George explained to me that we would hike in, maybe in the dark, and sleep in a "hut," I may have been a bit apprehensive. He sweetened the deal by saying that was the weekend Bob Duchesne was leading a winter bird watch. I hadn't been birding in so long, a winter bird hike sounded awesome to me.

Then George explained that all we needed to bring were sleeping bags, and that all the meals were prepared for the guests at the lodge. We could snowshoe in—no problem.

As it turned out, the gorgeous snowshoe in was extremely easy, even carrying in our gear. Walking up the well groomed Service Road was only 1 mile. A more scenic trial in along Flagstaff Lake is 1.8 miles. We decided to explore more trails once we unloaded our gear.

At the lodge we were met by friendly staff and noticed several guests taking advantage of the lounge area, including a family enjoying a game of dominoes. As more people arrived, guests visited, relaxed and enjoyed the fire.

Dinner was more than impressive. They try to use locally sourced ingredients and make everything right there. People gathered at the long tables and were served family style. The menu that night was shepherd's pie (featuring local beef), green beans in a mustard sauce (soooo good), and homemade focaccia bread, made with Maine Grains flour. I have to say I probably had more than my share.

They also served the best kale salad I have ever had, for certain. Fresh bright green kale was tossed with almonds, dried cranberries, and shaved parmesan cheese. It was so good that most of us had seconds. There is no excuse to leave the table hungry here. After a great day in the outdoors, appetites are big, and a hot home cooked meal is quite a treat.

After a fantastic breakfast of oatmeal, pancakes, egg scramble, bacon, coffee and juice, we were directed to a big table to make ourselves a bag lunch. Curried chickpea salad wrap was my choice and I made George a BBQ chicken sandwich. Fruit, granola bars and cookies rounded out a hearty lunch bag.

We rounded out our adventure learning more about bird identification with a slideshow by Bob on Friday night, and followed up with a walk around the grounds the next morning. I was pretty excited to see a Boreal Chickadee! I always learn something new when I go birding with Bob. A few of us die hard birdwatchers ventured out in our vehicles with him toward Cobb's Camps for two more hours of birding on Saturday afternoon. I learned a few more bird calls, saw a Black-Backed Woodpecker, and had great fun.

George

This is high adventure with an even higher comfort level. While the hikes and shared bunk rooms might discourage a few, the four huts and 50 miles of trails deliver a great experience in a family friendly environment. Some of the huts do offer private rooms, but all have bunk rooms holding from four to sixteen people. Shared bathrooms in the lodge feature composting toilets and hot showers.

The Flagstaff Hut is the easiest to reach, so of course we chose that one. Well, actually, we chose it because our friend and favorite birding guide, State Representative Bob Duchesne, was offering a birding adventure there that weekend.

The gathering/dining room in the lodge is gorgeous and welcoming. Everything in the room is Maine-made, including chairs by W.A Mitchell, tables by Native Woods LLC, and John Orcutt's awesome photographs which we first noticed at Coplin Dinner House in Stratton. The huts are heated by TARM wood gasification boilers.

We were joined at dinner on Friday night by Lani Cochran, Huts and Trails marketing director, who also owns Allagash Canoe Trips with her husband Chip. They guide canoe trips down the Allagash. Yes, Lani knows adventure!

Huts and Trails features special events every weekend. In May and June, guided fly-fishing retreats for beginners to advanced anglers at the Grand Falls Hut are offered. May 15–17, Chip Cochrane hosts a weekend of outdoor adventure. And May 29-31, retired U.S. Fish and Wildlife biologist Ron Joseph leads a birding adventure. Fun!

The Flagstaff Hut sits on the shore of Flagstaff Lake and features stunning views of Bigelow Mountain. The 22 mile ride from North New Portland to the Hut's parking lot was beautiful but very slow and bumpy thanks to frost heaves. Instead of Long Falls Dam Road, Linda suggested it should be called Long Dam Road. But really, it wasn't that bad. And it passes through some beautiful forests. This is the real Maine, the one that keeps us here.

Matagamon Wilderness

Adjacent to the swift-moving and beautiful East Branch of the Penobscot River, the cabins and campground here are near the north entrance to Baxter Park. Owners Joe and Sue Christianson totally renovated their store three years ago. On one side is a beautiful restaurant with many amazing wild animal mounts, and on the other a gift shop and store with everything from fishing flies to art to food and beverages. Joe offers lots of guided hunting and fishing opportunities while Sue, in "Momma Bear's Kitchen" cranks out very tasty food.

Owners: Joe and Sue Christianson; PO Box 220, Patten, ME 04765 (mailing address); www.matagamon.com, matagamon@hughes.net; (207) 446-4635.

Directions: T6 R8, 26 miles west on Route 159 out of Patten.

Description: Wilderness campsites and housekeeping cabins that sleep up to 12 people.

Meals: Offered to campers and the public in the campground restaurant; open daily from 7 a.m. to 7 p.m.

Prices: Campsites $22.50/family/night, cabins $30 to $40/night.

Activities: All outdoor activities, including hunting and fishing. Lots of folks camp here and enjoy the 200,000 acres in nearby Baxter State Park. They also provide space for private and public events in their dining room and along the shore of the river.

Other: Wifi in the store. No cell phone coverage.

Season: Open year-round.

MAYNARDS IN MAINE

MAYNARDS IN MAINE, OPEN YEAR-ROUND AND SERVING DELICIOUS meals to its guests and the public, is located in the celebrated Moosehead Lake Region, where an endless variety of outdoor sports can be enjoyed. The camps were established in 1919 with a rustic atmosphere that still exists today, thanks to the fourth generation of Mayards now running the camps. I loved the response the Maynards gave to my question asking what challenges sporting camp owners face today:

"The biggest (challenge) is technology. We are a rustic sporting camp. We have televisions in all cabins but they aren't the newest. They are older and only have cable. We have wifi but only in our main lodge. We live in a time where most people are too caught up in their electronic devices. Here at Maynards we believe that a vacation is a time to remove yourself from all of that craziness, from the things that cause stress and headaches. We have the limited ability for you to still be connected if you need to be, but we strongly suggest taking the time to put down your electronics. We have wildlife literally right in our backyard. We have a majestic mountain view out our front door. At night and early morning you can not only hear the loons calling, you can see them floating in our private cove. The beauty of nature and a peaceful life are at its finest here, so please come enjoy it with us."—The Maynard Family

Sounds lovely, doesn't it?

Owners: William and Gail Maynard; PO Box 220, Rockwood, ME 04478; www.maynardsinmaine.com; (888) 518-2055, (207) 534-7703.

Directions: Nearest town is Greenville. Paved roads.

Description: Camps were established in 1919 with rustic atmosphere that still runs true today, run by the fourth generation of Mayards. Sits on a hill overlooking the Moose River and Blue Ridge Mountain. Each cabin is unique, with some having kitchens. All have bathrooms. Main lodge is large, a place for meals and gathering, and a large front porch with rocking chairs. Interesting interior with artifacts from Maine to South America gathered by the founder, Walter Maynard. Above the large stone fireplace is the largest lake trout ever caught in Moosehead Lake, taken by Walter's great grandson, who now works alongside his wife and parents to run the family business.

Prices: Lodging without meals $45/person/night. American plan 3 meals/day $80/night. Children ages 4–12 with meals $50/child/night. Children age 3 and under no charge.

Meals: American plan option includes all meals, with breakfast and dinner in the lodge, and picnic packed lunches. Vegan and children's menus available upon request. Dietary needs when requested ahead of time. Some cabins have kitchens for those who wish to prepare their own meals.

Activities: Primarily fishing, hunting, sightseeing, secondary canoeing, kayaking, snowmobiling.

Other: Cell phone and Internet service, pets allowed.

Season: May 1–November 30. Restaurant is open May 1–October 15 (approximately).

McNally's Ross Stream Camps

FOR THE LAST THIRTY-ONE YEARS, THE OWNERS OF McNally's CAMPS have lived in the woods of northern Maine year-round. When many camps are closed, you will still find John and Regina hosting guests who want to explore northern Maine when the snow lies deep and the streams are hushed by a thick layer of ice. They operate the camps by themselves, serving homemade food and getting to know all their guests, many of whom return each year.

Owners: John Richardson and Regina Webster; PO Box 246, Ashland ME 04732; www.mcnallysrossstreamcamps.com, jgrichardson@hughes.net; (254) 241-1704 (satellite phone that rings right into camp), (207) 944-9995 (cell phone).

Directions: 8 miles northeast of Clayton Lake off the McNally Road (formerly known as the Cunliffe Road). Dirt road, access fees required from May until November. Behind the North Maine woods gates, 76 miles from Ashland, 120 miles from Millinocket, and 36 miles from St. Phamphile, Quebec. Some guests coming from the west or southern Maine choose to come up through Jackman and travel through Canada to the camps. It is an easier ride with just 36 miles of dirt road but does require having a passport, and guns have to be registered with a small fee attached.

Description: A big main lodge, where meals are served, and 5 guests cabins (4 log and 1 stick built), all with running water, flushes, bathroom sinks and showers. All have winterized water system to the cabins. Each cabin has an air tight Vermont Castings woodstove with glass fronts. The cabins have gaslights and are in good repair. They sit high on a bluff overlooking Ross Stream that runs into Long Lake, which is within the Allagash Wilderness Waterway. They are 1 mile upstream, just barely outside of the Waterway.

Prices: The cost is $120/person/day plus tax; includes three meals, cabin, linens during the spring and summer months. In the fall guests must bring sleeping bags and towels.

Meals: American plan only with all meals served in the lodge.

Activities: Primary are bird and moose hunting. Secondary is fishing. Canoe/kayak day trips and family reunions.

Other: Canoe and boat rentals are $20–$50/day depending on how long they are rented for. Free use of kayaks. Internet but no cell phone service.

Season: Usually open year-round but may be closed in the winter.

"I'm Just Happy to Be Here."
—by Trip McGarvey

That is what my dad said. That is all that needs to be said. Late May 2001 found us relaxed and content on the front porch of our cabin at McNally's Camps on Chemquasabamticook Stream (The Stream) in the North Maine Woods. Dad was about 80 years old. We made many memories during our annual fishing trips. Although we did not know it, this trip—our thirty-nineth—would be the last of our annual fishing trips. A year later he was called home to that great brook trout stream in the heavens.

Twenty-two of our trips were spent in the Allagash River region of the North Maine Woods. It all began in 1979. We arrived at the Allagash River with camping gear, fishing equipment, and maps. We went down river, set up camp and began exploring. That's how we discovered "The Stream."

One evening as we paddled back to camp we came upon a tall man with a staff walking the stream bank. He was Dana McNally who with his wife Mycki founded McNally's Sporting Camp in the late 1940's. In time we met Mycki and their partner Les Gardner. We did not know it at the time but that chance encounter with Dana, who passed away a few years later, was the beginning of a unique and cherished friendship.

Each year we would find Les guiding on the stream. He would share his wisdom of the waters with us and we would share stories of our fishing and camping adventures with him. Our bond deepened one very cold morning when he invited us into the camp for a hot cup of coffee. We shared our bounty of brookies with him and he shared his woodstove, hot coffee and friendship with us. The following year we were honored with a dinner invitation to meet Mycki. We felt we had been offered a wonderful and trusting relationship.

Our dinners together became an annual event—good food and trusted conversations in the company of friends. As we arrived for our third annual dinner Mycki met us at the door with towels and soap. Well, I guess we were like family now as we were instructed that "cleanliness is next to Godliness" and it is the preferred condition at Mycki's dinner table.

Eventually camping on the river became a little demanding for my dad so we decided to make McNally's our new base of operations. This was about the time that Mycki and Les decided it was time to retire and sold McNally's. Our friendship with them continued through correspondence as we started a new friendship with Reggie and John.

There are many camps in and around the North Maine Woods but McNally's Camps has become a haven for us. The camp is comfortable, the fishing is wonderful, the water is clean and fresh and the solitude renews our spirit. Most importantly our relationship with Reggie and John evolved from caring hosts to cherished and trusted friends. We keep in touch all year. John helps us know the best times to be there, clues us into where to find fish and shares his tools and workshop if we need to make repairs. Reggie makes certain that we are well cared for and organized. If we forget something it magically appears. One taste of her apple crisp and you will learn why our son declared her Saint Reggie.

McNally's has become a part of the McGarvey family story. It is a serene retreat shared by three generations to date. It is a tradition that I hope will continue into future generations.

As my dad said on his last visit, "I am just happy to be here!"

Moosehead Hills Cabins

You have a choice of two beautiful lakes when you visit Moosehead Hills Cabins. The log cabins at their home base are nestled on 50 acres of woods and nature trails with waterfront on Moosehead Lake. They also have two log cabins with private lakefronts on Loon Lake (aka Wilson Pond), a 7-mile long lake in Greenville. You can snowmobile from any of the cabins onto an extensive local and ITS trail network. And from their Loon Lake cabins you may ATV onto several hundred miles of trails.

Owners: Bill Foley and Sally Johnson; PO Box 936, Greenville, ME 04441; www.MooseheadHills.com; (207) 695-2514.

Directions: 418 Lily Bay Road, Greenville; 3 miles from the center of Greenville, all paved road until driveway, which is gravel.

Description: 3 cabins with 2 bedrooms, full baths, and kitchens, centered on 50 acres of nature trails and hillside including frontage on Moosehead Lake. The cabins are clustered, about 70 feet apart. Each cabin has an indoor woodstove/fireplace and a gas grill on the deck. 2 cabins are on Wilson Pond (also called Loon Lake). Sunrise Lodge has 3 bedrooms and 2 baths, plus a kitchen.

Loon Lodge has 3 bedrooms, 2½ baths. Master suite has king bed and private bath with Jacuzzi, plus a kitchen.

Prices: Range from a low of $144/night off peak for the smallest cabin to a high of $375 per night for the largest cabin.

Meals: Kitchens in each cabin. Grocery store and restaurants 3 miles away in Greenville.

Activities: Moose watching, hiking, swimming, canoeing/kayaking, whitewater rafting, ATVing, snowmobiling, downhill skiing nearby, cross-country skiing, ice fishing, snowshoeing.

Other: Free use of kayaks in the summer, 2 night minimum and 3 nights for holidays, 7 night minimum in summer. Cell phone service, Internet service at Greenville library. Pets allowed in some cabins.

Season: Year-round, but they say, "Don't come in mud season" (April)!

Hooked by Our First Trip
—by the Cataldo Family

Since our very first trip to Moosehead Hills Cabins in 2002, we were hooked and have been coming back every year! The location of all their cabins, both on Moosehead Lake and Lower Wilson Pond could not be any better. They are conveniently located to town and yet they are situated in such remote areas.

Upon arriving at Moosehead Hills Cabins, Bill and Sally greet us with open arms making our stay at Moosehead wonderful from the start. From the time we check in to the time we have to say goodbye again, we experience so many great times in between.

Arriving at the cabin, the first thing you notice is the panoramic view you will be enjoying during your stay at Moosehead Hills. It's spectacular! Each cabin is nestled between wooded areas giving you the privacy and seclusion from the other cabins. We have personally stayed at three of the five cabins that Bill and Sally offer, two of them on Moosehead Lake and the other on Lower Wilson Pond.

Looking back at my journal from 2002, my exact words upon arriving at our cabin were, "Wow, what a place!" and believe it or not, we still feel the same way every time we come here.

The three cabins on Moosehead Lake all have a covered front porch with adirondack chairs offering a breathtaking view of Moosehead Lake. You actually want to sit right down and take everything in before you even go into the cabin. When you do finally decide to go in, you will be just as pleased. The vaulted ceiling, the stone fireplace, large kitchen and charming bedrooms each with beautiful quilts on the beds, tile bathroom with a Jacuzzi tub and to top it off, a gentle breeze blowing through the cabin with the fragrance of spruce needles! It just doesn't get any better.

I think one of our most memorable experiences was when, after spending a fantastic week at the cabin and taking so many photographs of our adventures during the week, I decided to send some of the prints to Bill and Sally. When we came up the following year, to our surprise, Bill and Sally had framed some of photographs and had placed them in each of the cabins! It really made us feel like we weren't just another customer, but a friend.

Through the years at Moosehead Hills Cabins, we have always felt like it is our home away from home. Thank you Bill and Sally for always making us feel so welcomed!

MT. CHASE LODGE

MT. CHASE LODGE IS A LONG ESTABLISHED RECREATIONAL LANDMARK in Maine's Shin Pond/Patten area. I have stayed here and know Rick and Sara well, and can attest to their high level of hospitality. The uncrowded waterfront setting is very nice, on the shores of Upper Shin close to Baxter State Park and within sight of Mt. Katahdin with convenient access to Baxter State Park's less crowded northern entrance and Maine's great North Woods.

Owners: Rick and Sara Hill; 1517 Shin Pond Road, Mt. Chase, ME 04765; www.mtchaselodge.com, mtchaselodge@fairpoint.net; (207) 528-2183.

Directions: On Upper Shin Pond in the town of Mt. Chase. En-route to the Northern Entrance to Baxter State Park on Route 159 west. Driveway is ½ mile dirt road just off Route 159. Nearest town: Patten (10 miles).

Description: Main lodge with 8 private guest rooms. Fireplaced living room, dining area overlooking Upper Shin Pond. 4 full bathrooms, indoor hot tub, TV, wifi. Also 5 cabins with cooking facilities, full bathrooms, sleeping 4–8 people.

Prices: Costs range from $79/day/person to $139/day/person. Includes lodging and 2–3 meals. Housekeeping cabins range from $109 to $139/day for up to 3 persons; $20 additional for each additional adult. Weekly rates apply to in-season. Hunting guest prices are available upon request.

Meals: For lodge and cabin guests, meals are available and are served family style. Dietary issues can generally be handled with advance notice. Cabin guests can opt to prepare their own meals in cabin kitchen facilities.

Activities: Hunting, fishing, snowmobiling, hiking, mountain climbing, touring Baxter State Park, ice fishing, XC skiing, boat-ing, canoeing.

Other: Pets are welcome for cabin-only guests for a modest addi-tional charge. Cell phone signals are within walking distance, but are not available in lodge area buildings. Internet is available.

Season: Open ten months. Closed April and December unless special arrangements are made.

NAHMAKANTA LAKE CAMPS

NAHMAKANTA IS ONE OF MAINE'S LAST TRULY AUTHENTIC AND TRADI-tional wilderness sporting camps. Their historic nineteenth century dining lodge and beautifully restored lakefront guest cabins are the only buildings on sparkling, spring-fed Nahmakanta Lake. Except for these cabins, the Nahmakanta shoreline is entirely wild, with enormous granite boulders and natural sand beaches. Surrounding the camps is a vast wilderness preserve of mountains, forests and crystal clear lakes that is absolutely unique in the eastern United States.

Owners: Don and Angel Hibbs; PO Box 544, Millinocket, ME 04462; www.nahmakanta.com; (207) 731-8888; Facebook.

Directions: Although the mailing address is in Millinocket, you do not drive through Millinocket to reach the camps. The most direct route from points south of Bangor is via the town of Greenville (at the south end of Moosehead Lake).

To reach Greenville, exit I-95 at Newport, then take Route 7 north to Dexter, Route 23 to Guilford, then Routes 6/15 to Greenville. (For more details, see a state highway map of Maine.) From Greenville, drive 20 miles north along the east side of Moosehead Lake to the tiny village of Kokadjo. From Kokadjo store on left, it is 26 miles on gravel roads to Nahmakanta. Look for "NLC" signs at all turns. Check your odometer at the store.

The following mileage figures are measured from Kokadjo store (not to be added to previous figure): at 0.2 miles bear left, at 1.4 miles bear right, at 1.8 bear right, at 6.6 turn left, at 10.6 bear right, at 11.6 turn left, at 13.3 turn right, at 14.0 turn left, at 17.0 bear left, at 18.3 bear left, at 19.2 bear left, at 24.8 turn right, 25.8 arrive at camp.

From mid-coast Maine and the greater Bangor area, use state highways to reach Bangor, then take I-95 northbound about 15 miles to exit 199. Turn left (north) onto Route 16. After 25 miles, arrive in downtown Milo. Turn right (north) onto Route 11. Continue north on Route 11 for 25 miles, turn left onto gravel road at "Jo-Mary Lake Campground" sign. After ¼ mile, stop at checkpoint to register and pay road use fee (Maine residents $5 per adult; non-residents $10 per adult; no charge for kids 15 and under). Beyond gate follow "NLC" signs 27 miles to camp.

From Millinocket and Baxter State Park, head south out of Millinocket on Route 11. After 15 miles, turn right onto gravel road at "Jo-Mary Lake Campground" sign. After ¼ mile, stop at checkpoint to register and pay road use fee (Maine residents $5 per adult; non-residents $10 per adult; no charge for kids 15 and under). Beyond gate follow "NLC" signs 27 miles to camp.

Description: Nahmakanta is one of Maine's last truly authentic and traditional wilderness camps, situated in the heart of Maine's fabled North Woods. The historic, nineteenth-century dining lodge and beautifully restored lakefront guest cabins are the only buildings on sparkling, spring-fed Nahmakanta, often called Maine's most spectacular lake. Except for the wilderness cabins, the Nahmakanta shoreline is entirely wild, with enormous granite boulders and incredible natural sand beaches. Surrounding the camp is a vast wilderness preserve of mountains, forests and crystal clear lakes that is unique in the eastern United States. They offer comfortable, newly remodeled, private waterfront cabins. Their 9 lakefront cabins accommodate between 2 and 8 people. All have skylights, picture windows that face down the lake, screened porches with rockers, hardwood floors, gaslights, and woodstoves with plenty of dry firewood. The smaller cabins have at least 1 double and 1 single bed, and the larger cabins have separate bedrooms and toilets. Each cabin has its own designated bathroom, with a hot shower, flush toilet, and vanity, only a few steps away.

Prices: American plan—cabin and full home-cooked breakfast and supper served in lodge dining room and a packed lunch.

Meals begin with supper on the day of arrival and end with breakfast on the day of departure, $150/person/night. Modified American plan—cabin and home cooked supper. Guests furnish their own breakfast and lunch, $118/person/night. "Housekeeping plan" cabin with fully equipped kitchen as described above $85/person/night. Children's rates American plan—ages 1–17, $8 per year of age per night. Modified American plan—ages 1–17, $6 per year of age per night. Housekeeping plan—ages 1–17, $4 per year of age per night. All plans based on 2 adult minimum per cabin. Singles are charged 1.5 times the individual rate. 2-day minimum stay.

Meals: American plan guests enjoy home cooked meals served family-style in the warm atmosphere of the nineteenth-century log dining room overlooking Nahmakanta Lake. A variety of hearty full course meals are served, which include choice meats, seafood, rice, potato, pasta, fresh fruits and vegetables, baked breads and desserts, and beverages (no menu). Alternative diets can almost always be accommodated. For Housekeeping plan guests, kitchens are fully equipped with new gas ranges and refrigerators, cooking and eating utensils, and outdoor charcoal grills. Beds have new firm mattresses with fresh linens and blankets. Pure Nahmakanta well water is piped to each cabin.

Activities: Hiking, fishing, canoeing, kayaking, paddle boarding, sailing, swimming, moose tours, campfires at night, stargazing, bird watching, and just relaxing. There are also dogsledding tours in winter.

Other: Dogs are usually welcome but you must call first and pay $20/day. Cell phones "sometimes work." Internet service available in office and dining area. Guests must bring their own towels.

Season: May–October, January–March for dog sledding.

It's All about Wilderness
—by Mike Verville

It's the wildness that brings me back, the quiet of the all too scarce back-country. Nahmakanta is a special place. Coffee on the cabin porch, with sunrise through a thin fog. The loons calling back and forth . . . all quiet around camp.

The people you meet here are outdoors people. They show a respect and reverence for undisturbed wilderness. Some are fishermen, some photographers, some hikers, some families creating and passing on tradition. Many come back year after year. We have seen a few kids grow up here in annual increments. You'll hear them talk at dinner, about specific hikes they want to do again, or ponds they want to revisit . . . a lot of memories, old and new. They're all smiling too. Haven't met any curmudgeons.

The camp is surrounded by Nahmakanta Public Reserve Land and the Debsconeag Wilderness Area. It is some of the wildest country in Maine. It is circumscribed by the Applachian Trail . . . one of the prettiest sections of the trail. From the outlook on Nesuntabunt, (a short hike) you can see its northern end at Mt. Katahdin. In the fall you can catch the migration of the Thru-Hikers finishing the AT . . . some are chatty, some quiet, different reactions to the solitude of a 2,200 mile walk.

The ponds, within day-hike distance, are phenomenal brook trout fisheries. I'd like to stay a week at some. You are much more likely to share your fishing with moose, osprey or eagle, than another fisherman. The lake produces some great salmon and togue, and Nahmakanta Stream produces well in the spring.

Don and Angel Hibbs make Nahmakanta into your home. They are both the real deal. Don is a true woodsman. Look in his eyes and you'll know: paddler, dog-musher, fisherman, hunter, trapper. Angel is a capable and charming woman, comfortable handling a boat or fly rod, or talking about her travels in Europe. Her meals and hospitality are a big part of folks' traditions . . . cinnamon popovers! Oh my God! Over the past years, they've taken good care of us, but always let us have our own trips, our own space.

September is my favorite time. The fall foliage is truly a spectacle. Crisp air. Amazing stars. "God's country," we say here in Maine. Almost every day ends with the evening commute of the beaver in front of the camp. Occasional slap of the tail. Doesn't get any better!

Nicatous Lodge and Cabins

Established in 1929, Nicatous Lodge and Cabins is an authentic Maine sporting camp. I have stayed here and can report that this area of Maine is amazing. The rightful name for Nicatous is Kiasobeak, "Clear Water Lake," a perfect description of this lake with 34 miles of winding shores and sheltered coves, 76 unsettled islands and sandy beaches, and 20,000 acres of woodlands. With a history that began in the 1880s when logging families owned the islands and camps on Nicatous Lake, the region remains, to this day, a destination of pristine waters, recreations and solitude.

Owners: Dave Dane and Steve Schuster, managers; Jeff and Theresa Harriman; PO Box 100, Burlingon, ME 04417; www. nicatouslodge.com, nicatouslodge1@gmail.com; (207) 356-7506.

Directions: GPS coordinates: latitude 45.125N, longitude 68.125W; 65 miles north of Bangor. Take Route I-95 to exit 217, Howland, Route 155 North and 188 East. Go through Enfield, Lowell, and Burlington. Make a right at the stop signs in Howland and Enfield. Both are "T" intersections. Make a right at Ye Olde Tavern in Burlington. Stay on 188 East to the end, about 8 miles, then go another 6 miles on a well-maintained gravel road to Nicatous Lodge.

Description: The lodge was built in 1945 and new owners, as of January 2013, have been making lots of improvements, including new mattresses and furniture. The log cabins are authentic, handcrafted in the sporting camp tradition, and all are located on the lake and include a fireplace or woodstove, kitchen, bathroom with hot shower, and screened porch overlooking the water. Cabins accommodate 2–9 people. Only 1 cabin is fully winterized, but 4 others accommodate winter campers with meals and showers provided in the lodge.

Prices: Rooms in the lodge and cabin rentals are available for between $100/night and $200/night. 2-night minimum for cabins. Lodge rooms include a common bathroom.

Meals: Can be prepared by guests in the cabins or the lodge, and meals can be prepared for guests with advance notice. Seating for 30 guests in the lodge's dining room.

Activities: Ice and open-water fishing, cross-country skiing and snow shoeing, hiking, kayaking, canoeing, boating, river trips, swimming, seasonal special events, training, and workshops.

Other: Free use of canoes and kayaks and a sunfish boat and boats available for rent. Cell phone and Internet service is available. Pets are welcomed. Personal care devices that draw lots of power are not. Guests must bring their own towels.

Season: Year-round. Summer is the busiest time.

Where the Pavement and Power Lines End
—by Earl Brechlin of Bar Harbor, author, newspaper editor, and registered Maine guide

When it comes to really escaping the hustle and bustle of daily life there's no better place than a spot far from where the pavement and power lines end. One such place is in a corner of Hancock County that's so remote it doesn't even have a name, just a number—T3 ND.

That's where you'll find Nicatous Lodge at the north end of Nicatous Lake. For more than fifty years, the lodge and cabins have been a home base to a mix of visitors that can include fishermen, paddlers, hikers, hunters, ATV riders and snowmobilers. And many folks like to do nothing at all. Head down to the screened gazebo at the shore with a good book and see how fast the afternoon disappears.

The Native American name for the lake is Kiasobeak, which means "Clear Water Lake." With just a handful of private camps on the edges, the lake boasts some 34 miles of shoreline, numerous sandy beaches, and seventy-six islands devoid of evidence of human occupation.

Some 22,000 acres of the surrounding forest are now a preserve that allows rustic camping at established sites.

Established as a camp for boys in 1929, the lodge today features the authentic log main building containing a spacious lobby, small library, the dining room and restaurant-quality kitchen. Out front, a broad porch sports views miles down the lake. A large field stone fireplace is the building's centerpiece. There are several guest rooms located on the second level.

Out front are the docks that service fishing boats (bring your own or you can rent one or arrange for a guide), a handful of small pleasure craft, and the lodge's fleet of canoes, kayaks, a sunfish sailboat (free for use by guests) and the swimming beach and float.

Surrounding the main lodge and nestled in the trees are nine housekeeping cabins, in a variety of configurations. Most overlook the rushing waters of Nicatous Stream which arcs around the camp in a broad, sweeping curve where trophy trout can often be coaxed from a cool, deep eddy.

The decor is a unique blend of one part estate sale and another part L.L. Bean, with a pinch of grandma's attic. The floors creak and you can see all the pipes in the bathroom (the better to keep them from freezing in winter). Winter woodstoves are removed by summer so that the fireplaces can function.

In the cupboards are coffee cups that don't match and pots and pans that didn't begin life as part of an expensive set. What you will discover is that the sheets are crisp and clean, the blankets warm and anything you prepare in one of their vintage cast iron frying pans will be delicious—in short, utility and authenticity. There are no radios or televisions in the cabins although there is a satellite dish in the lodge.

When it comes to nightlife you'll have to settle for the calls of bearded owls, the breeze whispering in the tall pines overhead and the haunting cries of loons out on the lake. Be forewarned, however. The one thing you won't find anywhere, no matter how hard you look, is pretension.

Folks renting cabins can do their own cooking, although meals can be taken in the dining room which is also open to the public at various times of year. Electricity is provided by the camp's quiet generators that also charge a giant battery bank so no motors can be heard running at night or at times during the day.

While there are plenty of comforts at Nicatous Lodge, it's what they don't charge for that folks value the most. Waves lapping at the shore are the traditional way of marking time. Peace and solitude abound as sunlight filters through ancient pines to dance and play on the ground. At night, the brilliant arc of the Milky Way high overhead is the only bright light you'll see.

Cell phone service is spotty at best. But, for those who can't stand being off line for too long, there's free wifi in the lodge. The only guaranteed connection you'll find at Nicatous Lodge, however, will be with Mother Nature.

NORTH CAMPS

HERE YOU WILL FIND TWELVE RUSTIC HOUSEKEEPING CAMPS LOCATED on the northeast shore of Rangeley Lake, surrounded by 20 wooded acres and spacious lawns.

Owner: Elwin Gibson; PO Box 341, Oquossic, ME 04964; www.NorthCamps.com; (207) 864-2247.

Directions: Located off Route 4 to Mingo Loop Road to North Camps Road in the Oquossic section of Rangeley.

Description: 14 fully equipped camps built from 1890 to 1920 and updated with kitchens and baths, woodstoves and fireplaces, plus gas or oil heat. Views of Rangeley Lake from screened porches.

Prices: Range from $600 to $100 per week depending on cabin size and number of people. Nightly rentals when available from $95 up.

Meals: None, but coffee on the lodge porch every day.

Activities: Boating, fishing, hiking, tennis, bocce, horseshoes, nature watching.

Other: Cell and Internet service. No pets.

Season: Ice out in May–October.

A Family Vacation
—by Timothy Pearson

I first found North Camps in the late 1980s. My wife Soni and I with our two boys wanted to take a vacation on a lake with family. We decided on North Camps in Rangeley, sight unseen, through a brochure. We all fell in love with the place. The camps lined the shoreline. They had screened porches where we spent our evenings listening to the loons sing. The slamming screen doors were great and our cabin even had a clawfoot bath tub. Each cabin had that cozy feel and smell of camp.

We rented cabins 11 and 12 on the end with my brother in-law, Dana, and his wife Bonnie and their two boys. We had our own dock between the cabins, which was where we gathered from morning till dark fishing, lounging, swimming. A great place for morning coffee and the stars and moon at night were breathtaking. We grilled out when weather permitted, and on Fridays part owners Sonny and Dottie Gibson offered to cook lobsters and clams and deliver them to our camp.

We were welcomed by smiling faces from Sonny and Dottie and to this day I know their voices on the phone when they answer at North Camps. We have become good friends.

If I remember right, two of the camps were dragged up the frozen lake from town with heavy equipment and put in place. One was brought across the lake off the mountain with horses. I wish I could have grabbed a chair and watched that but it would have been short lived because Sonny would have said to me, "You gonna just sit there? Or give us a hand?"

Our family captured our time spent together on video. We love watching the movies of our boys growing up and having fun with their cousins at the lake. I started a fall fishing trip and then a spring fishing trip with my brothers and friends that has become a twenty-five-year tradition. I have never missed a year, spring or fall.

I've always felt strongly about doing everything I could to help keep North Camps going. Times are hard and the families running sporting camps are struggling to deal with the changing economy and taxes. I tell the guys "You want to try somewhere new, go ahead! I'm going to North Camps!" My bond with the Gibsons has grown deep over time and I just love the place. The family has worked so hard to keep the camps open. I hope the grandchildren will one day get involved in the family tradition of running the camps. I know there are others that feel the same way I do because I meet my friend Denny at camp every spring and fall.

Our group has a "Biggest Fish" trophy called the "Fitzy Fishing Award" named after my Uncle Fitzy who loved being at North Camps. One day he caught a 19½ inch salmon, 2½ pounds, off the dock. I had been trolling all day with my friend Bob and when we came into the docks Sonny said, "Hey, Tim, your uncle caught a nice salmon off the dock." I said "Thank you, God!" I mean all this money invested in a boat and motor and poles and my Uncle Fitzy catches a big fish with this ridiculous saltwater rigged pole, off the dock, on a worm! The story goes he was fishing with my brothers off the dock and a boat went by and made waves. All of a sudden his bobber disappeared. He gave all credit to the boat pushing the fish towards his bobber. I figure any fish that grabs a worm connected to a steel leader and saltwater pole is suicidal.

My brother Slugger always looked forward to being at North Camps. He, too, caught a big trout and salmon one weekend. Both my uncle and brother are gone now but our memories of both are in our hearts, minds, and our photo albums. We have a brick in downtown Rangeley at the park gazebo with their names engraved on it. We never forget our time spent with them at this special place.

We joke about the rule of the docks—"Don't forget the net!"—A few big fish have been lost at the dock's edge because someone forgot the net. One night my brother Mark was fishing off the dock with a bright red bobber that lights up in the dark. All of a sudden the bobber shot up in the air about 6 feet. I thought maybe a loon attacked it but a huge salmon grabbed his worm and came out of the water trying to spit the hook. He had hit the bobber, launching it skyward. We had the net and that fish didn't get away! I remember watching a fisherman from the next camp grab his pole with a dried up old worm on it, walk down to the dock, cast it in the lake and snag himself a 5½ pound hook jaw salmon. So our motto is "You never know."

One of my favorite things at North Camps would be the gazebo at the water's edge. This thing is awesome. It's just a great place to sit and relax. All handmade, great attention to detail. I just feel like I'm part of the place, especially at night, walking down the camp trail between cabins, or just sitting on the porch or dock. It's a very peaceful feeling and that is why I'm always the last one to leave. That's okay because I know I will be back soon. North Camps is a very special place; don't miss it.

NORTH COUNTRY LODGE

NO FAMILY IN THE SPORTING CAMP BUSINESS IS MORE HOSPITABLE than the Goodmans. I have known them for many years, stayed with them, walked the woods with them, fought ballot measure campaigns with them, and admired them. This is a hunting lodge with great food, superior guides, and lots of room to roam in the great north woods, where they have exclusive rights to bear baiting sites. While they once offered both bear and deer hunts, the loss of the deer herd in northern Maine forced them to focus strictly on bear hunting here a few years ago. To make up for the loss of deer hunters, they opened up their fishing camps in Canada to bear hunting.

Owners: Bert and Hank Goodman; PO Box 323, Patten, ME; www.northcountrylodge.com; (207) 528-2320.

Directions: 831 Aroostook Scenic Highway, Moro, Plantation.

Description: Lodge with 2 living rooms, dining room, and 9 rooms with capacity from 2 to 5 people, bathrooms on main and second floors.

Prices: $1,950/guest/week, Saturday to Sunday.

Meals: 3 per day in central dining room, served to the tables.

Activities: Hunting.

Other: Minimum one-week stay, no pets, cell and Internet service.

Season: Bear hunting season.

PENOBSCOT LAKE LODGE

A TRADITIONAL SPORTING CAMP, THIS LODGE IS THE ONLY FACILITY ON Penobscot Lake. The geographic location of the lake plays a large role in making this remote lodge a very relaxing place. You may fly in or choose to be ferried by boat to this remote location 60 miles northwest of Greenville and less than a mile east of the Quebec, Canada, border. As this book was being completed, the camps were for sale, so check the website for information about possible new owners. Or maybe there's still time for you to buy it!

Owner: Paul Fichtner; PO Box, Jackman, ME 04945 (summer), 40 Penobscot Ridge Road, Charleston, ME 04422 (winter); www.penobscotlakelodge.com; (207) 280-0280 (summer), (207) 280-3244 (winter).

Directions: T3 R5 within confines of West Branch easements and behind North Woods Gates (fees required).

Description: Large main lodge and 8 sleeping cabins, all with shower or tub, solar power.

Prices: See website.

Meals: Three per day in the kitchen or dining room.

Activities: Primarily fishing for brook trout and blue back trout. Kayaking and canoeing, swimming, hiking, shooting, birding.

Other: No cell or Internet service. Pets accepted.

Season: June–October, summers only.

THE PINES LODGE

THIS CAMP IS THE LAST REMAINING SPORTING CAMP OF SEVEN OWNED by one generation of the Norris family. That's a total of 108 years of sporting camps for one family. Yes, they know how to do sporting camps right!

Owners: Steve and Nancy Norris; 127 The Pines Road, Princeton, ME 04668; www.thepineslodge.com; (207) 557-7463.

Directions: 12 miles west of Grand Lake Stream on the shores of Sysladobsis Lake. Located on a gravel road maintained by the Downeast Lakes Land Trust.

Description: The lodge and 5 cabins are located on Norway point protruding into Sysladobsis Lake. The camp was built in 1884. Notable guests were President Calvin Coolidge and tycoon Andrew Carnegie. There are also two island cabins, each on their own private island only 5 minutes by boat.

Prices: Full American plan: $95/person/day mainland; island housekeeping: $700/week up to 4 persons.

Meals: Breakfast and dinner in the lodge, with pack lunch prepared for mid-day.

Activities: Quiet time and relaxation are the most popular pastimes. Fishing for salmon and small mouth bass rank high for many as well.

Other: Cell phone but no Internet service. Pets allowed.

Season: May 15–September 30.

Robinson's Cottages

Robinson's Log Cottages was started with one small cabin in 1920 by William Robinson and his wife Shirley. The cottages are located on the bank of the Dennys River on land owned by generations of Robinsons since 1875. Although the original camp has been replaced, several more modern log cottages with stone fireplaces and other amenities have been added over the years. The cottages have passed through several generations and are now owned and operated by the fourth generation of Robinsons, Bill Robinson (namesake of the original owner) and his wife Teresa.

Owners: Bill and Teresa Robinson; 253 King Street, Edmunds Twp, ME 04628; www.robinsonscottages.com, www.facebook.com/robinsonscottages, robinsonscottages@gmail.com; (207) 726-9546.

Directions: GPS coordinates: 44.898778, -67.257292.

Also, interactive map at https://www.google.com/maps/d/u/0/edit?mid=z355OUaqdvf8.kuCE_AVeGmmA. Directions are available at http://www.robinsonscottages.com/#!location/c1wln.

Located off a paved road on a gravel road. Route 86. No access fees; no gates.

Description: 3 log cottages on the Dennys River, 3 log cottages on Robinson's Pond. The cottages were all built between the 1930s and 1960s. All have running water, a single bathroom with sink, shower and toilet, and a fully equipped kitchen. Upkeep, maintenance, and improvements are continuous, with work being done every year.

All cottages have a fieldstone fireplace. Most have a woodstove and/or monitor heater.

Prices: Cottages range from $80–$115 per night for double occupancy depending on the season and cottage. There is a $10 additional per person fee for nightly stays (not for weekly).

Meals: No meals are provided. The kitchens are fully equipped for guests to prepare their own food.

Activities: Swimming in the river; canoeing on river or pond; fishing in river or pond; a swing set, horseshoes, and badminton for recreation; hiking along the Sunrise trail; bird watching; relaxing; reading (books in cottage); games in cottages. There are a variety of coastal towns nearby where guests can go whale-watching, shopping, hiking, ocean fishing, dining, kayaking, sight-seeing, and much more. Located only 30 minutes from the Canadian border in St. Stephen or Campobello. Passport is needed.

Other: All cottages include linens, towels, soap, use of canoes and lifejackets, complimentary firewood, 5 of the 6 have free wifi, modern appliances (electric stove, family-size fridge, microwave, coffee pot and filters, toaster); also a large library of DVDs at the office to borrow for free. Cell phone service can be spotty. Internet in 5 of the 6 cottages. Pets allowed.

Season: From late April into November.

Upland Bird Hunting
—by George Hodgson, Northumberland, New York

As a setter man and woodcock hunter, I was reaching out for new locations to pursue my upland bird hunting interests when I was contacted by

Ray Robinson during the summer of 1983. Following a warm and cordial telephone conversation with Ray, with his colorful Downeast humor, pictures of Cabin #1 arrived shortly thereafter.

That October was the beginning of a thirty-two year relationship with the Robinson family and their beautiful sporting camps located in Dennysville, Maine. Not a year has passed, since, that has not heard my setters' footsteps in the Robinson's log cabins during October, usually with several close friends and their setters who share my passion.

The six log cabins, the first being constructed in the 1930's, are rustic, beautifully sited along the Dennys River, and quite comfortable, with all the modern electrical conveniences and ample kitchen space. They are heated with woodstoves or kerosene fired furnaces (depending on your personal preference) and most of the cabins host beautiful stone fireplaces to accent this wonderful Downeast setting.

Located about one mile west of US Rt. 1 in Edmunds Township, Robinson's Cottages are in the heart of Downeast Maine and provide easy access to the nearby 85 mile Downeast Sunrise Trail. There are many excellent freshwater lakes and streams in the area which attract hikers, fishermen and paddlers, or like me, "sports" who may want to enjoy fall bird, moose or deer hunting opportunities nearby. Visits to remarkable natural phenomena such as Reversing Falls and The Whirlpool off Eastport Maine are also only a short drive away. The Roosevelt summer home at Campobello, just outside of Lubec, Maine, is another quite enjoyable destination for the less adventurous traveler.

I would be quite remiss in my comments about Robinson's Cottages if I did not say a few words about the Robinson family. Ever since that phone call in 1983, it was apparent to me that The Robinson family, besides possessing copious amounts of some of the best subtle Downeast humor, also displayed unwavering warmth and caring for other people, both of which are the cornerstones of fine hospitality. Ray, Evelyn, Jim and Bill—over the years these three generations of Robinsons have made all of their guests feel very comfortable at Robinson's Cottages, almost like family! There is never a lack of fine Robinson hospitality for guests at their cottages, as evidenced by the great number of long-term repeat clients such as myself who visit Robinson's Cottages each year.

So, if you want some of the best of Downeast Maine and a stay at a superior Maine sporting camp, it's hard to beat a stop at Robinson's Cottages, just outside of Dennysville, Maine!

Ross Lake Camps

Ross Lake Camps is located on Chemquasabamticook Lake in the North Maine Woods west of the Allagash Wilderness Waterway. This is a Maine hunting camp with remote cabins located deep within the North Maine Woods near the Allagash Wilderness Waterway. The camps have been operated commercially for many decades. They were originally very basic outpost cabins only accessible by float plane, but with the construction of a road system, customers can now drive right into the yard. And start hunting immediately!

Owner: Donald Lavoie; PO Box 140, Ashland, ME 04732; info@ rosslakecamps.com, www.rosslakecamps.com; (207) 227-7766, (603) 320-3208.

Directions: Inside the North Maine Woods gates (fees applied), in the unorganized territory T10 R15, in the tri-county corner of Piscataquis, Somerset, and Aroostook Counties. Approximately 83 miles of dirt and shale based logging roads (unless accessed via Canada). Nearest towns are Ashland (83 miles away) and Millinocket (109 miles away).

Description: On the shores of Chemquasabamticook (Ross) Lake, 9 cabins sleeping 3 to 9 people, all remodeled or newly constructed in the last 5 years. New propane lighting and appliances. Kitchens, woodstove for heat, but no running water. Water is supplied in 7-gallon dispensers from well that also serves the shower house (not available in winter). Outhouses located throughout the property. Main lodge with commercial kitchen and dining room seating up to 20 guests.

Prices: Depends on activity. Fully guided bear hunts with meals $1,750/hunter and $1,500 without meals for 6 nights/5 day hunts. Deer hunts $300/person/week, lodging only; $485/person/week with evening meals. Other packages available on website.

Meals: Most cabins have cook stoves and ovens, propane refrigerators. Breakfast is available for groups with minimum of 4 guests. Most packages give the option of some meals.

Activities: Primarily a hunting and fishing camp, specializing in moose hunting, black bear hunting over bait, deer and grouse hunting, and offering both ice and open water fishing (including for muskies).

Other: Boat rentals available in season, and snowmobile transport service for winter ice fishing season. 2-person/2-night minimum. Internet but no cell service.

Season: Closed from the end of the 3rd week in November through January 5. Again closed at the end of ice fishing season and reopened about May 20, weather dependent. Otherwise, open all year.

We Keep Coming Back
—by Michael and Roxann Kline

The sun is rising over the lake. There is a light fog on the water, and a pair of loons taking their morning swim. The quiet beauty of the mountain ridge in the background makes you believe in a higher power. I ask myself, "How did I get here and why did it take so long to do it?"

How did I get here? When a friend suggested a bear hunting trip to Maine, I thought "Why not." It will be an adventure. "Where in Maine?" I asked. "The North Maine Woods" was his reply. At the time I had no idea exactly how far north this was. I prepared for the hunt in the usual way. We made plans, plotted our course on map-quest and made reservations. What we did not prepare for, was the 80 miles of rough logging roads, the remoteness of this course that map-quest didn't provide, and the awesome beauty that was all around us.

It started with the drive past the base of Mt Katahdin and the start of the Appalachian trail. Everyone has heard of that. I had even walked on part of it myself in the southern mountains of Pennsylvania. It was not until I read on the sign of the miles to the end did it hit me how long it was. The majestic mountain in front of us and the river that runs alongside, and the stories that this trio inspired, are not realized until now. These are all things that we learned about in geography in elementary school, things in books that were now brought to life.

The directions we got from our outfitter gave us landmarks and mileage to follow. Landmarks such as the Allagash Waterway. What they did not give you was the different plants, the tall old trees and the random hunting camp along the route. The roads were rough at best. In some places, they were almost impassible because of water filled potholes. These are driving conditions we did not expect, but that just adds to the thrill. The thrill was almost lost in the pothole the size of a small farm pond, but we overcame the obstacle. Just watch the trip-meter and look for the next sign.

When we came to the edge of John's bridge, we stopped our truck and got out to investigate. Bridges that you drive over have guardrails of some sort. Not this bridge! No, this bridge was two wooden planks with more wood slats and it was open on both sides. Open with a 5-foot drop to the rushing water below. While the scene was breathtaking, the bridge was downright scary. Being true adventurers, we climbed back into the truck, and slowly, crossed the bridge. Once on the other side, we got out of the vehicle again and reveled in the beauty.

I guess the reality of how remote the North Maine woods didn't truly sink in until we arrived at the camp. Ross Lake Camps was one main house and a handful of guest cabins. The cabins have no running water, no electricity and no indoor plumbing. Not a five star resort, but the rooms are clean and we were here for hunting. What the camp did have is the lake. The beautiful, peaceful lake. This is where heaven was created. This is the exact spot. I stood on the rocky shoreline and gazed at water and the shore opposite me. More of the mountain ridge shown beyond. I was surrounded by water and trees and a quiet that I had never experienced before. There were colors and shapes and smells that overloaded my senses. I couldn't take it all in nor did I want to stop. This is Maine's North Woods. This is an untouched beautiful secret that I wanted for myself. This was worth the trip.

The camp was buzzing with activity. Other hunters arriving, gear being unloaded and introductions being made. A brand new camaraderie being forged by the lake. The peacefulness is shattered by the dinner bell. This bell will be the notice for all of our meals. An antique alarm so to speak. Everyone gathers in the lodge for dinner. The food was plentiful and delicious. The conversation light and sometimes all you could hear was the loons on the lake outside. This is when we meet our guides and a few of the camp rules are discussed. After dinner we retire to our cabins.

As night falls I find out what dark really is. The cabins are outfitted with propane lamps. These lamps are very hot and attract mosquitoes, so they don't stay on long. I break out the trusted flashlights and wander out to our small porch. Then I looked up and was completely speechless. If I live to be one hundred years old, I will never be able to describe the awe of that night sky. Thousands of stars twinkled above me. They were so dense, it looked as if it were a blanket. A satellite shoots across the sky and the moon looked as if it was close enough to touch. When I look out toward the lake, it is swallowed by darkness. This is an inky blackness only found in classic werewolf stories. I have never been this enveloped by darkness before, and it was a bit unnerving to say the least. I again look up to the starlit sky and listen. Now the quiet is pierced by the mournful howl of the coyote. How far off it sounded. That night I sleep more soundly than since childhood.

The sunrise wakes me. I blink in the half-light of morning wondering at my surroundings. Oh, that's right. I am in Maine. I step out into the cool morning air and look out onto the beautiful lake. I take in the silence and the fresh air and am filled with anticipation. The bell rings for breakfast and draws me out of my childlike need to explore. Again, we all gather at the lodge. We sit down to our morning meal. This is when the plans for the day are played out before us. Lunch at noon and then out to the bait sites for hunting. The morning is open for hiking, fishing in the lake or just sitting around. After sighting in our guns, my friends and I went for a hike. We explored a few neighboring camps out on the trail. I was just taking everything in. I did not want to miss a thing or forget any of what was seen.

Being out on stand is an entirely different story. The silence of the forest is only broken by an occasional jay. You are seated in a wood blind, surrounded by pine bough. You have been camouflaged and cover-scented and are now one with the woods. I can hear my own heartbeat and nothing else. Sit still and don't move around and be quiet were the instructions from my guide, so I did just that. I sat so still, a chipmunk sat on my foot. I was so quiet, a small bird perched on my blind. I was so quiet, a moose cow started to chew on the leaves of the tree beside me. I had to fight the urge to reach out and pet her, she was so close. Just another day in the Maine forest. As I sat and watched all of these activities, I ask myself, "How did I get here and why did I wait so long to do this?" At that very moment, other than my wedding day and the birth of my children, my life was perfect.

Even the perfection of the wilderness can be touched by the ugliness of the outside world. This trip was no exception. The remoteness brings along a delay in news. The date was September 12, 2001. One of our guides returns from the check station with the news of the attack on the World Trade Center and Pentagon. There is no television, so we gather around a battery operated radio and listen to the news accounts. It was then that I was comforted by the beauty around me and missed the modern amenities of a telephone all at once. I was saddened by what was happening and had no way to communicate to home.

The week bore on with same pattern. Breakfast, explore, lunch, hunt, sleep. Five days passed with the blink of an eye. It was now time to leave for home. After packing up the truck, I stand by the lake one last time. Looking around and saying goodbye to my new friend, the water, I feel the need to share this with my wife. "I have got to get her here!" I think to myself. As I turn to leave I vow to return.

Once at home, I told my wife and children of the beauty and the sights that I saw. I told my friends and co-workers about the adventure

I had embarked upon. I even started planning my next trip back to Ross Lake Camps. I returned again the following year with my same friends. We were surprised to find new owners of the camp. Everything else was the same. Same cabins, same schedule for the days and the same lake. The lake welcomed me like a longtime friend. I felt at home. Again, when my trip was over, I vowed to return and this time bring my wife. This is something she would love to see. I will find a way; I will talk her into this.

Talk her into it I did. Two years later, she joined me on the shoreline of Ross Lake. It was like bringing her home to meet my family. She fell in love with the lake and the mountain. She even fell in love with the cabin. That love affair ended at the outhouse, but she adapted. I know she loved it as much as I because she has joined me on the next six trips. Every trip feels the same and different. A new adventure is formed with the breaking dawn and a desire tor return on our last day here.

As I stand at the water's edge, looking at the mist covered mountain, I ask myself, "How did I get here and why did I wait so long?"

Russell Pond Camps

This is a hunting camp, with a special focus on bear hunting, but they welcome youth hunters. In 2007 they hosted five kids age twelve and under with their dads who bagged four nice bears. In 2009 hunters under age eighteen went three for three. The owners report, "We are very proud of our Junior Hunters!"

Owner: Owner Joe Cabral; contact Inga Cabral, PO Box 512, Maries, ID 83861; www.russellpondcamps.com, info@russell pondcamps.com; (208) 245 2458.

Directions: In the North Maine Woods. 3 miles north of the Golden road on the 490 road, right on Russell Pond in Russell Pond Township. *Delorme Atlas and Gazetteer*, p. 48.

Description: Rustic cabins sleep 2–8 right on Russell Pond (fly fishing only) commercial kitchen in main lodge dining room seats

40+. Each camp has wood heat, gaslights, and stove; dry sink, no running water in each camp. There is a central shower house with flush toilets and private shower rooms when under generator power only. Remote, private, historic hunting camp.

Prices: Fully guided bear hunting $1,600, includes all meals, lodging, guide service and hunting transport. Hunters must bring all license and permits, equipment, and gratuity; 5 full hunting days, arrive Sunday depart Saturday. Fully guided moose hunting $3,000, includes all meals, lodging, woods transport, and guide service for 2 guests guided to 1 moose ready for transport to tagging station. 5 full hunting days; if need be Saturday can be arranged. Fully guided 5-day deer hunt is $1,200; includes all meals, lodging, woods transport, and guide service for whitetail buck. Camp rentals up to 6 guests $550 up to 7 nights. Book in advance for popular seasons like grouse and moose, no bear season camps.

Meals: Fully guided hunters are served 3 hot cooked meals a day for bear hunts and 2 hot with bag lunches for deer, moose and grouse hunters. The food is home style till you're full: turkey, roast beef, meatloaf, pork loins ribs, plus soups, salads, and full breakfast with either french toast, eggs 'n' taters, or pancakes. Special dietary needs can be met. Camp rentals include no meals unless arranged; each camp has cooking facilities.

Activities: Fully guided hunting for bear, moose, deer, and grouse. Camp rentals in all seasons for all reasons.

Other: Cell phone service within a mile of camp but certainly not everywhere. No Internet. Pets allowed. Guests must bring all toiletries and towels, sleeping bags, and all gear if bear hunting or deer hunting. Safety belts. Camp rentals require their own food. These folks are exclusively hunting outfitters—it's all they do, and they have another big hunting outfit in Idaho.

Season: Year-round.

Bear Hunting
—by Bobby Nelms

About fourteen years ago give or take a year, a good friend of mine Steve Alexander asked me if I was interested in a fall bear hunt in Maine. Steve had been talking to me about hunting bear in Maine for some time with me typically ending the conversation by saying "Let me think about it."

You see Steve and I are like brothers and as brothers can do so well, Steve had finally convinced me it was time to get off my rump and book a Maine bear hunt. Steve had been hunting for years with Joe Cabral and Russell Pond Camps and enjoyed it so much he started guiding bear hunters. There is one thing Steve told me that I can still remember today "Once you hunt with this guy and his family you will be hooked." At that time I did not realize how true that statement would turn out to be.

I had never visited Maine prior to my first trip to Russell Pond Camps and was excited to see and hunt in a new state. Steve had put me in contact with Joe's wife Inga who explained everything up front and booked my hunt. From that phone conversation there is one thing learned about this outfitter: what they tell you is what to expect. Inga explained the state license and tag requirements, details of the hunt and most importantly how to properly prepare for hunting in Maine. I can honestly say there were no surprises; the information and details are provided right up front and they deliver on them.

The camp is situated on Russell Pond and has a great view. One thing I tell people to this day is there is nothing like standing outside brushing your teeth and have a moose standing in the pond right in front of you. The cabins are clean and comfortable with a roomy kitchen cabin centrally located; hot showers are available as well.

As far as food is concerned if you go hungry it's because you choose not to eat. When you wake up the smell of coffee and breakfast lingers in the air. The lunch prior to heading off to stand is a full course meal and is good. Dinner is waiting when you return to camp. In all my years now hunting with the Cabral family I have never once heard any hunter complain about the food.

I found the atmosphere in camp is laid back. Most of the hunting is done in the afternoon when the bear are most active and on the move so you have the morning to relax before the day's hunt. I have over the years hunted in the morning as well, based on scouting and trail cams set up by Joe and his guides. Joe will accommodate all day on stand as well if you wish.

One of my favorite things about being in "Maine Bear Camp" is the people. Joe, Inga and Company have a high rebook rate. When you have a family atmosphere like this, people will and do want to come back. I can tell you for me this has provided countless stories and laughs talking with guys who have hunted here for twenty years. If you ever meet anyone who has hunted with Joe before, ask them about the Sunday night speeches laying down the ground rules for the hunt. I have experienced a lot of them and can tell you they are legendary around camp.

A couple things I have learned since hunting with Russell Pond is they hunt in a remote area. You are not hunting near anyone else. This is probably what I enjoy most. Where I live in Pennsylvania you are typically hunting on top of other people; it has not always been that way but is getting progressively worse. I am very happy when I can get to the Maine woods. Joe maintains 100 plus bait sites. With that many potential hunting locations, you will not be placed or remain on a bait site that is not active.

For me I find participating in every aspect of the operation very re-warding; therefore I have become more involved with helping out than hunting. I enjoy running baits and setting up stand locations with Joe and his guides. One thing is for certain: the set up and care of 100 bait sites spread out across 400 square miles is a lot of work. Joe, his father Joe (Papa) and his son Joey start this tireless job thirty days prior to the first day of legal hunting. As I have learned firsthand it is easy to sit in a stand and hunt not realizing how much work it took to get to that point. Joe, his family, cooks and guides deserve a lot of credit as they really do work hard to ensure a client a memorable hunt.

As I said earlier my "brother" Steve told me once you go you will be hooked. As it turns out that was the truth. The only year I missed since my first hunt was the year my youngest son was sick. Since then I have been in camp every year. I have two sons, ages nineteen and fifteen who have both hunted in Maine with the Cabral family as well. For me these were the most rewarding hunts. My oldest boy was eleven when he harvested his first bear with Russell Pond. This also happened to be the year some of my buddies took their boys as well. There was a total of five boys under the age of fourteen in camp and four out of the five harvested bear. The picture of all those kids standing with their bears is priceless. My younger boy had his nerves get the best of him two years ago but will never forget the moment that bear appeared out of the woods.

Today my family and I head into bear camp with the Cabral family every year. This upcoming season my wife will be sitting on stand for her first bear hunt. I can already tell you I am afraid I created a monster. I hope to get my guide's license soon and continue enjoying our annual vacation to Russell Pond Outfitters. Based on my experience if you're looking for a Maine hunting trip with a family atmosphere where you will feel welcome right away give Russell Pond Outfitters a try; my bet is they won't disappoint you.

Sadulsky's Camps

Established in 1948 and located in Smithfield, Maine, Sadulsky's Camps has a tradition of fine, friendly, family vacationing. Nestled in a wide cove on the quiet north end of East Pond, the westerly view provides spectacular sunsets. East Pond is the first of the seven Belgrade Lakes chain, and while several species of fish inhabit the lake, it is the small and large mouth bass that draw the serious angler.

Owners: Dave and Sandy Marston; 1111 Barcelonia Drive, Lady Lakes, FL 32159; www.sadulskyscamps.com, sadulskyscamps@gmail.com; (207) 362-6337 (in season), (856) 231-9910 (off season).

Directions: On East Pond Road in Smithfield, on the northwest corner of East Pond. Private road.

Description: 16 camps with 1,200 feet of lake frontage. All camps have full kitchens and baths, and 2–3 bedrooms. Established in

1948, with continued upgrading. Each camp has a wood-burning stove.

Prices: $900/week for each camp, Saturday to Saturday.

Meals: All camps have full kitchens.

Activities: Swimming, boating, and fishing are primary activities.

Other: Small boats available for rent. Cell and Internet service. No pets.

Season: Memorial Day weekend through Labor Day weekend.

SALLY MOUNTAIN CABINS

THESE RUSTIC CABINS ON THE SHORES OF BIG WOOD LAKE IN THE Jackman-Moose River Valley region, are surrounded by 250,000 acres of unbroken forests with hundreds of miles of logging roads and trails, making it easy to explore the mountains, lakes, ponds, streams and wildlife of western Maine.

Owner: Corey Hegarty; 9 Elm Street, Jackman, ME 04945; www.sallymtcabins.com; (207) 668-5621, (800) 644-5621.

Directions: On Bigwood Lake, Jackman. Take Route 201 north from Skowhegan to Jackman. First street on left after railroad tracks.

Description: Year-round housekeeping cabins on lake. Cabins fully stocked with kitchens and bathrooms.

Prices: $38/person/night. $230/person/week. Kids under 5 are free.

Meals: All cabins have full kitchens.

Activities: ATV and snowmobiling, hunting, open water and ice fishing, hiking, moose watching.

Other: Cell and Internet service. Pets accepted. Free canoes and kayaks. Bait shop on site. Ice shack rentals available.

Season: Year-round.

SALMON POOL CAMPS

DON HELSTROM IS A VERY ACTIVE SPORTSMAN, GETTING TO THE AGE when he wants to reduce his work load. So he's now only offering bear hunting at his camps.

Owners: Don and Gail Helstrom; HCR69 Box 558, Medway, ME 04460; www.turnpikeridgeoutfitters.com; (207) 746-5860.

Directions: Gravel road 27 miles from Ashland in North Maine Woods (gate fees). Gate fees are paid for hunters staying at Salmon Pool.

Description: Cabins located on the Aroostook River at Salmon Pool. Most cabins built in early 1900s. Dining room with electricity from a generator, water, outhouse, shower available.

Prices: $1,700 to $2,200 full service. $500 for small game hunters and nonhunters.

Meals: Provided.

Activities: Fall hunting for bear.

Other: No cell or Internet service. Pets accepted.

Season: Fall only.

South Branch Lake Camps

These camps are nestled between Mattamiscontis Mountain and Bald Hill on a clear, spring fed lake full of smallmouth bass. You can also easily fish the Penobscot and Piscataquis Rivers and Seboeis Stream from here. The camps specialize in bass fishing and hunting for bear, deer, and grouse.

Owner: Russell Aldridge; 1174 Cove Road, Seboeis, ME 04448; www.southbranchlakecamps.com, sobranch@midmaine.com; (207) 732-3446.

Directions: I-95 north to exit 217, follow signs to Howland and then to Seboeis. Paved except for last mile of driveway.

Description: Traditional sporting camps build in the early 1900s. 3 housekeeping log cabins and 8 other cabins, updated with running water, toilets, electricity, and screened porches, all with views of the lake. Lodge with dining room and recreation hall.

Prices: American plan starts at $130/day or $745/week. Housekeeping plans start at $140/day or $795/week. Special packages available.

Meals: 3/day with bag lunch. 3 cabins have kitchens.

Activities: Fishing, family vacations, canoeing and kayaking trips, special events including weddings, fall hunting for bear, upland birds, moose, and deer.

Season: May to end of November. Cell and Internet service. Pets accepted.

Spencer Pond Camps

The first sporting camp to be certified as an environmental leader by Maine's Department of Environmental Protection, these remote cabins are the only ones on Spencer Lake, with a stunning view toward Little Spencer Mountain.

Owners: Christine Howe and Dana Black; 806 Spencer Pond Road, Beaver Cove, ME 04441 (winter address: 310 Bagaduce Road, Brooksville, ME 04617); www.spencerpond.com, spc@ spencerpond.com; (207) 745-1599; Facebook.

Directions: 14 miles from nearest neighbors, and only cabins on the pond. 34 miles north of Greenville, at the foot of Spencer Mountain, in the 22,000 acres of an unorganized township, to the east of Moosehead Lake. 1 hour from Greenville, the last 12 miles on well-maintained gravel roads with a sign at each intersection.

Description: 6 housekeeping cabins on the edge of Spencer Pond. The first cabin was built in 1901, and the newest cabins were built in the 1980s by the current owner's grandfather. Cabins do not have electricity and are "non-modernized." Each cabin has a fully equipped kitchen including propane refrigerator and gas stove and oven, shower stall, wood heat, and screened porch. Twinbeds that can be converted to king beds. Some cabins have futons that convert to double beds. Old-fashioned hand-pumps are in the kitchen and provide access to the spring-fed well. Kerosene and gaslights. Outhouses.

Prices: $62/person/night, $25/person/night ages 13–18 or college students under 21 traveling with parents. Children 12 and under are free. 5% discount for active military, seniors, and returning guests. Minimum nightly cabin charge $118 (double occupancy).

Meals: No food is served, and note that the refrigerators and freezers are small (freezer space is about a third the capacity of traditional freezers).

Activities: Hunting and fishing, hiking, kayaking, swimming.

> **Other:** Docks, canoes, and kayaks included, plus a sailboat and paddleboat. Motorboats can be rented. Alcohol prohibited except inside cabins. Phone service available, but no Internet or cell service. Pets accepted.
>
> **Season:** May–November.

Family Friendly
—by Christine Howe

We strive to be family friendly and since we reside on the premises with our two young children, that is our utmost priority. (Most guests) are self-sufficient, low maintenance, and generally in love with the mountain and area and comfortable being separated form creature comforts for a few days, weeks, or months. These camps are not for everyone. It is not for someone expecting a pristine, sterile, upscale environment. It is not a hotel and we do not cater to the high maintenance.

Along with the rustic beauty and authentic and quirky cabin ambience comes grim reality of washing dishes and body by hand, using outhouses, and going days without power or cell service. This is too much for some folks. It is more like camping, with the convenience of a sturdy roof and comfy bed. We meet the most fascinating individuals, from the lifelong native Mainer who is comfortable trudging off over a ridge with compass and fly pole in hand in search of a remote brookie pool or a shotgun to find a treasure trove of grouse, to the European family looking to experience the big woods of Maine, to couples vacationing from up and down the east coast.

SUNRISE RIDGE GUIDE SERVICE AND SPORTING CAMPS
TWO MAINE GUIDES OWN THESE CAMPS LOCATED IN BINGHAM AND offer a selection of guided and semi-guided Maine hunts and hunting trip package for all species including bears, rabbits, deer, moose, coyotes, turkeys, and grouse.

Owners: Troy and Cheree Conrad; PO Box 435, Bingham, ME 04920; www.sunriseridgeguide.com, info@sunriseridgeguide.com; (207) 672-5551; Facebook.

Directions: 117 Donigan Road, Moscow, half mile off Route 201 on gravel road, 20 minutes from Skowhegan.

Description: Cabins spaced out for privacy. Fully equipped kitchens. Large cabin has 12 beds, sleeping 16 with 2 bathrooms. Full bath. Fire pits.

Prices: $40/adult and $20/child/night.

Meals: Fully equipped kitchens. Meal package are available.

Activities: Hunting for deer, hare, turkey, coyote, moose, and bear. Whitewater rafting. Moose safaris and foliage tours. Snowmobiling and ATVing.

Other: Two-night minimum. Cell and Internet service. Pets accepted.

Season: Year-round.

Hunting the Hare
—by John Gilpin

Our group of ten to fifteen hunters has been making the trip in March to Maine since 2004 to hunt snowshoe hare. We started using the services of Sunrise Ridge in 2011. What we like about Sunrise Ridge is that they always go the extra mile. If a road is not plowed Troy will find a way to get us there. Cheree is a high energy person who will not be satisfied till we are. When we are there, we are truly treated like family.

In today's world that is not always the case but at Sunrise they are grateful that we use their services. We have used other outfitters in Maine and none compare to the service that Troy and Cheree give us, from the clean cabins, to the hot lunches in the woods to the outstanding dinners we are served at night. The most special time I've had there is the year I was able to have both my sons with me. Those memories are ones that won't be forgotten. Maine is a beautiful state with so much to enjoy and our group always looks forward to the next trip.

Tomhegan Wilderness Camps

Tomhegan Wilderness Camps features rentals of privately owned cabins and a lodge, available year-round, on Moosehead Lake.

Owners: Each camp is privately owned. PO Box 310, Rockwood, ME 04478; www.tomhegan.com, info@tomhegan.com; (207) 534-7712.

Directions: 832 Spinney Road, Tomhegan Township. Nearest town is Rockwood, 20 minutes away.

Description: Lodge and 10 privately owned 4-season camps, all with 2 or 3 bedrooms. Lodge sleeps 26. Built in 1910 with recent renovations. Some have inside bathrooms and some have outhouses. All are on the water on Moosehead Lake with a shared dock.

Prices: Start at $140/night and $850/week and go up depending on camp and time of year.

Meals: All camps and the lodge have full kitchens with gas stoves and woodstoves, refrigerators, coffee-makers, and outdoor grills.

Activities: Fishing, hunting (off site), snowmobiling, boating, canoeing, kayaking, downhill and cross-country skiing, wildlife watching, whitewater rafting, golfing.

Other: Camps are located in a Maine State Game Sanctuary. Boat, canoe, kayak, snowshoe, bicycle, and ice shack rents available. 2-night minimum in off season. Rented weekly (Saturday to Saturday) in February, July, and August. No pets. Cell and Internet service.

Season: Year-round.

UMCOLCUS SPORTING CAMPS

IN THE NORTHERN PART OF PENOBSCOT COUNTY, UMCOLCUS IS A TRA-ditional sporting camp, focused on hunting of deer, moose, and birds, with some fishing and family outings. The name is an Indian word meaning "whistling duck." The Curriers, the third generation to welcome guests here, advertise their camps this way: "The Maine reason for the way life used to be."

Owners: Al and Audrey Currier; 1243 Oxbow Road, Oxbow 04764; www.umcolcus.com, umcolcuscamps@gmail.com; (207) 435-8000, (207) 435-8227.

Directions: T8 R6, 6 miles off Oxbow Road before North Maine Woods gage. Nearest town is Ashland.

Description: 4 log camps, 2 board and batten camps, log dining room, located on a stream and deadwater. Camps are 17–30 years old. Separate shower house and 3 outhouses.

Prices: $50/person/night lodging, $110/person/night with 3 meals/day, $750/week lodging and meals. Family rates for camps.

Meals: Kitchens in each camp, and meals also available in the dining room.

Activities: Hunting, fishing, kayaking and canoeing.

Other: Cell phone but no Internet service. Sporting dogs allowed during hunting season.

Season: Mid-May–November.

WEATHERBY'S

A WELL-KNOWN TRADITIONAL SPORTING CAMP, IN BUSINESS FOR MORE than 100 years, and focused on hunting and fishing, Weatherby's is an Orvis dealer.

Owner: Jeff McEvoy; 112 Milford Road, Grand Lake Stream, ME 04668; www.weatherbys.com, info@weatherbys.com; (877) 796-5558; Facebook.

Directions: Located Down East in Grand Lake Stream. Nearest town is Princeton.

Description: 15 "comfortable but rustic cabins," each with a bathroom, with dining in the lodge. Solar hot water and photovoltaic power, new electrical systems, new bathrooms, hot water heaters, and more.

Prices: $189/person/night in peak season, $159/person/night otherwise. Kids are free in July and August.

Meals: All meals provided in the lodge. 2 cabins have full kitchens.

Activities: Primarily fishing and bird hunting.

Season: May–October.

A Sporting Destination
—by King Montgomery, outdoor travel writer and photographer, www .kingmontgomery.com

"Sports" have been coming to the bucolic 125-person village and the unique stream, both named Grand Lake Stream (GLS), since the early 1800s and in real force since the turn of the twentieth century when railroads pushed through to the more far flung reaches of Maine. Once GLS, located about 90-minutes northeast of Bangor, was home to the largest tannery in the world, and was in the heart of serious logging operations. Trees were felled and the logs rafted in the many lakes and driven downstream to the St. Croix River, which opened to the Atlantic Ocean and the timber/lumber markets beyond. GLS served as a 3-mile log sluice from West Grand Lake (WGL) into Big Lake (BL).

By the late 1800s, after the tannery closed and logging slowed greatly, the town was reachable by boat from Princeton, some 10 miles from GLS at the headwaters of the West Branch of the St. Croix River. As time progressed, an ever increasing number of anglers and hunters could take a train to nearby Princeton from the more developed New England states, hop on a small steamer, and head to GLS where sporting camps began to flourish. A rough road from the Princeton area to GLS eventually was completed as well.

It is said that GLS is home to more Maine guides than other location in Maine—about fifty fishing, hunting, and recreational guides work here. Some of the guides work out of Weatherby's Lodge to help anglers catch GLS landlocks; cruise and float the smallmouth bass rivers and lakes; troll for *togue* (lake trout) in their beautiful and stable square-stern, outboard-driven Grand Lake Canoes; or chase brook trout in the clear, cool streams. The angling possibilities are such that modern sports, like their predecessors of old, can fish for different species during a visit.

Historic Weatherby's Lodge is one the oldest and best known camps where a number of famous people—Ted Williams, Joe Brooks, A. J. McLean, Curt Gowdy, to name a few—stayed to fish for brookies, salmon, togue, and smallmouth bass in the stream, the many lakes and ponds, and the nearby rivers including the St. Croix, and to hunt American woodcock and ruffed grouse in the fall. Weatherby's, extant for over a century, is an Orvis-Endorsed Lodge, located just above the state fish hatchery, a short downhill walk in waders to GLS.

Weatherby's has fifteen cabins with all the conveniences, including continuous electricity, and serves three meals a day—or you may take a nice lunch basket out on the water. Owner Jeff McEvoy is head guide and an all-around outdoorsman who can take you fishing or bird hunting, or tell you where to go on the stream and in the field.

Landlocked salmon—called *tagewahnahn* by the indigenous Passamaquoddy tribe—rule the fishing in the stream. The salmon season runs from April 1 to October 20 in this gorgeous tailwater. The fish are late fall spawners—hence the season closure in October.

These marvelous and engaging fish are the same species as the vaunted Atlantic salmon: *Salmo salar*—the leaper. As the ice sheets retreated after the last Ice Age, salmon were trapped inland and adapted over the millennia to their new, more sedentary lifestyle. No longer anadromous, they plied the lakes and streams throughout Maine, and some of those stocks exist today. It is Maine's state fish.

Eastern brook trout have a similar evolutionary history as the salmon, and some of their kind still run out to sea and back to fresh water today, but most are landlocked as well. They live in GLS, chase the same flies as the salmon, and it's not unusual to take a brookie while fishing for landlocks. Brook trout are Maine's Heritage Fish.

I brought my old friend Lefty Kreh to Weatherby's in summer 2013 to fish for smallmouth bass in the St. Croix, just as his mentor, outdoors writer Joe Brooks, had done decades before. He declared the experience "outstanding," and we hope to make another trip there someday soon.

West Branch Pond Camps

Owned by the same family since the camps opened in 1881, the current owners take a lot of pride in that, and in the fact they still offer the traditional sporting camp experiences, with lots of repeat guests who treasure this place.

Owners: Eric Stirling and Mildred Kennedy-Stirling; PO Box 1153, Greenville, ME 04441; www.westbranchpondcamps.com, ecstirling@hughest.net; (207) 695-2561.

Directions: 30 miles from Greenville; 18 miles north on Lily Bay Road and 10 miles on Frenchtown Road.

Description: Lodge and 9 cabins on 125-acre pond. Dining room and kitchen in the lodge. Newest cabin was built in 1935, oldest in 1881. Private bathrooms in summer. Outhouses in winter. Shower house.

Prices: $120/person/night, children 5–11 $50/person/night. Single occupancy $175/person/night.

Meals: American plan only with all meals provided.

Activities: Hiking, fishing, birding, cross-country skiing.

Other: Minimum stay of 3 nights for single and 2 nights for double. No cell or Internet service. Pets accepted.

Season: January 22–March 20, May 8–October 12.

Lost in the North Woods
—by Dick Landon

We were turned around in the north woods. Five miles north and east of West Branch Pond Camps, we stood under the dense canopy of trees at the edge of a small clearing. July sun filtered down to dry matted roots and moss and a snake-like green fern I did not recognize. But surrounding the clearing, the woods grew thick again, and with this, came the paralyzing dread of feeling lost.

In the clearing were tufts of a stiff grass and grey, dead trees leaned at angles along the edges. Just beyond, were stumps of larger trees, cut level at a height of 3 feet. A foot wide, dark stream twisted slowly under the sun. Was this the place? Was this the deep, cold beaver bog where we would find brook trout "thick as a cant dog handle"?

Cliff Kealiher, then owner of the Camps, had held his own forearm out as another, clearer measure of the size. But I did not have an answer. We knew so very little. Suburban boys from Rhode Island, this was just our second trip to the Camps. My younger brothers, ages nine and five, looked to me for some sort of guidance or maybe just reassurance. I was twelve years old that summer. And now, at the remnant edges of a once great boreal forest, and the Camps far off, I was lost. Or maybe just "turned around," as they like to say.

That was fifty-five years ago. Over this time, the Camps, this collection of log cabins on the shore of a remote pond, has been a vacation spot, a refuge, a work place, almost a second home, and the family there often feels much like my own. I have returned each year since, sometimes five or six times in all seasons, and it is hard not to feel lost again, this time in reverie and memory.

Much has changed over the years, and some things remain unchanged. But neither the landscape nor Camps are untouched or pristine: the human hand is everywhere in these woods. This is no wilderness. But in those first years, the Camps had an illusionary, permanent sense of remoteness, the most recent lumbering operations having ended in the 1940s and 50s. Logging roads had become trails with balsam fir and blueberry shooting up between the truck ruts, bridges had failed. To star struck boys, the sense of remoteness felt both attractive and enduring. And we returned each year to learn, to explore, to get lost in the wild terrain, and then slowly, to put a name on things and places.

In the winter months through the 70s and early 80s, the Camps grew all but inaccessible, and still we came. In the 80s and 90s, lumbering operations began anew, the hardwoods and spruce having matured another time, and miles of new roads were introduced, often on or across the beds of old ones. Silver culverts were dug into the stream beds and plantations of larch and red pine installed, an unusual green patchwork quilt across the face of mountains.

Now again as I write, with the purchase of surrounding lands by AMC and as part of a "Hundred Mile Wilderness," the earlier feel of remoteness could once more return. Plantations have been harvested and a few culverts pulled from mountain feeder streams. Through all of this, the Camps have remained very much intact. Ownership has remained in one family for four generations: Chadwicks, Kealihers, Stirlings.

Not enough can be said about this family. It is their stewardship and their sense of place, sometimes through the most difficult of circumstances, that has kept these Camps and alive and well. But there is no wilderness here; no vast, untouched, unknowable forest stretching to the horizon. It is a traveled, peopled, storied place, a landscape always in progress. And so what remains, always, is just how is this place—these Camps and this landscape—to be used, worked, enjoyed, loved. This is this family's legacy, and maybe ours.

Later that day long ago, I stood with my brothers at the edge of a second, wider clearing high along a shoulder of White Cap Mountain.

We had wandered uphill, jumped a swift stream and then crossed two woods roads, one with a still intact cedar bridge. Machine parts—gear sprockets—and Shell oil cans lay at our feet. Out ahead of us was the wide panoramic, postcard-like view of forest and hillside and gleaming waters.

Had we followed that first lazy tannic stream, still in the low country, we would have come to Third Roach Pond far in the distance, and this eventually to Kokado-jo and Moosehead Lake a dozen miles away. And had we taken the quick mountain brook, we would have found the East Branch of the Pleasant River, this winding north and around the backside of White Cap, merging later with the West Branch. This second clearing overlooked the headwaters of two great drainages, the Kennebec and the Penobscot. We did not know this then.

Behind us, hidden beyond a stand of white birch and poplars, was Scott Paper's Lumber Camp 4, still active into the 1950s. In later winters we would ski and picnic among the fallen buildings. Out ahead of us, in both distance and time, were dozens of adventures, great and small.

From the hermit Joe Budreau's cabin on a bend in Logan Brook, we would scavenge a woodstove and lantern from 1930. A state trapping tag from 1918 belonging to Charles Randall, first owner of West Branch Camps, was a surface find. On the shore of First Roach Pond, we would pocket Late Woodland artifacts chipped from fine grained Kineo flint. And there, too, on this modern shore, we would find amalgams of fossilized clam shells in a hard dark mud, these from a time before this was forest and or lake water, when all this territory was a storm tossed inland salt sea, to be covered and exposed by nature and then by human hands.

Years later, below where this second clearing once existed, and standing to the side on a newly cut road, I heard first a bicycle and then a kind of music. And coming around a slash pile of birch and alder by the new road was young Jack Stirling, and he was singing, singing aloud and bravely as only those who think themselves alone can sing. Driving the bike pedals hard with young legs, his voice carried over the whirrr of tires and the kicking up of fresh gravel. And for sometime, I could hear him biking and singing loudly out over the newly opened country ahead of him.

That afternoon, my brothers and I found our way back to the Camps. Following the ridges of White Cap, I would see Third West Branch Pond, and then recognize Second, and soon, below us, were docks and cabins and dining hall at First West Branch Pond. And I understood we were home.

Wheaton's Lodge and Camps
The Wheaton family is well-known and highly respected in Maine, and the new owners have a great heritage to protect into the future.

Owners: Patrick and Sandy Patterson; 22 Grove Road, Forest City Twp., ME 04413; www.wheatonslodge.com info@wheatons lodge.com; (207) 448-7723.

Directions: By car: Take I-95 north to Lincoln (exit 227), proceed to Route 2 (4 miles) and turn left, continuing through 2 lights into downtown Lincoln. From Main Street, take a right on Route 6 to Topsfield (40 miles), left on US Route 1 to Brookton (8 miles), and right to Forest City (12 miles). All paved roads. No access fees. Nearest towns: Danforth (20 miles); Houlton (1 hour); Calais (1 hour); Lincoln (1 hour).

Description: Ten private cabins/cottages graciously spaced on the shore of East Grand Lake. 20-plus year old, very well maintained, very clean, private bathrooms with hot showers, spacious living areas, private bedrooms, screened in porches; varying in size. Sleep from 2 to 6 persons.

Prices: American plan—$158/adult/night includes 3 meals each day. No charge for bikes, kayaks, canoe, paddleboat, unlimited ice, firewood. No charge for stories, tall fishing tales, jokes (some really good!). Minimum 3-day stay requested.

Meals: Breakfast and dinner served from a menu out of the lodge. Lunch is packed to go, cold if you're on your own or a hot shore lunch if you've hired a guide for the day. Breakfast is cooked to order including fresh made muffins (each morning) pancakes, french toast, homemade waffles, eggs any style, bacon, sausage, ham, fruit, hot and cold cereals. Dinner is served out of the dining room from a menu. The meal begins with cracker and relish trays with a salad. The next course is soup and fresh baked bread. Next course is your main meal such as prime rib or lobster rolls (Monday), pulled pork (Tuesday), turkey dinner (Sunday), baby back ribs (Saturday) and more. Finish with your choice of 2 homemade desserts and ice cream is always available. There are 3 main meal choices every night. Guests are seated in the dining room at private tables; wait staff handles the rest.

Activities: Guests primarily fish with a registered Maine guide out of a traditional Grand Laker canoe built specifically for Wheaton's lake system for salmon, lake trout, small mouth bass, and white perch. Enjoy crystal clear waters by kayak, canoe, swimming and other lake activities. Hike, bike, and explore unspoiled nature.

Other: Cell phone and Internet service available. Pets allowed.

Season: Year-round.

Look Back and into the Future
—by Dale Wheaton

In early 2013, Patrick and Sandy Patterson became the new owners of Wheaton's Lodge. They have quickly shown an attentiveness to the comfort and enjoyment of their guests and commitment to a long sporting camp tradition.

Wheaton's follows a strong guide heritage, using a cadre of experienced Maine guides who ply this expanse of large lakes and interconnected streams along the Canadian border in their locally built Grand Lakers, cook a full shore lunch for their sports at some remote campsite, and pursue broad-shouldered smallmouths far from the noise of humanity. The camp proudly uses more fishing guides than any other Maine camp, all in the Washington County tradition. As one guest once said, "We come up here each year for a change and a rest. The lodge gets the change, and the guide gets the rest!"

In the fall of 1952, Ruth and Woodie Wheaton purchased a white pine grove on the shore of East Grand Lake and began construction of a main lodge and four cabins. On a wing and a prayer and with three small boys underfoot, prospects were scary. A few of Woodie's sports followed him from Grand Lake Stream, and they told others about it. Like other successful camp owners, Ruth and Woodie were willing to work long days and had a sincere interest in the pleasure of their guests. The business grew, and a terrific fishery helped.

"Best Smallmouth Lake in the World," a feature article in *Outdoor Life* (July, 1960) by Wynn Davis, put Wheaton's on the map of anglers nationwide. It was the first of many articles by Davis, Ben East, Charlie Elliot, Al McLain, Bill Rae, Bud Leavitt, and other prominent writers of the day that verified a good thing and drew fishermen from afar. The sports returned year after year, bringing their wives and friends.

The lodge was sold in 1976 to a young couple from New Jersey, but faltered in their third year along with their marriage. The fellow's aversion to physical labor, clumsy people skills, and indiscretions with the camp waitress may have had something to do with it.

The camp was brought back into the family in early 1979 when Dale and Jana Wheaton purchased what was left of the business and began to put the pieces back together. Hoodwinked by the pledge to "give it five years and re-assess," Jana gave up her lesson plans and grade books to tackle something new. It was not always pleasant, with an overburdened electrical system and an archaic water supply. And, then another young family. Her dire threats provoked a string of physical improvements.

Jana grew to enjoy the dimensions of operating a family business well off the beaten path. Her high standards for meal preparation and attention to detail, supported by a reliable and conscientious staff, added some polish to an establishment otherwise consumed by fish stories.

The fish continued to cooperate. An abundance of rugged small-mouths, aerial landlocks, and heavy togue offered combat for savvy anglers on the lakes. And a busy stream just a stone's throw from the lodge provided opportunity for those with a prejudice for waders and a fly rod. A new generation of guides was developed in the early 1980s, exhorted to high standards of professionalism, an ethic that respected the fishery and waters, and the goal of shaping each outing around the skill sets and expectations of their clients. Guide/client relationships grew and became part of the lodge experience.

Feature articles by Jerome Robinson in *Sports Afield* and Tom Davis in *Sporting Classics* began another era of media recognition. Two world record smallmouths on fly rod, later eclipsed, spoke to the quality of the fishery.

Wheaton's made *North America's Greatest Fishing Lodges* by John Ross and Katie Anders, *Fishing Vacations for All Budgets* by H. Lee Simpson, and "The 25 Best Fishing Lodges in North America" in *Field and Stream* by John Merwin. There were kudos in Kevin Tracewski's *A Fisherman's Guide to Maine* and other books. There were unsolicited television programs. "It was a lot of hot air, as you know," says Dale Wheaton, looking back. "But it's great for the ego during blackfly season."

With the development rage of the late 1980s and early 1990s, guides began to see some of their cherished places nibbled away by cottages and subdivision. In 1994 Dale approached several of his guides for their support in creating a land trust, with the initial goal of preserving a parcel of land on Mud Lake that had been offered to him. The Woodie Wheaton Land Trust, leveraging the generous financial support of Wheaton's Lodge guests, has grown into one of Maine's strong conservation organizations. The Trust has protected over a hundred miles of shoreline, thousands of acres, numerous islands, and many special places along the border for public benefit. The group now provides public outreach, children's programs, a public speaker series, nature outings, and a community center in Forest City.

"The guide passion for wild places, along with the generosity of our many guests and lakes residents has accomplished a lot," says Dale, proudly. "Future generations will have these wild places to explore, and will learn to love them as we do. I am grateful to so many for making it happen."

Patrick and Sandy appreciate the special landscape in which they carry on, and their inherited responsibility to defend it. After thirty-four years, Dale and Jana realized they were not young any more. But the lodge and stewardship of over sixty miles of lightly fished boundary waters appears to be in good hands. And new generations of fishermen and outdoor enthusiasts can enjoy quiet, bountiful, unspoiled waters as others did before them.

Each Maine lodge has its own unique personality, defined by the loyal clientele. So it is with Wheaton's. These folks understand that a nasty wind or a day of lousy fishing is not the end of the world; that a pan full of white perch fillets and a cup of guide coffee under a leaky tarp will do just fine until the serious fish decide to bite. And that many of life's problems can be solved on the camp porch over a little snort of bourbon or in the lobby after dinner. That the host will just smirk attentively when you describe how the big one got away is pretty much assured.

WHISPERWOOD LODGE AND COTTAGES

DOUG AND CANDEE MCCAFFERTY HAVE OWNED WHISPERWOOD FOR sixteen years, and while many of their guests, especially in May and June, are there to fish, they have made the necessary transition to offer lots of other activities for those who do not fish. The camps are located on a beautiful lake in the famous Belgrades, just a short drive from the state capital, with the 6,000-acre Kennebec Highlands nearby, public lands that offer wonderful hiking and backcountry adventures. I live ten minutes from the Highlands and spend a lot of time there.

Owners: Doug and Candee McCafferty; 103 Taylor Woods Road, Belgrade, ME 04917; www.whisperwoodlodge.com, info@whisper woodlodge.com; (207) 465-3983.

Directions: Just north of Augusta, off Route 8 about 13 miles from Belgrade.

Description: A traditional sporting camp with a main house and dining lodge and 11 cottages on 11 acres overlooking the south end of Salmon Lake. Each cottage has a living room with 1 or 2 bedrooms, a bathroom with shower, small refrigerator, and automatic heating unit. Some cottages have wood burning stoves and screen porches. A 20-slip docking facility with electrical power outlets is available. Daily housekeeping.

Prices: $83/person/day/double occupancy, $88 single occupancy, $93/person/day/double occupancy in prime season, $98 single occupancy.

Meals: American plan three meals/day. Breakfast and dinner in the central dining room. Lunches packed in a cooler to go.

Activities: Fishing, motor boating, kayaking, birding, swimming, hiking, golf.

Other: Boats with motors available, gasoline, fishing licenses, and a fishing tackle shop. 3-night minimum for a reservation. Last minute single night stays according to availability. Cell phone and Internet service. Pets accepted.

Season: May–September.

The Early Years
—by Mike Polakoff

Fifty-two years ago my father first brought me to Whisperwood Lodge and Cottages in Belgrade, Maine. I was 13 years old. Dad and I fished throughout New England and I have so many wonderful memories of fishing with my father. Our fishing trips, local or overnight adventures, were always very special and my father taught me to appreciate nature and the outdoors. Our first trip to Whisperwood was magical and being in the "wilds" of Maine and being able to fish with my dad for the week was as good as it gets.

Those early years at Whisperwood were truly adventurous because we were in the wilderness—not much worked and hot showers were spotty at best. My father kept his 6 HP Evinrude in the trunk of his Chevy and we rented a small 12-foot aluminum boat for the week; our only boating comfort was our red seat preserver cushion tossed on the bench seats. We were in that little boat at least eight to ten hours a day but catching bass and being with my father for the week were cherished times. Dad caught his biggest bass in June of 1974 and the mount is proudly displayed on my office wall along with a Belgrade Lakes trophy I received for catching the largest trout in August of 1979. We continued our weeks at Whisperwood for many years.

Dad's last visit to Whisperwood was in 1985. He was very ill and I knew this would be our last fishing trip together and I wanted to make sure it was a memorable one. When I told him I wanted to take him to Whisperwood for a few days of fishing, he lit right up and I saw that glow in his eyes return once again. Seeing him catch bass and enjoy those last fishing days with his son embedded Whisperwood in my soul forever. I continued going to Whisperwood with friends and every trip reminded me of my favorite times there with my father.

In 2000 a major change occurred at Whisperwood. Doug and Candee McCafferty became the owners and it was immediately clear that big changes were in store for this fishing camp in Belgrade, Maine. From their opening weekend in May of 2000 until today, I have been there every year and Whisperwood Lodge and Cottages is better than ever—by far. Doug and Candee have spent an incredible amount of time and effort transforming Whisperwood into the quintessential Maine fishing camp. Staying at Whisperwood is like visiting family, a very enjoyable experience with home cooked meals, clean and comfortable accommodations and Salmon and McGrath lakes providing some of the best bass fishing in New England.

If you like bass fishing, you truly have an opportunity to catch your bass of a lifetime here and if you check the webpage at www.Whisper woodlodge.com, you will see the quality bass caught year after year by the Whisperwood guests. The Father's Day and August Bass Fishing tournaments have become very popular and with so many attractions within an hour's ride, there are plenty of enjoyable activities for everyone. I can't imagine a spring, summer or fall without Doug, Candee and Whisperwood.

Anglers Gather Here
—by Tim Padgett

Whisperwood Lodge and Cottages is located in the beautiful Belgrade Lake Region of Maine on Salmon Lake. Salmon Lake is connected to McGrath Pond by a navigable channel which means fishermen have access to approximately 1,152 acres of water in total. I've enjoyed good days on the water there catching both smallmouth and largemouth bass.

I first stayed at Whisperwoods several years ago when I lived in Massachusetts and I was a member of Cabin Fever Bass Club out of Waltham. We booked a club trip there for a long weekend. The club had been there several times as a group even before my first visit and we all continue to go there to this day. I've gone back about half a dozen times, both with the Bass club but also with my family. It's a place that is very accommodating for both groups of friends or for a family getaway.

Repeat customers are always a good sign and they certainly have no shortage of repeat business. Whisperwood is an annual tradition for several people that I've met there during my stays, and for good reason.

Owners and operators Candee and Doug McCafferty are what make the Whisperwood experience such a good one. Granted the lake itself makes for a beautiful setting but the service and attention to detail provided by both Doug, Candee and their staff is what puts them over the top in my opinion. Upon check-in Candee can set you up with a Maine fishing license and a required Maine lake and river protection sticker for your boat ("Milfoil sticker"). I live in Maine now and always have the proper licensing ahead of time, but when living out-of-state that was very convenient. They also have a bait and tackle shop on premise with a good selection of artificial bait as well as live bait. I tow my own boat up when I go and Doug will have you simply unhook at the top of the driveway when you pull in, then he takes care of the rest.

The gravel road to the ramp is a bit steep so Doug makes it a policy to use his tractor to tow you down to the water and launch you; then he parks the trailer and you don't have to worry about it until departure. You'll have a slip dedicated to you and you can simply drive over and tie up with the ropes provided. The docks are in great shape, well bumpered to protect your boat and all have power, which makes it easy if you need to charge your trolling motor batteries. The dock is also well illuminated at night so the diehards can make their way back. They also maintain a fleet of rental fishing boats should you need to rent one. Doug is always happy to share the latest successful fishing pattern for the lake and will give you pointers to put you on fish. Whisperwood encourages a strict policy of catch and release.

The cabins are either lakeside or close to the water. They are comfortable, well maintained and very clean. They are cabins by a lake, so as long as you aren't expecting luxury, you won't be disappointed. There are various options with different sleeping arrangements and I've found it comfortable staying with both a group of friends/fishermen, as well as family. Candee will work with you to find the best option for your family/group when you book your trip.

They have the "American plan" which includes three meals per day. The food has always been great and the schedule works for fishermen, which is no accident. There is plenty of time to go out and fish before breakfast, which is served in the dining hall. The lunches are pre-ordered and packed to go in coolers and ready for you to take with you after breakfast, so you can stay out of the water the rest of day and fish uninterrupted. Dinner is back in the dining hall at the end of the day, with time left to still hit the water after dinner before dark.

Typically you hear several fish stories being traded during dinner. They also have a game room for kids and/or adults and they have a fire pit down by the water for a late evening campfire. I look forward to my next visit there and I'd recommend you check it out as well.

WILDERNESS ESCAPE OUTFITTERS

THIS IS A FAMILY BUILT, FAMILY RUN SPORTING CAMP AND WILDERNESS retreat. The lodge and cabins are on the shore of Upper Hot Brook Lake with a mile of lake frontage. They specialize in four seasons of hunting and fishing adventures, wilderness canoe and kayak trips, winter time snowmobiling fun, and relaxing family vacations in the lake front cabins. The Flannerys are well known in the hunting field, with at least one article about them in *Field and Stream* each of the last twelve years, and they have also been featured in *Outdoor Life*, *Deer and Deer Hunting*, and other magazines. *Field and Stream*'s latest book, *The Total Deer Hunter Manual*, also features them.

Owners: Randy and Sharon Flannery; PO Box 10, Upper Hot Brook Lake, Danforth, ME 04424; www.wildernessescape.com; (207) 448-3238; Facebook.

Directions: From the southern Maine border. Follow Route 95 north to exit 227 Lincoln/Mattawamkeag. Bear right off the exit ramp. Follow approximately 4 miles to traffic light and take a left onto Route 6 east. Follow Route 6 east approximately 25 miles to Route 169 north toward Danforth. The entrance is 19½ miles on the left side of Route 169.

Description: The lodge and cabins are located on the shore of beautiful Upper Hot Brook Lake, where they have a mile of lake frontage. The lodge has 2 large living rooms, 7 bedrooms, 5 bathrooms, 3 fully equipped kitchens, a commercial kitchen and dining room, and 2 covered porches overlooking the lake. The cabins have a large living room, 3 bedrooms, 2 full bathrooms, a fully equipped kitchen, and a covered porch overlooking the lake.

They are also in the process of building more cabins on the lakeshore. The lodge and cabins also are fully equipped with all the modern conveniences, including satellite TV and wifi.

Prices: Packages start at $395 and go up as high $2,500 for moose. Minimum stay of 3 days.

Meals: Both American plan and Housekeeping cabin rentals offered.

Activities: Wilderness Escape Outfitters is a family built, family run sporting camp and four-season outfitter. They specialize in four seasons of hunting and fishing adventures. They hunt big game, bear, deer, moose, coyote, bobcat, and small game, grouse and woodcock, snowshoe hare, duck, and turkey. They fish over a dozen lakes, 5 rivers, and many remote streams. They fish for small-mouth bass, salmon, lake trout, brook trout, brown trout, chain pickerel, cusk, white perch, yellow perch, sun fish. They also offer wilderness canoe and kayak trips from 1-day to 6-day trips. They offer river float fishing trips. And they offer wintertime snowmobile, ice fishing, snowshoeing fun as well as guided tours. They also offer year-round family vacations and have two large boat docks, full of boats to rent. Their guests are welcome to bring their own boat. They have two swimming docks with spring-boards, motorboats, canoes, and kayaks, plus their own boat ramp, horse shoe pits, volley ball/bat mitten nets. There's a campfire each night out in front of the lodge, by the lakeshore. There is nothing quite like sitting around the campfire under a star-filled sky, on the shore of a Maine wilderness lake, listening to loons and enjoying great conversations with new friends. They own several hundred acres on Upper Hot Brook Lake and there are snowmobile trails and hiking trails that cross the property and go beyond. Their driveway is also a mile long and between the driveway, snowmobile trails, and hiking trails, there are great opportunities for hiking, biking, bird watching, viewing wildlife, nature photography and more. They also have kennel facilities.

Season: Year-round.

WILSON'S ON MOOSEHEAD LAKE

SERVING GUESTS SINCE 1865, WILSON'S IS STRATEGICALLY LOCATED FOR those whose passion if fishing. I have stayed here, partly because the camps are alongside the East Outlet of Moosehead Lake, a fantastic river in which to cast a fly. And the East Outlet is open to fishing all year long!

Owners: Scott and Alison Snell; Route 15, Rockwood Road, Greenville Junction, ME 04442; www.wilsonsonmooseheadlake .com; (207) 695-2549, (800) 817-2549.

Directions: Take I-95 to Newport, exit 156; take Route 7-11 to Corinna; take Route 7 to Dexter; take Route 23 North to Guilford; and then take Route 15 North to Greenville. Turn left at the light and continue north on Route 15 for about 15 minutes. Wilson's is 6 miles past Squaw Mountain on Rockwood Road, Route 15. As you come down a long hill, you will see the sign for Wilson's on the right. It is located at the headwaters of the Kennebec River. If you go over a bridge crossing the river, you've gone too far.

Description: Wilson's village of fully equipped housekeeping is nestled in the woods half a mile off Route 15 (Rockwood Road) right on Moosehead Lake and the Kennebec River. All the cottages have a screened porch with views of Moosehead Lake and surrounding mountains. The cottages range from 1 to 5 bedrooms all with full bathrooms. Facilities include: fully equipped kitchen, full bathroom, hot and cold water, electricity, gas stove, propane furnace, refrigerator, dishes, utensils, pots and pans, toaster, coffee maker, linens and towels at no additional charge. All guests have access to launching and docking facilities, beach, picnic areas, and fire pits. Boats and motors, canoes, and tandem kayak rentals available. Master Maine guide available for hunting and fishing. Direct access to ITS snowmobile and ATV trails at the end of the driveway. Gas and small store on premises.

Prices: Ranges from $80 to $425/night and $590 to $2,400/week depending on cabin and season.

Meals: All cabins include kitchens.

Activities: All outdoor activities.

Other: Internet service.

Season: Year-round.

Wilson's Is Historic
—by Don Wilson

Don Wilson was born in Greenville in 1941 and resided at East Outlet until 1974. While at Moosehead, he helped his father, also Don, in operating these camps. He has authored many books, including one of my favorites, *The History of East Outlet Moosehead Lake, Maine* and *Wilson's on Moosehead Lake*. Don wrote the following article for my book on sporting camps. It includes a fascinating account of everything from log driving on the rivers to the heyday of Maine's sporting camps.

Prior to and during World War II, my grandmother operated a post office in what we called the Big Camp, now known as Ski Lodge. She was a postmaster for 29 years, and ran the office from the hotel during the summer months. The hotel was the center of the operation, with guest rooms on the second floor, guides' quarters on the third floor and wait staff on the top floor. During the winter months, my grandparents lived in the Big Camp.

In the mid-50s they bought a place in Greenville and during the week, my grandfather commuted every day to work, while my parents, who now had a house on site built by my father, took care of things at the place. Attending the Greenville school presented a challenge, especially during the winter months when the road was snowy and icy. My father used to drive me, along with some of the neighbor kids, until my grandparents purchased the house in Greenville, where I then lived during the week. When more families moved to the area, Moosehead and Squaw Brook, the state instituted school bus service, which later expanded to Rockwood since the school there did not include high school grades.

When I was growing up in the 1950s and 1960s, we had a number of cottages, and during that time added two more. Going down the row from the hotel to the dam, there was what was called the First Camp, Second Camp, Third Camp, then the Big Camp. These are now known as Penobscot, and Piscataquis, while the Third Camp was destroyed by fire shortly after we sold the property in 1974. After the Big Camp came Hate to Quit It, Riverside (as that was on the river and below the dam before the last reconstruction), then Hiawatha and Love Nest the name of which was changed to Pocahontas. After that were two longer camps, known as First Long and Second Long.

These camp were part of the original log lodge built as an addition to the hotel. It was known as Fisherman's Lodge, and existed as early as 1901. The middle portion was removed, resulting in three smaller camps, the middle one being known as Antlers, now called Kennebec, and set in back of the first two camps. Toward the dam from this camp my uncle, Alfred J. Wilson Jr., who drowned in the lake in 1936, built a cottage for him and his wife. The camp is now known as Sequoia.

Out on the point in front of the hotel was a camp known as Canabas, the name being one of the native American names for Kennebec. On the other side of the hotel was a camp known as Camp Burton, now called Lakeside. In back of this camp on the same side of the hotel was Chesb'm, a native American name for Moosehead. The camp is now known as Katahdin, behind which is a camp added after the Wilsons' sold, called Somerset. Behind this camp, at the shore, are Driftwood and Spencer, both built during the late 1950s and early 1960s, respectively.

In total, at its height, Wilson's had forty buildings on site, including the four-story hotel, seventeen cottages, two homes, two sets of garages, an ice house, a chicken coop and a stable, a power house, two shops, large wood shed, a pump house for filling the gravity-feed water tank, and a motor house which serviced the boats and the dock area and another shed. Besides two generations of Wilson family, there were employed a staff of thirteen, which included two cabin women, a laundry woman, a cabin and grounds maintenance man, a dock man, three waitresses, two cooks, two dishwashers and a receptionist. Depending on the part of the season, there were as many as a dozen guides, some of whom spent the entire summer, living in the hotel and eating with the staff. A second dining room was for the guests and could seat as many as sixty people at a time.

Wilson's offered three meals a day, each with an extensive menu that included several choices of entrees, vegetables, homemade breads and desserts. For fully one hundred years, until 1965, Wilson's operated on the American plan serving three meals a day, and provided either box lunches or shore dinners for those who chose to be away for the noon meal. In addition, Wilson's continued to offer meals upon request to those not on the American plan, as well as transients from elsewhere.

Due to rising labor costs and taxes, the decision was made in 1965 to offer either American plan or make your own meals, and a number of cottages were converted to include a kitchen. During the early 1960s, with the construction of the Squaw Mountain Ski Area, the decision was made to winterize several cottages and remain open through the winter, making Wilson's a year-round operation. In addition to skiers, Wilson's offered accommodations to snow mobilers and ice fishermen during the winter, as well as hunters during the fall months.

Before my time, guests would arrive in one of three ways, the latter two being the most popular: by car, by rail often embarking at the Moosehead station, or by boat from either Greenville or Rockwood. Like many establishments, Wilson's had their own boat for ferrying guests to the establishment from wherever they landed. Railroad travel was popular enough up until the 1950s that a set of rails existed running from the station to the hotel which accommodated a platform on wheels moveable by hand, upon which to move baggage, goods, and, in season, game from the various hunts.

After the highway was completed c. 1927, the preferred travel by sports and vacationers was by automobile. Many of the patrons would stay for extended periods of time, often a month or more, particularly prior to the construction of Route 15, when the establishment was more isolated and less accessible.

Wilson's always maintained a fleet of boats, smaller ones with low horsepower motors for rent in the earlier years, along with one large boat which could accommodate over a dozen passengers with their guides trailing a string of canoes to fish from once arriving at their destination. Generally a noontime cookout was part of such a trip. In later years, beginning in the 1950's, guests started bringing their own boats, and fishing on their own rather than the traditional way of hiring a guide for the day or longer.

Early in the season, especially just after ice-out, the establishment would be full and the early morning dock scene a hubbub of activity with guides getting ready to take their parties fishing. Frequently, at a spot on the lake known for good fishing, there would be a dozen or more boats trolling around, all catching fish. During the 50s and into the 60s most sports would return from a day's fishing with their limit of fish.

Wilson's maintained two large walk-in coolers to accommodate the catches, and most parties went home with a limit of fish which, back then was 15 lbs. per license, changed in the late 50s or early 60s to 7½ pounds. There have been several changes to the law since that time, always less, or more restrictive.

Like a lot of young sportsmen who lived around the lake, I became a guide as soon as I was allowed. Since I was in school during the fall and winter months, my guiding was confined to the summer season, fishing not hunting, although I did my share of hunting myself. I guided mostly on the lake, but occasionally on the river, at the dam, or trout fishing in remote ponds and streams. A couple of trips to the Allagash, and to a few of the larger lakes like Seboomook, Chesuncook, and Lobster, served to round out my exposure to the area. I guided for ten years, the last two of which I spent the season operating a cabin cruiser for Mr. Cannon, a regular guest who spent a month or more with us. I still retain a guide's license, but mostly, when I do guide, it is for family and friends.

A number of sportsmen, sometimes with their wives, came to fish the river and the famous East Outlet dam. Most of them were fly fishermen, although until the late 60s or early 70s when the law was changed to fly fishing only, a number of repeat anglers were either bait fishermen or spin fisherman. Up to the 1940s, the dam was made entirely of wood, held in place by several rock cribs. During the 40s, the northerly half was reconstructed to a more modern and more permanent concrete structure. The dam remained that way until the mid-1950s when the southerly portion was also replaced with a concrete structure as well as being moved a considerable distance down river, thus eliminating one of the deepest and best fishing pools on the entire river.

About this same time, Harris Dam at the lower end of Indian Pond was constructed, also eliminating not only a sizeable section of the Kennebec River both upriver and down, but also enlarging Indian Pond to over twice its original size. This impoundment also served to flood over a sizeable section of the old Somerset Railroad bed, but also one of Wilson's neighbors and close friends, the Marr's establishment, which was at the junction of the East and West Outlet branches of the Kennebec at the head of the Pond.

The stories that persisted about the fishing and hunting prior to these events have not since been equaled. To make matters worse, bass were illegally introduced into Indian Pond during the 1960s, turning the pond into a tremendous bass fishery, but to the detriment of its tributaries, as now the invasive species has found its way into the branches of the Kennebec River, but also into Moosehead Lake. This has caused a noticeable effect on the overall fishery, with a scarcity of baitfish and, in some areas of the lake, fewer brook trout than in the past.

During this time, a number of dignitaries and famous persons frequented the establishment. Many newspaper articles and stories in national sporting magazines appeared from well known writers and promoters. A number of local people were also promoters, appearing at, and sometimes hosting, sportsmens shows and like events. My father, Don Wilson, was an exhibition fly caster numerous times, and spent many hours with the sportsmens and local groups. He also served on the Governor's Fish and Game Advisory Council.

From very early times until the late 1960s the dam was a scene of spring logging activity. At first, logs, then later, pulpwood, was towed in large rafts known as booms, from all over the lake to the dam, where it was sluiced down the river, then through more dams after being collected at and towed across Indian Pond and Wyman Lake farther down river. The rafts assembled at Moosehead collected wood from other lakes and tributaries around the region, including the Moose River, Tomhegan Stream and the Roach River, as well as several smaller ones. Hundreds of thousands of board feet of sawlogs and thousands of cords of pulpwood were sent through the dam and down the river to the mills, having been delivered to the East Outlet by steamboat at first and later diesel-operated towboat, from around the lake where it had been collected.

The dam and Wilsons once again became a center of attention as the dock at Wilsons made a convenient location to tie up the *Katahdin*, the prime towboat of booms of logs, along with its smaller craft. The dock was therefore used by the paper companies as a hub to come and go from, since by the 1930s it was accessible by highway from either Greenville or Rockwood. Around the early 1970s, environmentalists helped put a stop to this long-standing practice by many logging companies on many rivers, but not before the companies harvested as much wood as they could, and built a network of roads traversing hundreds of miles and accessing thousands of acres of woodland previously relatively inaccessible.

This last big harvest was not the first, however, as earlier in the twentieth century hundreds of dams were constructed throughout Maine, for the purpose of moving wood down every imaginable trickle of running water, delivered streamside by horses as well as mechanized machines such as log haulers, and later, tractors and skidders. The Moosehead Lake Region was no exception. By the 1950s, many of these access roads provided avenues for hunting as the forests recovered, and a way to reach many of the rotting dams where trout fishing was at its best. Such resources remained until the dams finally fully deteriorated, or were totally destroyed by spring freshets.

In 1974, after a period of continual operation for 109 years, for a variety of reasons Wilson's decided to sell, insisting the name be retained. This name had gone through an evolution of its own, from Wilson's Tavern, to the Outlet House and Camps, to Wilson's Camps, to Wilson's on Moosehead Lake, to finally just Wilson's.

Wilson Pond Camps
The Youngs have owned these camps since 1995 and are justifiably proud that 90 percent of their guests are repeats.

Owners: Robert and Martine Young; PO Box 1354, Greenville, ME 04441; www.WilsonPondCamps.com, info@wilsonpond camps.com; (207) 695-2860, (877) 695-2860; Facebook.

Directions: Located on the west shore of Lower Wilson Pond, 3½ miles from downtown Greenville. In Greenville, turn right onto Pleasant Street that takes you right to the camps.

Description: Cottages are modern, finished in tongue-n-groove pine with wooden or carpeted floors, have bathrooms with showers, and drinkable water from the tap. Most cottages have 2 bedrooms and a kitchen/dining-living area. BBQ grills, picnic tables, and Adirondack chairs are available outside. Each cottage has its own dock and private waterfront space. Most have screened-in porches overlooking the 7-mile-long pond.

Prices: January 1–June 13 and September 19–December 31: Weekly $850 for up to three people, $120 each additional person, $60 children under age 5. Daily $135 for 2 people, $35 each additional person. June 14–September 19: Weekly $900 up to 3 people, $120 each additional person, $60 children under age 5. Daily $150 for 2 people, $35 each additional person.

Meals: Cottages have fully equipped kitchens with full size refrigerators.

Activities: fishing, swimming, canoeing, hiking, wildlife watching, boating, horseback riding, hunting, cruise ship and seaplane tours, birding, snowshoeing, and other outdoor adventures

Other: 2-day minimum off season and 3-day peak season. Linens and towels supplied for $20/person; boat and canoe rentals.

Season: Year-round.

MORE INFORMATION

NORTH MAINE WOODS—
GATED ACCESS TO 3 MILLION ACRES

THE NORTH MAINE WOODS (NMW) OFFERS ACCESS TO MANY MAINE sporting camps, camp sites, and recreational opportunities on 3 million acres of forests, lakes, ponds, rivers, and streams. I don't believe there is anything like this anywhere else in the country, a place where private landowners are so welcoming to recreational uses of their property.

NMW's mission is "to provide the visiting public with high quality, traditional outdoor recreation experiences that are compatible with providing renewable forest resources which sustain approximately 20% of Maine's economy. Forest recreation, when managed properly, is compatible with harvesting forest products."

In the early 1970s, user fees were initiated to help landowners recover part of the management costs related to accommodating public visitors on their lands. Before the North Maine Woods organization was created, separate landowners had their own regulations and fee schedule for use of their lands. Travelers might have passed through two or three gates or checkpoints to get to their destinations and paid separate fees on each stop.

In 1971, with the agreement between landowners to form NWM, a day use season registration for Maine residents was set at $2. Landowners also imposed a self-assessment to fund the startup of the North Maine Woods program. The self-assessment share was based on the owner's percentage of acres within the designated North Maine Woods area. During the period between 1971 and 1986, these assessments amounted to nearly three quarters of a million dollars. Since then, increased usage, prudent management and modest fee increases have allowed the program to become self-sufficient.

Although annual assessments have ceased, landowners still absorb many costs. They provide staff time on various operating committees; donate professional services of draftsmen, soil evaluators, and others; donate use of construction equipment; and maintain thousands of miles of roads which receive wear and tear from public travel.

Fees for each activity pay for the management of that activity. In general, all day use collections offset costs of operating the checkpoint facilities. Receptionists are available at convenient times for visitors to enter the area. Guidance, brochures and information are provided. Trash bags are provided to help control litter in the area. Receptionists also assist parties with emergencies and provide information to game wardens looking for sportsmen to relay emergency messages from home.

Camping fees collected are dedicated to maintaining and developing facilities used by campers. NMW's travel costs, to maintain these sites, are expensive, requiring staff to frequently travel 30 to 40 miles between sites.

Amazingly, visitor use has always occurred without any advertising by NMW, due in part to the favorable experiences of recreational users who spread the word and often return themselves. NMW does not promote the area, because it is not a park. It is private property which we are blessed to have access to.

Management contracts established over the years with the Allagash Wilderness Waterway, the Bureau of Parks and Lands, Jo-Mary Campground, and members of the KI Jo-Mary Use Forest provide just enough income to offset costs for management.

The NMW website contains lots of good information, and you are encouraged to check it out before accessing this area: www.northmaine woods.org.

Resources
Maine Sporting Camp Foundation, www.sportingcampfoundation.org. The Maine Sporting Camp Foundation was founded to preserve Maine's traditional sporting camps and the natural resources they rely upon The Foundation's core mission is to preserve this part of Maine's cultural heritage so that future generations will continue to have access to some

of Maine's most wild and scenic locations and will be able to enjoy the outdoor experiences that sporting camps offer.

The Maine Sporting Camp Association, www.mainesportingcamps.com. A diverse coalition of sporting camp owners from across the state dedicated to keeping the Maine sporting tradition alive for future generations.

www.visitmaine.com; includes a list of sporting camps.

www.georgesmithmaine.com; for outdoor news, "Travelin' Maine(rs)" columns on Maine's best restaurants and inns, book reviews, and more.

OTHER SPORTING CAMPS
Alden Camps, Oakland, www.aldencamps.com
Allagash Wilderness Camps, North Woods, www.allagashwildernesscamps.com
Bear Mountain Lodge, Herman, www.bmlmaine.com
Blackwater Outfitters, Marsaridis, www.maineblackwateroutfitters.com
Bosebuck Mountain Camps, Magalloway Plt, www.bosebuck.com
Camp Wapiti, Mt. Chase, www.campwapiti.com
Casey's Spencer Bay Camps, Greenville, www.caseysspencerbaycamps.com
Coles Moosehorn Cabin, Millinocket, www.colesmoosehorncabins.com
Conklins Lodge and Camps, Patten, www.conklinslodge.com
Cowger's Lakefront Cabins, East Grand Lake, www.cowgerscabins.com
Cozy Cove Cabins, Jackman, www.cozycovecabins.com
Down River Camps, Princeton, www.downrivercamps.com
East Branch Lodge, Haynesville, www.eastbranchlodge.com
Grants Kennebago Camps, Oquossic, www.grantscamps.com
Great Pond Wilderness Lodge, Otis, www.greatpondwildernesslodge.com
Greenland Cove Cabins, East Grand Lake, www.greenlandcovecabins.com
Homestead Lodge, Oxbow, www.homesteadlodgemaine.com
Katahdin Lake Wilderness Camp, Millinocket, www.katahdinlakewildernesscamps.com
Katahdin Lodge, Moro Plantation, www.katahdinlodge.com
Kokadjo Cabins and Trading Post, Kokadjo, www.kokadjo.com
Lake Molunkus Sporting Camps, T1 R5, www.lakemolunkus.com
Lawrence's Lakeside Cabins and Guide Service, Rockwood, www.lawrencescabins.com
Long Pond Camps, Jackman, www.mainbearoutfitters.com
Lugdon Lodge, Eagle Lake, www.lugdonlodge.wordpress.com
Maine Wilderness Camps, Kossuth Township, www.mainewildernesscamps.com
Merchant Camps and Lodge, Garfield PLT, www.merchantcampsandlodge.com
Niboban Sporting Camps, Rangeley, www.niboban.com
9 Lake Outfitters, Bridgewater, www.9lakeoutfitters.com

Northern Hideaway Camps, Fort Kent, www.northernhideawaysportingcamps.com
Patten Hunting Lodge, Patten, www.pattenhuntinglodge.com
Penobscot River Cabins, Howland, www.penobscotrivercabins.com
Portage Lakeside Cabins, Portage Lake, www.portagelakesidecabins.com
Porter Point Camps, Nicatous Lake, www.porterpointcamps.com
Rideouts Lodge, Weston, www.rideouts.com
Sam-O-Set Four Seasons, Rangeley, www.samosetfourseasons.com
Shoreline Camps, Grand Lake Stream, www.shorelinecamps.com
Smoldering Lake Outfitters, Bridgewater, www.smoldering-lake-outfitters.com
Sunny Shore Camps, Oakland, www.sunnyshorecamps.com
Sunset Camps, Smithfield, www.sunsetcamps.com
The Village Camps, Forest City Township, www.thevillagecamps.com
Willard Jalbert Camps, Allagash Waterway, no website, email atpj@wbhinc.com
Woodrest Cottages, Belgrade, www.woodrest.com

ABOUT THE AUTHOR

George A. Smith of Mount Vernon, Maine, has done a lot of things in his life, from writing comprehensive plans for rural towns to managing statewide referendum campaigns. He served as executive director of the Sportsman's Alliance of Maine for eighteen years, growing the membership from 4,000 to 14,000 and making it one of the state's most influential organizations. George left SAM at the end of 2010 to write full-time.

He writes an outdoor news blog posted on his website and the website of the *Bangor Daily News*, cited by the Maine Press Association in 2014 as the state's best sports blog. He has written a weekly editorial column published in the *Kennebec Journal* and *Morning Sentinel* for twenty-five years, columns for *The Maine Sportsman* magazine since 1977, and lots of special columns for the newsletters of various Maine organizations. You can access many of George's columns at www.georgesmithmaine.com. George and his wife Linda, a recently retired first grade teacher, have written a weekly travel column for the *Kennebec Journal* and *Morning Sentinel* for five years, focused on Maine inns, restaurants, events and activities.

For thirteen years, George hosted, with his friend Harry Vanderweide, a unique television talk show called *Wildfire*, focused on hunting, fishing, conservation, and environmental issues. Smith was part of the management team that successfully defended Maine's moose hunt in a 1983 referendum, and managed a successful campaign in 1992 that placed the Department of Inland Fisheries and Wildlife in the Maine Constitution and protected its revenues. He also led a successful campaign in 2004 to defeat an animal rights referendum that sought to end Maine's bear hunt. He also worked on many political campaigns and served on the staff of Congressman David Emery for eight years.

Among his many ideas, Smith conceived the Maine Outdoor Heritage Fund, funded by an instant lottery game that has provided over $18 million for wildlife conservation and outdoor recreation programs in Maine. George served five years on the Winthrop Town Council, three terms as Mount Vernon Selectman, one term as Kennebec County Commissioner, seven years on the Mount Vernon Planning Board, and thirty-six years as a Trustee of the Dr. Shaw Memorial Library. At the state level, George served on the Forest Legacy Advisory Committee, Maine Outdoor Heritage Fund Board, Commission to Study Trespass Laws, Hatchery Commission, Submerged Lands Task Force, Great Ponds Task Force, and many other task forces and study groups.

In 2014 George's book *A Life Lived Outdoors* was published, gathering his favorite writings about home, camp, family, faith, travel, hunting, fishing, and other outdoor activities. George is a Winthrop, Maine, native, a graduate of the University of Maine, and has lived in Mount Vernon for thirty-seven years. He and Linda have three children and three grandchildren.

You can reach George by email or online at: georgesmithmaine@gmail.com, www.georgesmithmaine.com.